YOUR COLLEGE EXPERIENCE

Strategies for Success

Eighth Edition

John N. Gardner

Distinguished Professor Emeritus, Library and Information Science
Senior Fellow, National Resource Center for the First-Year Experience
and Students in Transition
University of South Carolina, Columbia

A. Jerome Jewler

Distinguished Professor Emeritus, School of Journalism and
Mass Communications, College of Mass Communications and
Information Studies
University of South Carolina, Columbia

Betsy O. Barefoot

Co-Director and Senior Scholar
Policy Center on the First Year of College
Brevard, North Carolina

 WADSWORTH
CENGAGE Learning™

Australia • Brazil • Japan • Korea • Mexico • Singapore • Spain • United Kingdom • United States

WADSWORTH
CENGAGE Learning™

Your College Experience: Strategies for Success, **Eighth Edition**
John N. Gardner, A. Jerome Jewler, Betsy O. Barefoot

Director, Developmental English & College Success: Annie Todd

Development Editor: Marita Sermolins

Editorial Assistant: Daniel DeBonis

Technology Project Manager: Stephanie Gregoire

Marketing Manager: Kirsten Stoller

Marketing Assistant: Kate Remsberg

Marketing Communications Manager: Darlene Amidon-Brent

Content Project Manager: Tiffany Kayes

Creative Director: Rob Hugel

Art Director: Linda Helcher

Print Buyer: Elizabeth Donaghey

Permissions Editor: Margaret Chamberlain-Gaston

Production Service/Compositor: Pre-Press PMG

Text Designer: Diane Beasley

Photo Researcher: Cheri Throop

Photo Manager: Sheri Blaney

Copy Editor: Kristina Pinto

Cover Image: *Background:* © istockphot.com; *Bulletin Board:*
 © Gary Regaglia

For product information and technology assistance,
contact us at
Cengage Learning Academic Resource Center
1-800-423-0563
For permission to use material from this text or product,
submit all requests online at
www.cengage.com/permissions.
Further permissions questions can be e-mailed to
permissionrequest@cengage.com.

Library of Congress Control Number: 2007942368

ISBN 13: 978-1-413-03377-9

ISBN 10: 1-413-03377-6

Wadsworth Cengage Learning
25 Thomson Place
Boston, MA 02210-1202
USA

Cengage Learning products are represented in Canada by
Nelson Education, Ltd.

For your course and learning solutions, visit
academic.cengage.com

Purchase any of our products at your local college store
or at our preferred online store **www.ichapters.com**

Printed in the United States of America
1 2 3 4 5 6 7 12 11 10 09 08

About the Authors

John N. Gardner brings unparalleled experience to this authoritative text for first-year seminar courses. John is the recipient of his institution's highest award for teaching excellence. He has twenty-five years of experience directing and teaching in the most respected and widely emulated first-year seminar in the country, the University 101 course at the University of South Carolina. John is universally recognized as one of the country's leading educators for his role in initiating and orchestrating an international reform movement to improve the beginning college experience, a concept he coined as "the first-year experience." He is the founding executive director of two influential higher education centers that support campuses in their efforts to improve the learning and retention of beginning college students: the National Resource Center for The First-Year Experience and Students in Transition at the University of South Carolina (www.sc.edu/fye), and the Policy Center on the First Year of College in Brevard, NC (www.firstyear.org). The experiential basis for all of his work is his own miserable first year of college on academic probation, an experience he hopes to prevent for this book's readers. Today, as a much happier adult, John is married to fellow author of this book, Betsy Barefoot.

A. Jerome Jewler is a best-selling author, educator, and friend to students. As distinguished professor emeritus of the College of Mass Communications and Information Studies as well as co-director of the University 101 first-year seminar, including its faculty development component, at the University of South Carolina, Columbia, he has guided advertising students through the creative and writing processes, taught doctoral candidates how to teach mass communication courses, and has helped hundreds of new students determine their goals. As University 101 co-director, he planned and conducted training workshops for first-year seminar instructors, has won a Mortar Board award for teaching excellence, and was recognized as USC Advisor of the Year and nationally as the Distinguished Advertising Educator in 2000. Currently, he is teaching younger children anything from Napoleon to dinosaurs to art as a volunteer docent for the South Carolina State Museum.

Betsy O. Barefoot is a writer, researcher, and teacher whose special area of scholarship is the first year of college. During her tenure at the University of South Carolina from 1988 to 1999, she served as co-director for research and publications at the National Resource Center for The First-Year Experience and Students in Transition. She taught University 101, in addition to special-topics graduate courses on the "first-year experience" and the principles of college teaching. She conducts first-year seminar faculty training workshops around the U.S. and in other countries and is frequently called on to evaluate first-year seminar outcomes. Betsy currently serves as co-director and senior scholar in the Policy Center on the First Year of College in Brevard, NC. In this role she led a major national research project to identify "institutions of excellence" in the first college year. She currently works with both two- and four-year campuses in evaluating all components of the first year.

Brief Contents

Contents

Chapter 5 Listening, Taking Notes, and Being Engaged in Class.........................83

Chapter 10   Research and College Libraries 191

Chapter 13   Diversity: Appreciating Differences Among Us..........................261

Chapter 14   Staying Healthy...277

Preface to Students

Question:
How many American colleges and universities offer a first-year seminar or student success course?

a) I think my campus is the only one.

b) Maybe about half – I really don't know.

c) I've heard that almost all colleges and universities offer a special course to help students like me be successful.

If you picked answer "C," you're right. Recent research conducted by the Policy Center on the First Year of College found that over 90 percent of higher education institutions in the U. S. offer such a course.

First-year seminars/student success courses are different from other courses you will take in your first year. And this book is different from all your other textbooks. In fact, it may be the most important book you read as you begin your college experience because it's about you and improving your chances for success in college and beyond.

The very fact that you even have this book means that your campus offers a course designed to help first-year college students. One thing we know is that if you successfully complete this course, your chances of continuing in college and completing your degree are greater than those for students who do not take advantage of this opportunity.

We know that college can be very difficult and that you will face many challenges ahead. But we also know that many experiences you have in college will be really enjoyable. This book will help you take advantage of all that college has to offer.

Why listen to us? For one thing, all three of us have dedicated our higher education careers to helping improve what educators have come to call "the first-year experience." Many professionals in our field would probably agree that we are three of the country's leading experts on promoting student success in college as well as champions for all new college students. All three of us met and became friends and coworkers at the University of South Carolina. All three of us taught USC's internationally known University 101 first-year seminar, where we developed and practiced many of the strategies we provide in this book. In our current work, we help colleges and universities around the U. S. investigate and improve the way they design experiences in the first year, both in and out of the classroom.

You probably have some questions you would like answered before you even start reading this book. Here are some of the most common questions we hear from students across the country.

▶ Why should I take this course?

Research conducted by colleges and universities all over the world has found that first-year students are far more likely to be successful and to graduate if they participate in courses, programs, and activities designed to teach them "how to do college." That is the basic purpose of this course. It isn't a course for dummies, but one that is intentionally designed to help you avoid some of the pitfalls that trip up many beginning students.

▶ Aren't all the topics covered in this book common sense? I know how to read and study and have lots of experience with relationships and wellness.

Although you have probably been exposed to some of the information you'll learn in this course, college is a totally different environment. Topics such as relationships and personal health become even more important when you're living away from home in an apartment or campus residence hall. Even if you're living with your family, college will challenge you to manage your time, feel comfortable interacting with professors, and study effectively. All of these skills will be a focus of this course.

▶ What am I going to get out of this course?

Most importantly, this course will be a supportive environment where you will be able to share your successes and your frustrations, get to know others who are beginning college, and develop a lasting relationship with your instructor. You will feel more knowledgeable about and secure in your present environment, but you'll also be encouraged to think about the future and begin making plans for life after college, whether that is a job or additional education in graduate or professional school.

Doing everything this book suggests might seem easy while you are reading about it, but putting this information into action is a different matter—and that's what we are going to show you how to do. Generally speaking, if you can apply the ideas in this book to your everyday life, especially the 25 suggestions in the "Formula for Success," you will be more likely to graduate and achieve your life goals. Welcome to college!

John N. Gardner
A. Jerome Jewler
Betsy O. Barefoot

Preface to Instructors

Anyone who teaches beginning college students knows how they are changing from year to year. Today's students are increasingly job focused, technologically adept, and unevenly prepared for the academic expectations of college. Engaging and retaining students is a challenge at all levels, but particularly in the first year.

Since the early 1980s, college and university educators have recognized that the first-year seminar is a powerful tool in an overall plan to improve student success. But as students themselves change, so do these courses. Helping students develop a clear sense of purpose for college, assisting them in making the right choice of an academic major, and engaging them in learning, especially through the use of technology, are goals of today's seminar courses.

This new edition of *Your College Experience* responds to the changing needs of first-year students. It continues discussion of some of the timeless issues—learning strategies, critical thinking, time management, relationships, personal health, and so forth. But it adds a new focus on purpose and life planning. Each chapter includes an electronic portfolio component to engage students more effectively, and through a new chapter feature, "Wired Window," this edition develops students' awareness of the implications of technology.

While this edition of *Your College Experience* has been significantly revised, it is still based on our collective knowledge and experience in teaching first-year students. It is also grounded in the growing body of research on student success and retention, and we are confident that if students read and heed the information herein, they will be more likely to become engaged in the college experience, to learn more, and to persist to graduation.

This book is designed for students of any age, race, or ethnicity in both two- and four-year, residential and commuter, institutions. Our intent always has been to write in a way that conveys both respect and admiration for students by treating them as the adults we know they are, while recognizing their continued need for challenge and support.

Whether you are considering this textbook for use in your first-year seminar or already have made a decision to adopt it, we thank you for your interest and trust that you will find *Your College Experience: Strategies for Success* a valuable teaching aid. While our text was written primarily for students in first-year seminar courses, we hope it will also guide you and your campus in understanding the range of issues that, for better or for worse, can affect student success. Whether you are a first-time adopter of *Your College Experience* or someone who has used previous editions, we want you to know the essential features of this text and the major differences between this edition and the previous ones:

Chapter Features

Each chapter includes a number of distinctive features designed to actively engage your students and encourage them to become self-directed learners:

▶ Opening Quiz

WHAT: These are brief student quizzes about expectations of chapter content that are modeled on popular magazine pop quizzes.

WHY: They engage students by giving them a sneak peek of what the chapter is about. Armed with their responses, students can quickly see what they know and what they stand to gain from reading the chapter.

HOW TO USE: Instructors can use the quizzes as a way to get students interested at the beginning of class, as a launching pad for discussion, or as a preview assignment before the next class.

▶ Wired Window

WHAT: Wired Window provides practical advice on how to make use of technology within the context of each chapter topic.

WHY: Although today's students are tech-savvy, they might not have considered how technology can and will be implemented in college. This feature gives instructors tips that are useful in exploring the integration of technology into the college experience.

HOW TO USE: Wired Window provides good discussion topics for class to get students interested in the chapter.

▶ Confessions of a College Student

WHAT: These are real student profiles revealing students' fears or failures and subsequent paths to success.

WHY: Students are interested to learn about their peers and learn from their peers' mistakes and successes. Students then see how the practical skills detailed in *Your College Experience* can be applied.

HOW TO USE: Confessions of a College Student can be used to help students understand the relevance of topics to their everyday lives. You may also want to encourage students to create their own confessions throughout the term.

▶ Building Your Portfolio

WHAT: These are assignments, provided both in the book and online, that help engage students through the use of technology while building a body of student work.

WHY: Students will leave the course with an electronic record of their ideas and accomplishments. They can continue to add to the portfolio so it becomes a record that can be shared with future employers.

HOW TO USE: Instructors can use the Building Your Portfolio feature online or as a traditional pen and paper activity.

▶ Where to Go for Help

WHAT: This important feature directs students to helpful resources on campus and online and gives them a place to write in notes on resources specific to your campus.

WHY: Students often don't know where to get help when they need it. This feature provides a handy reference list of valid sources of information and assistance.

HOW TO USE: This feature provides a good wrap-up to a chapter to reinforce how your institution provides the services discussed in the chapter.

▶ **Write • Discuss • Compare • Ask • Blog • Answer • Journal Prompts**

WHAT: These are quick questions intended to provide students and instructors options for discussing, writing, blogging, or journaling about issues related to the chapter content.

WHY: Students should begin to think about how chapter topics relate to them personally and what prior knowledge they have about the topic. Likewise, instructors should get to know where their students stand on the chapter topics and where further emphasis might be needed.

HOW TO USE: As explained in the title, these prompts are ideal for a variety of classroom or out-of-class uses.

What's New in this Edition

Chapter 1: Exploring Your Purpose in Attending College

▶ Encourages students to think about their purpose in going to college and how to apply that purpose to goal-setting, both short- and long-term.

▶ Includes a brief explanation of why college is important to our society and the tangible and intangible benefits of earning a college degree.

▶ Emphasizes the motivation and commitment required of first-year students to succeed.

Chapter 2: Time and Money Management

▶ Includes financial management along with time management to streamline students' overall management of these finite resources.

▶ Features a strong emphasis on procrastination, including a quick true or false quiz to help students understand how procrastination is a barrier to success. The chapter also provides tactics for combating this common problem.

▶ Offers a clear presentation of how to manage time for the term, the week, and day to day via a planner and term assignment preview, a weekly timetable, and daily to-do lists.

▶ Presents revised section on respecting others' time and how students should be mindful of how others choose to use their time.

▶ Focuses on the popular usage of credit and debit cards and offers students tips on using these wisely.

Chapter 3: How We Learn

▶ Includes the popular and widely used VARK Learning Styles Inventory at the beginning of the chapter.

▶ Provides advice for students on how to adapt their learning styles to instructors who may have different teaching styles.

▶ Introduces attention disorders, the most prevalent learning disorders among today's students.

Chapter 4:   Critical Thinking

▶ Provides a comprehensive description of critical thinking.

▶ Offers examples to illustrate critical thinking in action, which then translates into practical application of critical thinking in the student's life.

▶ Includes application of critical thinking skills to everyday life and the Internet.

Chapter 5:   Listening, Note-Taking, and Being Engaged in Class

▶ Links student engagement to listening and note-taking so that students can see their success is dependent upon their own actions.

▶ Shows students how collaborative learning teams can increase success in school and how collaboration is a large part of the world of work.

Chapter 6:   Reading Strategies

▶ Helps students understand how reading college textbooks requires different skills and behaviors.

▶ Emphasizes how to prepare for reading.

▶ Gives students a step-by-step approach to effective reading.

Chapter 7:   Learning to Study, Comprehend, and Remember

▶ Focuses on study methods and how comprehension and memory are integral components of effective studying.

▶ Connects how memory works with comprehension and critical thinking when studying for tests.

Chapter 8:   Taking Exams and Tests

▶ Presents new, in-depth advice for studying specifically for math and science exams.

▶ Provides suggestions on how students can use exams as study aids even after they have received their grades.

▶ Offers a revised section on academic dishonesty that defines cheating and plagiarism, consequences of such actions, and how to avoid committing such offenses.

Chapter 9:   Effective Writing and Speaking

▶ Presents all the stages of writing succinctly, including freewriting, narrowing topics, writing a thesis statement, peer editing, and rewriting.

▶ Includes a new section entitled "Choosing the Best Way to Communicate with Your Audience." This section alerts students to the important differences between the informal writing they do when writing or instant messaging with their friends and the formal writing they will do in their courses.

Chapter 10:   Research and College Libraries

▶ Includes the five best practices of information literacy as outlined by the Association of College and Research Libraries, which help students focus on essential activities associated with each step of library research.

▶ Presents an updated section on using electronic resources.

Chapter 11:   Majors and Careers: Making the Right Choices

▶ Focuses on connecting one's purpose in college to starting a career and finding a job and applying skills learned to college to a job after college.

▶ Presents a new section entitled "Getting Off to a Good Start in the Workplace" that identifies behaviors employers are looking for in new employees and what behaviors can be the reason for termination.

Chapter 12:   Relationships

▶ Includes new information about relationships students forge online and how to manage those types of relationships while in college.

▶ Emphasizes personal and online safety so that students know what to do in troublesome situations.

Chapter 13:   Diversity: Appreciating Differences among Us

▶ Examines values and why individuals view diversity in different ways.

▶ Provides expanded coverage of diversity that now includes age, learning and physical ability, gender, and sexual orientation.

Chapter 14:   Staying Healthy

▶ Updated to ensure accuracy of all facts and statistics.

▶ Includes a new table that shows students how to calculate target heart rate zone.

▶ Provides information on the new Human Papillomavirus (HPV) vaccine, Gardasil.

Supplements

Instructor Resources

▶ Annotated Instructor's Edition, *Your College Experience: Strategies for Success, Eighth Edition (1428229949)*

This full textbook includes annotations and suggestions for teaching, updated and revised by Heidi Jung of Southern Illinois University, Carbondale. Heidi has been providing instructional support to faculty as an Instructional Designer at SIUC for over 12 years and consults with faculty to identify instructional needs and strategies to improve teaching and learning, which makes her a good fit to guide users of *Your College Experience* through the teaching experience.

▶ Instructor's Manual and Test Bank, *Your College Experience: Strategies for Success, Eighth Edition (1428229922)*

Revised by Heidi Jung of Southern Illinois University, Carbondale, the Instructor's Manual and Test Bank includes chapter objectives, teaching suggestions, additional exercises, test questions, a list of common concerns of first-year students, an introduction to the first-year experience course, a sample lesson plan for each chapter, and various case studies relevant to the topics covered. Heidi teaches the New Student Seminar course on the SIUC campus using *Your College Experience* and has provided this edition of the Instructor's Manual with her plentiful ideas of how to effectively teach alongside the book. In addition, she has written new test bank questions for every chapter to update them according to the book and today's students.

▶ PowerLecture™: A 1-Stop Microsoft® PowerPoint® Tool (1413033776)

Following the organization of the book, this easy-to-use tool helps you assemble, edit, and present tailored multimedia lectures. Create a lecture from scratch, customize the provided templates, or use the readymade Microsoft® PowerPoint® slides as they are. This CD-ROM also features software and image-specific JoinIn™ on TurningPoint® content for Audience Response Systems, allowing you to transform your classroom and assess your students' progress with instant in-class quizzes and polls. PowerLecture also includes the Instructor's Manual,Test Bank in electronic format, video clips, and web links.

▶ Videos

See your local Wadsworth/Cengage sales representative for more information.

▶ 10 Things Every Student Needs to Know to Study (1413015336)
This 60-minute video covers such practical skills as note-taking, test-taking, and listening, among others.

▶ 10 Things Every Student Needs to Succeed in College (1413029078)
This 60-minute video compilation illustrates ten valuable and highly effective practices every student needs in order to engage in a successful college experience. Topics include successful time management, recognizing and understanding learning styles, and written/spoken communication.

▶ ABC News Video on DVD for College Success: Life Skills (1413033008)
For many students, college brings with it added financial responsibility, the
pressure of finding a career, and the stress of unforeseen challenges. Here are
reports on what students across the country are facing, interviews with experts
on college life, and up-to-the-minute advice on what students of all ages need to
know about life outside the classroom—all taken from the award-winning coverage of ABC News.

Student Resources

▶ *Your College Experience* Online Resource Center offers a variety of rich learning
resources designed to enhance the student experience. These resources include
self assessments, portfolio blogs (online journals), Web resources, and video. All
resources are mapped to key discipline learning concepts and students can browse
or search for content in the Resource Center library. The Resource Center also provides communication tools, content authoring capabilities, and the ability to share
resources with others.

▶ The College Success Factors Index (CSFI), accessible via the iLrn College Success
website. This exclusive student assessment tool measures eight indices that can
affect student adjustment to college life. This program is an excellent pre- and
post-test for incoming students and helps individual instructors tailor their course
topics to appropriately address student needs. For more information about the CSFI,
please visit www.success.wadsworth.com and click on the link to the College Success
Factors Index website.

Acknowledgments

We would like to thank the numerous colleagues who have contributed to this book
in its previous editions, as well as this edition:

Chapters 2, 5, 6, 7, 8: Jeanne L. Higbee, University of Minnesota, Twin Cities
Chapter 3: Tom Carskadon, Mississippi State University
Chapter 6: Mary Ellen O'Leary, University of South Carolina, Columbia
Chapter 8: Christel Taylor, University of Wisconsin, Waukesha
Chapter 9: Constance Staley, University of Colorado, Colorado Springs; and Robert
　　Stephen Staley II, Colorado Technical University
Chapter 10: Charles Curran, Rose Parkman Marshall, University of South Carolina,
　　Columbia; Margit Watts, University of Hawaii, Manoa
Chapter 11: Philip Gardner, Michigan State University
Chapter 12: Tom Carskadon, Mississippi State University; Reynol Junco, Lock Haven
　　University
Chapter 13: Juan Flores, Folsom Lake College
Chapter 16: Michelle Murphy Burcin, University of South Carolina, Columbia

Special thanks also to reviewers of this edition whose wisdom and suggestions guided the creation of this edition of the text:

Eunie Alsaker, Winona State University

Marianne Auten, Paradise Valley Community College

Joanne Baird Giordano, University of Wisconsin, Marathon County

Julia Brown, Northern Virginia Community College

Kara Craig, University of Southern Mississippi

Anne Dawson, Eastern Connecticut State University

Rosie DuBose, Century College

Melissa Gomez, Austin Peay State University

Laurene M. Grimes, Lorain County Community College

Kathleen Hangac, State University of New York at Oswego

Elizabeth H Hicks, Central Connecticut State University

Claudette Jackson, Baylor University

Rebecca Jordan, University of Kentucky

Elizabeth Kennedy, Florida Atlantic University

Mary P. Lovelidge, Blinn College

Marty Marty, formerly of Missouri State University

Karen Mitchell, Northern Essex Community College

Kate Pandolpho, Ocean County College

Margaret Puckett, North Central State College

Christel Taylor, University of Wisconsin, Waukesha

Janice Waltz, Harrisburg Area Community College

Jodi E. Webb, Bowling Green State University

Nicole Weir, Montclair State University

Erika Wimby May, Dillard University

Michael B. Wood, Missouri State University

Janice E. Woods, Mohave Community College

We'd also like to continue to thank our reviewers from the sixth and seventh editions as they have helped to shape the text you see today.

Seventh Edition

Richard Conway, Nassau Community College

Joyce Deaton, Jackson State Community College

Gigi Derballa, Asheville Buncombe Technical Community College

Lisa Donato, Essex Community College

Diane Frazier, Colby Community College

Charles Frederick, Indiana University

Melanie Harring, University of Wisconsin, Oshkosh

Judy Jackman, Amarillo College

Rebecca Jordan, University of Kentucky

Harriet McQueen, Austin Peay State University

Jaseon Outlaw, Arizona State University

Bea Rogers, Monmouth University

Christel Taylor, University of Wisconsin, Waukesha

Susan M. Vladika, Marywood University

Linda S. York, Wallace Community College

Sixth Edition

Anne Hawthorne, Cuyahoga Community College

Bill Horstman, Mesa State College

Elizabeth S. Kennedy, Florida Atlantic University

Karen M. Kus, East Carolina University

Judith M. Lang, Whitworth College

Polly McMahon, Spokane Falls Community College

Anna Roope, Virginia Tech University

Diane L. Savoca, St. Louis Community College

Vicki Stieha, Northern Kentucky University

Mary Walz-Chojnacki, University of Wisconsin, Milwaukee

Phyllis N. Weatherly, Floyd College

Finally, all this could not have happened without the Thomson Wadsworth team that supported our text, guided us through the writing and production, and worked at least as hard as we did to make *Your College Experience* the premier text in its field. Our special thanks to:

Annie Todd, Director of College Success

Marita Sermolins, Associate Development Editor

Kirsten Stoller, Marketing Manager

Daniel DeBonis, Editorial Assistant

Stephanie Gregoire, Technology Project Manager

Tiffany Kayes, Content Project Manager

Heidi Jung, Instructor's Manual and AIE annotations

Julie Alexander, Building Your Portfolio Activities

Reynol Junco, Wired Window feature

Maggie Barbieri, Editor for Confessions of a College Student

Most of all, we thank you, the users of our book, for you are the true inspirations for this work.

Exploring Your Purpose for Attending College

In this chapter YOU WILL LEARN

▶ What college is all about

▶ The many purposes of college

▶ The importance of thinking about your own purpose for college

▶ How college "levels the playing field" for students from different backgrounds

▶ The many differences between high school and college

▶ The challenges of being an adult or returning student

▶ The benefits of a college education

College gives you many opportunities to meet people and explore ideas.

© John Boykin/PhotoEdit

What Is Your PURPOSE FOR ATTENDING College?

Read the following questions and choose the answer that most fits you.

1 What is the reason you decided to come to college?

A I have a lot of reasons—some are related to what I plan to do when I graduate, but I also just want to learn about different things and have lots of different experiences.

B I think that if you want a good job when you graduate, you have to go to college. That's the real reason I'm here from high school.

C I really don't know why I'm here. All of my other friends were applying to colleges so I thought I should. It seemed like a good idea when I applied—it's better than working or joining the military.

2 Why do you think there are so many colleges and universities in the United States?

A I think the U. S. and most other countries really value education and believe it's important for everyone.

B I didn't know there were many colleges and universities. I only know of about ten of them.

C How would I know? Maybe it has something to do with needing a lot of football teams.

3 Do you think college will help you change in positive ways?

A I'm looking forward to learning, meeting people, and having new experiences. I know I'll change for the better.

B I'm not sure whether I'll change for the better or for the worse. My parents are concerned that I won't be the same person.

C Change? What do you mean? I have no intention of changing anything I think or believe.

4 Do you understand the importance of critical thinking?

A There are so many false claims everywhere you look; it's really important to learn how to analyze evidence by thinking critically and to arrive at logical conclusions.

B Well, some things can be debated, but others are absolutely the truth. I don't need to think critically about everything.

C Why do I need to learn more about critical thinking? I'm already pretty critical.

5 What do you think it means to be a responsible college student?

A I think being responsible means managing my new freedom, keeping up with my work, and making the most of all my opportunities.

B I know what my parents would say: it's important for me to be a good student. But, I also think it's my responsibility to take advantage of all the new social opportunities.

C Not flunking out.

Review your responses. **A** responses indicate that you have a good beginning understanding of what's important in college, but you'll still need to work on maintaining those skills. **B** responses indicate that you're a good student who is thinking about the purpose of college, but there's always room for improvement. **C** responses indicate that you need some help in understanding college and why you're here. This course and this book can help you develop the understanding and motivation you need to be a successful college student.

In 1900 fewer than 2 percent of Americans of traditional college age attended college. Today, new technologies and the information explosion are changing the workplace so drastically that few people can support themselves and their families adequately without some education beyond high school. College is so important that more than 60 percent of high school graduates (more than 15 million students) attend. Because higher education can be essential to your future earning power and your overall well-being, we are committed to providing a set of strategies for you to do your best. That's what this book is all about.

As you're settling into your new college routine, we would like to welcome you to the world of higher education. The fact that you are reading this textbook probably means that you are enrolled in a first-year seminar or "college success" course designed to introduce you to college and help you make the most of it. In this chapter, we'll discuss how you fit into the whole idea of college. We'll consider

◀ **Each of these students probably defines the purpose of college differently.**

why the U. S. has more colleges and universities than any other country in the world. We'll also help you explore the purposes of college—many that your college might define for you. But even more importantly, we'll help you define *your* purposes for being here.

The College Experience

So what is the college experience? Depending on who you are, your life circumstances, and why you decided to enroll, college can mean different things. College is often portrayed in books and film as a place where young people live away from home in ivy-covered residence halls and "find" themselves. Many students do find out a lot about themselves, and we hope you will, too. But today, most students don't move away from home, don't live on campus, and don't see much ivy. We often see college portrayed as a place with a major focus on big-time sports, heavy drinking, and partying. And yes, there is some of that at some colleges. But college is really far more than any single image you might carry around in your head.

Write • DISCUSS • Compare • Ask • BLOG • Answer • *Journal*

So far, is life at your college or university what you expected or hoped for? Why or why not?

There are many ways to define college. For starters, college is an established process designed by our society to further formal education, so that students who attend and graduate will be prepared for roles in what has become known as "the information economy." Basically, that means that most college graduates are going to be earning their living by creating, managing, and using information. Because the amount of available information expands all the time, your college classes can't possibly teach you all you need to know for years to come. The most important skill you'll need to learn in college is how to keep learning throughout your life.

Why College Is Important to Our Society

American society obviously values higher education, which explains why the U.S. has so many colleges and universities—more than 4,100. College is the primary way that people achieve "upward social mobility," or the ability to attain a higher standard of living. In earlier centuries, a high standard of living was almost always a function of family background. You were either born into power and money or you spent your life working for others who had power and money. But in most countries today, receiving a college degree helps "level the playing field" for everyone. A college degree equalizes differences due to background, race, ethnicity, national origin, immigration status, family lineage, and personal connections. Simply put, college participation is about ensuring that more people have the opportunity to be evaluated on the basis of merit rather than by family status, money, or other forms of privilege. It makes achieving the "American dream" more possible.

Write • DISCUSS • Compare • Ask • BLOG • Answer • *Journal*

> When you hear the phrase "American dream," what do you think of?
> How would you describe the meaning of these words to someone else?

College is also important because it is society's primary means for preparing citizens for leadership roles. Without a college degree, it is much more difficult to be a leader in a community, company, profession, or the military.

A four-year college degree also prepares students for continuing their education in a graduate or professional school. If you want to become a medical doctor, dentist, lawyer, or a college professor, four years of college are just the beginning.

Why College Is Important for You

College is about thinking and will help you understand how to become a "critical thinker"—someone who doesn't believe everything he or she hears or reads, but who looks for evidence before forming an opinion. Developing critical thinking skills will empower you to make sound decisions throughout your life.

Although college is often thought of as a time when traditional-age students become young adults, we realize that many of you are already adults. Whatever your age, college can also be a time when you take some risks, learn new things, and meet new and different people—all in a relatively safe environment. It's okay to experiment in college, within limits, because that's what college is designed for.

WIRED WINDOW

THE INTERNET OFFERS a number of ways to get connected online. As you might already know, social networking websites like Facebook and MySpace are a great way to connect to your friends. Is Facebook popular at your college? If so, take advantage of its networking potential. Through Facebook, you can find new schoolmates with similar interests, join clubs or interest groups, and find friends in your classes. Keep in mind that the information that you post on Facebook is available to everyone in your network unless you adjust your privacy settings. While most students use Facebook and MySpace appropriately, some students have faced institutional (and sometimes legal) sanctions for pictures and information they posted online. Therefore, it is important that you review your profile to make sure that you are only including information that you want the public to know about you.

Another way you can learn about your specific college is by taking advantage of official and unofficial online campus resources. Your institution's website is one official resource that you might find useful for finding a range of information from how to get help with your writing to when the semester break begins. Unofficial resources include websites that rate professors and student-run wikis to help you find answers to common questions about your college or university. A popular website for rating professors is http://www.RateMyProfessor.com. Keep in mind that ratings on these websites are not reviewed for accuracy, so use them only as a starting point to learn about a professor.

College will provide you with many opportunities for developing a variety of networks. You will find both formal and informal networking opportunities that will help you make friends and develop alliances with faculty and other students who share your interests and goals.

College, for many students, is also a good time. College definitely can be fun, and we hope it will be for you. You will meet new people, go to athletic events and parties, build camaraderie with new friends, and feel a sense of school spirit. Many college graduates relive memories of college days throughout their lives, fanatically root for their institution's athletic teams, return to homecoming year after year, and encourage their own children to attend their alma mater. In fact, you might be a "legacy," someone whose parents or grandparents attended the same institution.

In addition to being fun, college is also a lot of work. Being a college student means hours studying each week, late nights, high-stakes exams, and working harder than you thought you could. For many students, college becomes much like another job with defined duties, expectations, and obligations.

But most importantly, college will be a set of experiences designed to help you further define and achieve your own purpose. Right now, you might feel that you know exactly what you want to do with your life—where you want to go from here. Or if you're like many students, you might be struggling to find where you fit into life and work. It is possible that as you discover more about yourself and your abilities, your current ideas about your purpose for coming to college will change. In fact, the vast majority of college students will change their academic major at least once during their college years, and some students will find they need to transfer to another institution in order to meet their academic goals.

But first, how would you define your reasons for being in college and at this particular college? Perhaps you, like the vast majority of other college students, see college as the pathway to a good job. Maybe you are in college to train or retrain for an occupation or because you have recently experienced an upheaval in your life. Perhaps you are here to fulfill a lifelong dream of getting an education. Or maybe you are bored or in a rut and looking for more pizzazz in your life. College should provide some of that. Many students enter without a purpose that is clearly thought out. They have just been swept along by life's events and, now, here they are.

Write • DISCUSS • Compare • Ask • BLOG • Answer • *Journal*

> How would you describe your reasons for coming to college at this time in your life? Do you think your reasons will change during your college career? Why or why not?

Your college or university might require that you select a major during or prior to the first year, even before you've figured out your own purpose for college. Some institutions will allow you to be "undecided" or "no preference" for a year or two. Even if you're ready to select a major, it's a good idea to keep an open mind. There are so many avenues to pursue while you're in college—many that you might not have even considered. Or, you might learn that the career you always dreamed of isn't what you thought at all. You'll learn more about choosing a major and a career later in this book, but you ought to use your first year to explore and think about your purpose for college and how that might connect with the rest of your life.

Outcomes of College

Although a college degree will clearly make you more professionally marketable, the college experience can enrich your life in many other ways. We hope you will take advantage of the many opportunities you'll have to learn the skills of leadership, experience diversity, explore other countries and cultures, clarify your beliefs and values, and make decisions about the rest of your life—not just what you want to do, but more importantly, how you want to live.

Many college graduates report higher education changed them for the better. Based on their experiences, you can anticipate the following outcomes of the college experience:

▶ You will understand how to accumulate knowledge.

▶ You will be more likely to seek appropriate information before making a decision. Such information will also help you realize how our lives are shaped by global and local, political, social, psychological, economic, environmental, and physical forces.

▶ You will grow intellectually through interactions with cultures, languages, ethnic groups, religions, nationalities, and socioeconomic groups other than your own.

◀ **College is a place where you can make new friends and maybe even meet a life partner.**

© Michael Newman/PhotoEdit

▶ You will gain self-esteem and self-confidence which will help you realize how you might make a difference in the world.

▶ You will tend to be more flexible in your views, more future oriented, more willing to appreciate differences of opinion, and more interested in political and public affairs.

▶ You will have children who are more likely to have greater learning potential, which, in turn, will help them achieve more in life.

▶ You will be an efficient consumer, save more money, make better investments, and spend more money on home, intellectual, and cultural interests, as well as on your children.

▶ You will be able to deal with bureaucracies, the legal system, tax laws, and advertising claims.

▶ You will spend more time and money on education, hobbies, and civic and community affairs.

▶ Finally, you will be more concerned with wellness and preventive health care, and live longer and suffer fewer disabilities and, through diet, exercise, stress management, a positive attitude, and other factors, suffer fewer disabilities.

When you made the decision to come to college, you probably didn't think about all of the positive ways that college could affect the rest of your life. Your reasons for coming might have been more personal and more immediate. There are all sorts of reasons, circumstances, events, and pressures that bring students to college, and when you put different people with different motivations and purposes together, it creates an interesting mix from which to learn.

How College Graduates Are Different

We know without a doubt that, college makes it possible for your life to be different from the one you would have had if you had never been a college student. Consider the list below. You'll note that the first item on the list is that college graduates earn more money. Look at Table 1.1 to see exactly how much more. However, note that these differences go far beyond making more money. When compared to non-college graduates, those who graduate from college are more likely to:

▶ earn more money

▶ have a less erratic job history

▶ earn more promotions

▶ have fewer children

▶ be more involved in their children's school lives

▶ have more discretionary time and money to raise their children

▶ become leaders in their communities and employment settings

▶ stay married longer to the same person

▶ be elected to public office

▶ participate in and enjoy the arts

When compared to non-graduates, college graduates are less likely to:

▶ be imprisoned

▶ become dependent on alcohol or drugs

▶ be duped, conned, or swindled

▶ be involuntarily unemployed

▶ use tobacco products

These outcomes dramatically increase the value of your investment in college.

Table 1.1 Median* Earnings by Educational Attainment for Year-Round, Full-Time Workers Age 25+

Advanced degree	63,076
Bachelor's degree	50,960
Associate degree	36,764
High school graduate	31,148
Less than high school diploma	22,568

* These are median earnings, meaning half the group earned less and half the group earned more. These figures are annualized based on weekly data through the second quarter of 2007.

Source: U.S. Department of Labor, Bureau of Labor Statistics, 2007. (http://data.bls.gov/cgi-bin/surveymost)

How College Differs from High School

As you think about your new life in college, it will help you to be clear from the outset on some of the ways that college is unique. If you just graduated from high school, you'll find some distinct differences. For instance, you will probably be part of a more diverse student body, not just in terms of race, but also in terms of age, religion, political opinions, and life experiences. If you attend a large college or university, you might feel like a number—not as unique as you felt in high school. You will have more potential friends to choose from, but your old ways of categorizing potential friends might not work for you. Familiar assumptions about people based on where they live, where they go to church, or what high school they attend might no longer apply to the new people you're meeting.

You will be able to choose from many more types of courses, but managing your time is sure to be more complex because your classes will meet on various days and times and you will have additional commitments, including work, family, activities,

© image100/Alamy

◀ **Managing your time in college can be a major challenge.**

and sports. You might live away from home, which means that no one will check to make sure you're out of bed and on your way to class.

Your college classes might have many more students in them and meet longer. College tests are given less frequently—sometimes only twice a term—and you will probably be required to do more writing in college. You will be encouraged to do original research and to investigate differing points of view on a topic. You will be expected to study out of class, to prepare assignments, do assigned reading, and be ready for in-class discussions. Your instructors might rely far less on textbooks and far more on lectures than your high school teachers. They will rarely monitor your progress; you're on your own. But, you will have more freedom to express views that are different from your instructors. They will usually have private offices and keep regular office hours.

> *Write* • DISCUSS • Compare • Ask • BLOG • Answer • *Journal*
>
> In what ways are you already finding that college is different from high school? Did you anticipate these differences? Why or why not?

Challenges and Opportunities for Adult and Returning Students

If you're a "returning" student, or someone who might have experienced some college before, or if you are an adult living and working off campus, you might also find that college presents new challenges and opportunities. For instance, college might feel liberating, like a new beginning or a stimulating challenge, or a path to a career. However, working full-time and attending college at night, on weekends, or both can add stress, especially with a family at home.

You will tend to work harder than younger students because you realize how important an education can be. Consequently, you will probably earn higher grades, even though you might believe you won't be able to keep up with your younger classmates. Your age and life experience will give you a unique and rich perspective on what you're learning, a perspective that most 18-year-olds lack.

First-Year Motivation and Commitment

What attitudes and behaviors will help you achieve your goals and be successful in college? If you are fresh out of high school, it will be important for you to learn to deal with newfound freedom. Your college professors are not going to tell you what, how, or when to study. If you live on campus, your parents won't be able to wake you in the morning, see that you eat properly and get enough sleep, monitor whether or how well you do your homework, or remind you to allow enough time to get to class. In almost every aspect of your life, you will have to assume primary responsibility for your own attitudes and behaviors.

If you are an adult student, the opposite is true: You might experience a daunting lack of freedom. Working, caring for a family, and meeting other adult commitments and responsibilities will compete for the time and attention it takes to do your best or even simply to stay in college.

Whatever challenges you are facing, what will motivate you to be successful? And what about the enormous investment of time and money that getting a college degree requires? Are you convinced that the investment will pay off? The following list might include some of your thoughts:

▶ This is the first time someone has not been there to tell me I had to do something. Will I be able to handle all this freedom? Or will I just waste time?

▶ I've never been away from home before, and I don't know anybody. How am I going to make friends? How can I get involved in some activities? Who do I go to for help when I need it?

▶ I have responsibilities at home. Can I get through college and still manage to take care of my family? What will my family think of all the time I'll have to spend in classes and studying?

▶ As a minority, will I be in for any unpleasant experiences?

▶ Maybe college will be too difficult for me. I hear college teachers are much more demanding than high school teachers.

▶ I hope I won't disappoint the people I care about and who expect so much of me.

▶ In high school, I got by without working too hard. Now I'll really have to study. Will I be tempted to cut corners, or maybe even cheat?

▶ Will I like my roommate? What if he or she is from a different culture?

▶ How will I know if I've picked the right major? What if I don't know which major is right for me?

▶ Can I afford college? Can my parents afford it? I wouldn't want them to spend this much and then have me fail.

▶ Maybe I'm the only one who's feeling like this. Maybe everyone else is just smarter than I am.

▶ Looking around class makes me feel so old! Will I be able to keep up at my age?

Thoughts like these are very common. Although your classmates might not say it out loud, many of them share your concerns, doubts, and fears. This course will be a safe place for you to talk about all of these issues with people who care about you and your success in college.

Write • DISCUSS • Compare • Ask • BLOG • Answer • *Journal*

> On a scale of 1 to 5 with 5 being high, rate your own level of motivation for college. What do you think accounts for your current motivation level? If you don't think you are motivated, what strategies can you think of that would help motivate you?

Confessions of a College Student

Name: Valeria Maya Fernandez

Age: 18

University: University of Texas at El Paso (UTEP)

Hometown: El Paso, TX

Major: Business: Computer Information Systems

Favorite book(s): *The Alchemist, Pride and Prejudice, Harry Potter* series

Favorite college courses: Art Appreciation and Intro to Cultural Anthropology

The person who inspires me the most or who I would most like to meet: Queen Elizabeth I

Favorite way to relax: With a cup of hot tea and good book

Your proudest moment or biggest accomplishment: Becoming the godmother to my nephew

Favorite food: Green Chile Chicken Enchiladas

Starting college confession: When I first started college, I thought I'd just attend for the standard 4 years so I could get a degree and a good job. But now I realize college is a place for growing and learning and discovering. I discovered that I wanted more than a job; I wanted a career. My ideal career would be one in which I would be in a position to help people and have a positive impact on their lives.

I've learned so much from all my classes, and there is still much to be learned. I've learned so much about myself as well. I now realize that getting involved and making new friends are just as important as "making the grade."

College is not a quick stop in life. It is where you can expand horizons and learn, not just about math and history, but also about yourself. I believe that college is a place where you can figure out who you are and become the person you want to be.

What's Your Purpose in College?

Consider these differences in the way you might feel about college:

I belong in college. . . . . vs. . . . . .What am I doing here?

Where would you fall between these opposite attitudes? You might find that your exact position shifts, depending on what's going on in your academic and personal life. But no matter how you feel on any given day, as you begin college you will need to spend time sorting out your own sense of purpose and level of motivation. The clearer you are about why you're in college, the easier it will be to stay motivated, even when times are tough.

To build a clearer sense of purpose, look around you and get to know other students who work hard to be successful. Identify students who have the same major or career interests and learn about the courses they have taken, work experiences they have had, and their plans for the future. Look for courses that are relevant to your interests, but don't stop there. Seek relevance in those required general education courses that might seem to be a waste of time or energy at first. Remember that general education courses are designed to give you the kinds of knowledge and skills you need for the rest of your life. Visit your career center, your library, and the Internet to investigate your interests and how to develop and apply them in college and beyond. Talk to your residence hall advisors, as well as your professors, academic advisors, and campus chaplains. College is designed to give you all the tools you need to find and achieve your purpose. It's all at your fingertips—but the rest is up to you.

WHERE TO GO FOR HELP

On Campus

To find the college support services you need, ask your academic advisor or counselor or consult your college catalog, phone book, and college website. Or, call or visit student services (or student affairs). Most of these services are free. In subsequent chapters, we will include a "Where to Go for Help" feature that is specific to the chapter topic.

Academic Advisement Center Help in choosing courses; information on degree requirements.

Academic Skills Center Tutoring; help in study and memory skills; help in studying for exams.

Adult Reentry Center Programs for returning students; supportive contacts with other adult students; information about services such as child care.

Career Center Career library; interest assessments; counseling; help in finding a major; job and internship listings; co-op listings; interviews with prospective employers; help with resumes and interview skills.

Chaplains Worship services; fellowship; personal counseling.

Commuter Services List of off-campus housing, roommate lists, orientation to community, maps, public transportation guides, child care listings.

Computer Center Minicourses, handouts on campus computer resources.

Counseling Center Confidential counseling on personal concerns, stress management programs.

Disabled Student Services Assistance in overcoming physical barriers or learning disabilities.

Financial Aid and Scholarship Office Information on financial aid programs, scholarships, and grants.

Health Center Help in personal nutrition, weight control, exercise, and sexuality; information on substance abuse programs and other health issues; often includes a pharmacy.

Housing Office Help in locating on- or off-campus housing.

Legal Services Legal aid for students. If your campus has a law school, possible assistance by senior law students.

Math Center Help with math skills.

Physical Education Center Facilities and equipment for exercise and recreational sports.

Writing Center Help with writing assignments.

My Institution's Resources

_____

_____

_____

_____

_____

_____

_____

_____

_____

▶▶▶ BUILDING YOUR PORTFOLIO
What's in it for Me? Skills Matrix

Life is what happens to you while you're busy making other plans.

-John Lennon

To complete this portfolio activity electronically, please visit
academic.cengage.com/collsucc/Gardner/YCE8e.

How might the courses you are enrolled in right now affect your future? While it might be hard to imagine that there is a direct connection to your career or lifestyle after college, the classes and experiences you are engaged in now can play an important role in your future.

Developing a skills matrix will help you to reflect on your college experiences and track the skills that will help you land a great summer job, the hard-to-get internship, a scholarship, and one day, a career.

1. Create a new entry in you portfolio with the title "Skills Matrix." Record your work for this assignment there.

2. Begin by making a list of the skills you think you are acquiring or enhancing in the courses you are currently taking (e.g., critical thinking, writing, analysis).

   Tip: Course syllabi often list specific course goals—this is a good place to start.

3. Next, develop a skills matrix to identify courses and experiences that enhance the following skills: communications, creativity, critical thinking, leadership, research, social responsibility, and teamwork. You might try using Microsoft Excel for the matrix. Identify three additional skill categories that you would like to track.

   ▶ Include a "references" or "reflections" section for each course or experience.

   ▶ Include important assignments/reflections in your portfolio for future reference.

   ▶ Reflect on important experiences, noting what you learned, how the experience changed your thinking, your personal reaction, etc.

1. Save your skills matrix on your computer or external storage device.

2. Write a brief description of your skills matrix and then attach your worksheet to your description in your portfolio. Consider allowing your instructor and classmates to review the matrix and give you feedback.

3. Update your matrix often and include the revised version in your portfolio.

4. Use your reflections to connect knowledge with experiences in and out of class, on and off campus.

My First Semester {2008}

Skill Categories	Example (English 101)	Example (References)	(Course 2)	References	(Course 3)	References	(Out-of-Class Experience)	References	(Out-of-class activity 1)	References	(Out-of-class activity 2)	References	(Out-of-class activity 3)	References
Communications	X	Essay on Reading One: "Training on Real Life"												
Creativity	X	Creative writing project												
Critical Thinking														
Leadership														
Research	X	PowerPoint Presentation on Type Theory												
Social Responsibility														
Teamwork														
(new category)														
(new category)														

Managing Your Time and Money

In this chapter YOU WILL LEARN the following:

- ▶ How to take control of your time and your life
- ▶ How to use goals and objectives to guide your planning
- ▶ How to prioritize your use of time
- ▶ How to combat procrastination
- ▶ How to use a daily planner and other tools
- ▶ How to organize your day, your week, your school term

- ▶ The value of a to-do list
- ▶ How to avoid distractions
- ▶ How values, time, and money are all related
- ▶ How to set up a budget
- ▶ The pros and cons of credit and debit cards

How do you finish everything in your day?

© Gary Gerovac/Masterfile

Jeanne L. Higbee of the University of Minnesota Twin Cities contributed her valuable and considerable expertise to the writing of this chapter.

How Do You MANAGE YOUR TIME and MONEY?

A?B?C?A?B?C?A?B?C?

Read the following questions and choose the answer that most fits you:

1   How do you stay in control of your time?

A   I religiously schedule my everyday tasks in my hand-held personal digital assistant (PDA).

B   I sometimes use the task reminder on my cell phone.

C   I just go and do whatever I want, whenever I want.

2   How do you set academic and personal goals to prioritize your time?

A   At the beginning of a term, I schedule my larger academic tasks and then find time for personal activities that help keep me sane.

B   I try to keep my academics balanced with my personal goals, but I tend to forget about assignments when there's something to do with my friends.

C   What academic goals? I only pay attention to myself.

3   What, if anything, distracts you or causes you to procrastinate?

A   I never let that happen—I focus on studying by going to a quiet place like the library.

B   I try to study in my room with my iPod, but someone always knocks on my door and I wind up talking to people while I'm trying to study.

C   TV shows always draw me in and I wind up studying an hour before the test.

4   What does your to-do list look like?

A   Very detailed, with everything I expect to accomplish that day—I even schedule in meals.

B   I usually just write in school stuff and tend to forget about my personal appointments.

C   Should I have a list? I usually just do whatever my roommate's doing.

5   How do you develop a budget for the term?

A   I think about everything that will cost me money during the term and create a budget that I live by.

B   I write down a budget, but I occasionally reward myself and buy something I really want.

C   I don't live on a budget—I buy whatever I want until I run out of money.

6   How do you use credit cards?

A   I have a credit card, but I only charge what I can pay off every month.

B   I try to use my credit card wisely, but every now and then I charge more than I should.

C   I have more than one credit card and they're pretty much maxed out. I try to make the minimum payments every month when I can.

Review your responses. **A** responses indicate that you have a good beginning understanding of how to manage your time and money, but you'll still need to work on maintaining those skills. **B** responses indicate that you're doing fairly well with resource management, but there's always room for improvement. **C** responses indicate that you need some help with getting control of your time and money. This course and this book can help you develop the knowledge and skills you need.

How do you approach time? How do you approach money? You might find that you view these important resources differently than your classmates. Some of these differences might have to do with your personality and background. And often, these differences are so automatic and ingrained that you don't even think about them. For example, if you're a natural organizer, you probably enter all due dates for assignments on your calendar or PDA as soon as you receive each syllabus. If you are careful with your money, you likely adopt and stick to a strict budget. On the other hand, if you take a more laidback approach to life, you might prefer to be more flexible and go with the flow. You might be good at dealing with the unexpected, but you also might occasionally find yourself in trouble because you have wasted either time or money.

Most fundamentally, how you manage time and money reflects what you value—what's most important to you and what consequences you're willing to accept when you make certain choices. For instance, when you value friendships above everything else, your academic work can take a back seat to social activities. Or, when you can't resist the latest expensive electronic gadget, you might be willing to spend money you don't have.

What you value most and how that relates to the way you spend your time and your money often changes in college. Importantly, how you manage these resources corresponds to how successful you will be in college and throughout life.

Taking Control of Your Time

Time management involves:

- ▶ Knowing your goals
- ▶ Setting priorities to meet your goals
- ▶ Anticipating the unexpected
- ▶ Taking control of your time
- ▶ Making a commitment to punctuality
- ▶ Carrying out your plans

The first step to effective time management is recognizing that you can be in control. How often do you find yourself saying, "I don't have time?" Once a week? Once a day? Several times per day? The next time you find yourself saying this, stop and ask yourself whether it is really true. Do you really not have time, or have you made a choice, whether consciously or unconsciously, not to make time for that particular task or activity? When we say that we don't have time, we imply that we do not have a choice. But we do have a choice. We do have control over how we use our time. We do have control over many of the commitments we choose to make. And we also have control over many small decisions, such as the time we get up in the morning, how much sleep we get, what we eat, how much time we study, and whether we get exercise. All of these small decisions add up to have a big impact on our success in college and in life.

Being in control means that you make your own decisions. Two of the most often cited differences between high school and college are increased autonomy, or independence, and greater responsibility. If you are not a recent high school graduate, you have most likely already experienced a higher level of independence, but returning to school creates additional responsibilities above and beyond those you already have, whether those include employment, family, community service, or other activities.

Whether you are beginning college immediately after high school or are continuing your education after a break, make sure that the way you spend your time aligns with your most important values. For instance, if you value becoming an expert in a particular academic area, you'll want to learn everything you can in that field by taking related classes and participating in internships. If you value learning about many things and postponing a specific decision about your major, you might want to spend your time exploring many different areas of interest and taking as many different courses as possible. Begin by setting some goals for the future in order to take control of your life and your time and to guide your decisions.

Overcoming Procrastination

To get you thinking about procrastination, a serious impediment to college success, consider this short quiz. Which scenarios represent the kind of procrastination that could interfere with college success?

1. You have a major exam tomorrow. Instead of studying all afternoon when you have no classes, you spend part of the afternoon going for a 5-mile run. YES or NO

2. You have a U.S. History exam in three weeks. You take notes in class each day and review them for the first time the night before the exam. YES or NO

3. You come to college with a significant other from high school. You know the relationship isn't working but you can't bring yourself to break it off, so you pretend that things are the same. YES or NO

4. You have a term paper assigned on August 28 that is due December 1. You don't select a topic until November 15, which still leaves you two weeks to write the paper. YES or NO

All of the above scenarios illustrate procrastination. For instance, a 5-mile run is a great way to spend some time, but when a major exam is right around the corner, you should postpone or shorten that run until after you have studied. And although it's a good idea to review notes just before an exam, you should never wait until the last minute to start studying.

Procrastination is a serious problem that trips up many otherwise capable people. There are numerous reasons why students procrastinate. In the book, *Procrastination: Why You Do It, What to Do About It,* psychologists Jane Burka and Lenora Yuen summarize a number of research studies about procrastination.[1] According to these authors, even students who are highly motivated often fear failure, and some students even fear success (although that sounds counterintuitive). Some students procrastinate because they are perfectionists; not doing a task might be easier than having to live up to your own very high expectations—or those of your parents, teachers, or peers. Others procrastinate because they find an assigned task boring, irrelevant, or consider it "busy work," believing that they can learn the material just as effectively without doing the homework.

Simply not enjoying an assignment is not a good reason to put it off; it's an *excuse,* not a valid *reason.* Throughout life you'll be faced with tasks that you don't find interesting, and in many cases, you won't have the option to not do them. However, procrastinating can signal that it's time to reassess your goals and objectives; maybe you are not ready to make a commitment to academic priorities at this

[1]Burka, Jane B. and Lenora M. Yuen. *Procrastination: Why You Do It, What to Do About It,* Reading, MA: Addison-Wesley Publishing Co., 1983.

WIRED WINDOW

THE TECHNOLOGY we use daily is a catch-22. On the one hand, technology helps us to be more productive and organize our time efficiently. On the other hand, technology becomes a colossal distraction and a time-waster. College students spend a lot of time chatting online by using instant messaging software. Think about how you use instant messaging. How often do you use it while doing something else on the computer? Generally, this kind of multitasking is harmless and often helpful when you are trying to do your "digital errands" like paying bills, buying books, and so on. However, because it is so easy to multitask, many students also try to do their school work while surfing the web or IM'ing. Have you ever completed your school work while actively sending and receiving instant messages or while surfing the web? If so, what was the quality of your work? A recent nationwide survey found that over 40 percent of students reported that their school work suffered because of multitasking on the web. Are you in that 40 percent? If so, what are some ways that you can disconnect in order to get your work done? One suggestion is to find a quiet study spot and leave your computer in your room. If you can't leave your computer, room, or your Internet connection, consider purchasing software that will block digital distractions.

point in your life. Only you can decide, but a counselor or academic advisor can help you sort it out.

Here are some ways to beat procrastination:

▶ Remind yourself of the possible consequences if you do not get down to work, then get started.

▶ Create a to-do list. Check off things as you get them done. Use the list to focus on the things that aren't getting done. Move them to the top of the next day's list, and make up your mind to do them. Working from a list will give you a feeling of accomplishment.

▶ Break big jobs into smaller steps. Tackle short, easy-to-accomplish tasks first.

▶ Promise yourself a reward for finishing the task, such as watching your favorite TV show or going to a sports event. For more substantial tasks, give yourself bigger and better rewards, for example a night out with friends at your favorite club or restaurant.

▶ Find a place to study that's comfortable and doesn't allow for distractions and interruptions. Say "No" to friends and family who want your attention, and agree to spend time with them later.

▶ Don't make or take phone calls, text message, e-mail, or surf the web during planned study sessions. If you study in your room, close your door.

If these ideas fail to sufficiently motivate you to get to work, you might want to reexamine your purposes, values, and priorities. Keep coming back to some basic questions. Why am I in college here and now? Why am I in this course? What is really important to me? Are these values important enough to forgo some temporary fun or laziness in order to get down to work? Are my academic goals really my own, or were they imposed on me by family members, my employer, or societal expectations? If you are not willing to stop procrastinating and get to work on the tasks at hand, perhaps you should reconsider why you are in college and if this is the right time to pursue higher education.

Researchers at Carleton University in Canada have found that college students who procrastinate in their studies also avoid confronting other tasks and problems and are more likely to develop unhealthy habits, such as higher alcohol consumption, smoking, insomnia, a poor diet, or lack of exercise.[2]

If you cannot get procrastination under control, it is in your best interest to seek help at your campus counseling service before you begin to feel as if you are also losing control over other aspects of your life.

Setting Priorities

To help combat the urge to procrastinate, you should think about how to prioritize your tasks, goals, and values. Which goals and objectives are most important to you and most consistent with your values? Which are the most urgent? For example, studying in order to get a good grade on tomorrow's test might have to take priority over attending a job fair today. However, don't ignore long-term goals in order to meet short-term goals. With good time management you can study during the week prior to the test so that you can attend the job fair the day before. One way that skilled time managers establish priorities is to maintain a to-do list (discussed in more detail later in this chapter), ranking the items on the list to determine schedules and deadlines for each task.

Another aspect of setting priorities while in college is finding an appropriate way to balance your academic schedule with the rest of your life. Social activities are an important part of the college experience. Similarly, time alone and time to think are essential to your overall well-being.

For many students, the greatest challenge of prioritizing will be balancing school with work and family obligations that are equally important and do not feel optional. If you have work or family obligations, you are becoming the norm, not the exception, in American colleges and universities. Good advanced planning will help you meet these challenges. But you will also need to talk with your family members and your employer to make sure that they understand your academic responsibilities. Most professors will work with you when conflicts arise, but if you have problems that can't be easily resolved, be sure to seek support from the professionals in your college's counseling center. They will understand your challenges and help you manage and prioritize your many responsibilities.

Write • DISCUSS • Compare • Ask • BLOG • Answer • *Journal*

> What are your most pressing obligations, other than your studies,
> that will have to fit into your time management plan? Are any of them
> more important to you than doing well in college? Why or why not?

[2]Timothy A. Pychyl & Fuschia M. Sirois. *Procrastination: Costs to Health and Well-being.* Presentation at the APA Convention, August 22, 2002, Chicago.

◀ **Some college students have to juggle taking care of children and pursuing a degree.**

© Erin Gilcrest

Staying Focused

Many of the decisions you make today are reversible. You can change your major, and your career and life goals can change as well. But it is important to take control of your life by establishing your own goals for the future, setting your priorities, and managing your time accordingly. Many first-year students, especially recent high school graduates, might temporarily forget their primary purposes for coming to college, lose sight of their goals, and spend their first term of college engaging in a wide array of new experiences. While this is okay to do within limits, some students spend the next four or five years trying to make up for poor decisions made early in their college careers, such as skipping class and not taking their assignments seriously, decisions that can lead to plummeting grade point averages (GPAs) and the threat of academic probation or, worse, academic dismissal. Staying focused means always keeping your eyes on your most important purposes for being in college. Ask yourself whether what you are doing at any moment contributes to, or detracts from, those purposes.

Many students, whether young or old, question their decision to attend college and might temporarily feel overwhelmed by the additional responsibilities of college. Prioritizing, rethinking some commitments, letting some things go, and weighing the advantages and disadvantages of attending school part-time versus full-time can help you work through this adjustment period. Again, keep your long-term goals in mind and find ways to manage your stress, rather than react to it. While this book is full of suggestions for enhancing academic success, the bottom line is to stay focused and take control of your time and your life. Make a plan that begins with your priorities: attending classes, studying, working, and spending time with the people who are important to you. Then think about the necessities of life: sleeping, eating, bathing, exercising, and relaxing. Leave time for fun things like talking with friends, watching TV, going out for the evening, and so forth. But finish what needs to be done before you move from work to pleasure. And don't forget about personal time. Depending on your personality and cultural background, you might require more or less time to be alone. If you live in a residence hall or share an apartment with other college students, talk with your roommates about how you can coordinate your class schedules so that you each have some privacy. If you live at home with your family, particularly if you are a parent, work together to create special family times as well as quiet study times.

Write • DISCUSS • Compare • Ask • BLOG • Answer • *Journal*

List your current priorities in order of importance. What does your list suggest about why you consider some things more important? Less important? Have you put any items in the wrong place? What should you change, and why?

Creating a Workable Class Schedule

As a first-year student, you might not have had much flexibility in determining your course schedule; by the time you were allowed to register for classes, some sections of the courses you needed might already have been closed. You also might not have known whether you would prefer taking classes back to back or giving yourself a break between classes.

How might you wisely use time between classes? This might have been your first opportunity to take classes that do not meet five days a week. Do you prefer spreading your classes over five or six days of the week, or would you like to go to class just two or thee days a week, or even once a week for a longer class period? Your attention span and other commitments should influence your decision. In the future, you might have more control over how you schedule your classes.

Write • DISCUSS • Compare • Ask • BLOG • Answer • *Journal*

Knowing what you know now about your schedule, what will you do differently next term? Will you try to schedule classes close together or spread them apart? Why?

Before you register, think about how to make your class schedule work for you—how you can create a schedule that allows you to use your time more efficiently. Also consider your own biorhythms by recognizing what part of the day or evening you are most alert and engaged.

Get Organized Using a Planner

In college, as in life, you will quickly learn that managing time is important to success. Almost all successful people use some sort of calendar or planner, either paper or electronic, to help them keep up with their appointments, assignments or tasks, and other important activities. Many campuses design and sell a calendar in the campus bookstore designed specifically for your school, with important dates and deadlines already provided. Or you might prefer to use the calendar that comes on your computer or PDA. Regardless of the format you prefer (electronic or hard copy), it's a good idea to begin the term by completing the term assignment preview (Figure 2.1). This is a template you can use to map your schedule for an entire term.

To use the term assignment preview, begin by entering all of your commitments for each week: classes, assignment due dates, work hours, family commitments, and so on. Examine your toughest weeks during the term. If paper deadlines and test dates fall during the same week, find time to finish some assignments early to free up study time for tests. Note this in your PDA or calendar. Break large assignments (like term papers) into smaller steps, such as choosing a topic, doing research, creating an outline, learning necessary computer skills, writing a first draft, and so on. Add deadlines in your term assignment preview for each of the smaller portions of the project. Breaking a large project into smaller steps is something you'll probably have to do for yourself. Most professors won't provide this level of detailed assistance for you.

After you complete the term assignment preview, enter important dates and notes from the preview sheets into your calendar or planner and continue to enter all due dates as soon as you know them. Write down meeting times and locations, scheduled social events (including phone numbers in case you need to cancel), study time for each class you're taking, and so forth. It's best not to rely solely on an electronic calendar. Keep a back-up copy on paper in case your PDA or computer crashes. It's also a good idea to carry your calendar or planner with you (just like your cell phone) in a place where you're not likely to lose it. Your first term of college is the time to get into the habit of using a planner to help you keep track of commitments and maintain control of your schedule. This practice will become invaluable to you in your career. Check your notes daily at the same time of day for the current week, as well as the coming week. It takes just a moment to be certain that you aren't forgetting something important, and it helps relieve stress.

Write • DISCUSS • Compare • Ask • BLOG • Answer • *Journal*

> What kind of planner do you currently use, if any? Does your method of planning work for you? Why or why not?

	Monday	Tuesday	Wednesday	Thursday	Friday
Week 1					
Week 2					
Week 3					
Week 4					

	Monday	Tuesday	Wednesday	Thursday	Friday
Week 5					
Week 6					
Week 7					
Week 8					

▲ **Figure 2.1** Term Assignment Preview. Using the course syllabi provided by your instructors, enter all due dates on this term calendar. For longer assignments, such as term papers, divide the task into smaller parts and establish your own deadline for each part of the assignment, such as deadlines for choosing a topic, completing your library research, developing an outline of the paper, writing a first draft, and so on.

	Monday	Tuesday	Wednesday	Thursday	Friday
Week 9					
Week 10					
Week 11					
Week 12					

	Monday	Tuesday	Wednesday	Thursday	Friday
Week 13					
Week 14					
Week 15					
Week 16					

▲ **Figure 2.1** (Continued)

Charting a Weekly Timetable

Now that you've created a term preview, the weekly timetable chart in Figure 2.2 can help you tentatively plan how to spend your hours in a typical week. Here are some tips for creating a weekly schedule:

▶ As you create your schedule, try to reserve at least 2 hours of study time for each hour spent in class. This universally accepted "two-for-one" rule reflects faculty members' expectations for how much work you should be doing to earn a good grade in their classes. This means that if you take a typical full-time class load of 15 credits, for example, you should plan to study an additional 30 hours per week. Think of this 45-hour-per-week commitment as comparable to a full-time job. If you are also working, reconsider how many hours per week it will be reasonable for you to be employed above and beyond this commitment, or consider reducing your credit load.

▶ Depending on your biorhythms, obligations, and potential distractions, decide whether you will study more effectively in the day or in the evening, or a combination of both. Determine whether you are capable of getting up very early in the morning to study, or how late you can stay up at night and still wake up for morning classes.

▶ All assignments are not equal. Estimate how much time you will need for each one, and begin your work early. A good time manager frequently finishes assignments before actual due dates to allow for emergencies.

Keep track of how much time it takes you to complete different kinds of tasks. For example, depending on your skills and interests, it might take longer to read a chapter in a biology text than one in a literature text. Keeping track of your time will help you estimate how much time to allocate for similar tasks in the future. How long does it really take you to complete a set of 20 math problems or to write up a chemistry lab? Use your weekly timetable to track how you actually spend your time for an entire week.

> *Write* • DISCUSS • Compare • Ask • BLOG • Answer • *Journal*
>
> What are the best and worst times for you to study, and why? Have you found a particular time when it's easier for you to concentrate or be creative?

Maintaining a To-Do List

Once you've plotted your future commitments with a term planner and decided how your time will be spent each week, you can stay on top of your obligations with a to-do list, which is especially handy for last-minute reminders. It can help you keep track of errands you need to run, appointments you need to make, e-mail messages you need to send, and so on—anything you're prone to forget. You can keep this list in your notebook or post it on your bulletin board. Some people start a new

	Sunday	Monday	Tuesday	Wednesday	Thursday	Friday	Saturday
6:00							
7:00							
8:00							
9:00							
10:00							
11:00							
12:00							
1:00							
2:00							
3:00							
4:00							
5:00							
6:00							
7:00							
8:00							
9:00							
10:00							
11:00							

▲ **Figure 2.2** Weekly Timetable. This chart has several uses. Using the suggestions in this chapter, create your perfect schedule for next term. Do you want your classes back-to-back or with breaks in between? How early in the morning are you willing to start classes? Do you prefer—or do work or family commitments require you—to take evening classes? Are there times of day when you are more alert? Less alert? How many days per week do you want to attend classes? At some institutions you can go to school full-time by exclusively attending classes on Saturday. Plan how you will spend your time for the coming week. Track all of your activities for a full week by entering into this schedule form everything you do and how much time each task requires. Use this record to help you estimate the time needed for similar activities in the future.

list every day or once a week. Others keep a running list, and only throw a page away when everything on the list is done. Whichever method you prefer, use your to-do list to keep track of all the tasks you need to remember, not just academics. You might want to develop a system for prioritizing the items on your list: highlight; different colors of ink; one, two, or three stars; or lettered tasks with A, B, C. As you complete each task, cross it off your list. You might be surprised by how much you have accomplished, and how good you feel about it.

▶ WHERE TO GO FOR HELP

On Campus

Academic Skills Center Along with assistance studying for exams, reading textbooks, and taking notes, your campus academic skills center has specialists in time management who can offer advice for your specific problems.

Counseling Center If your problems with time management involve emotional issues you are unable to resolve, consider visiting your school's counseling office.

Your Academic Advisor/Counselor If you have a good relationship with this person, he or she might be able to offer advice or to refer you to another person on campus, including those in the offices mentioned above.

A Fellow Student A friend who is a good student and willing to help you with time management can be one of your most valuable resources.

My Institution's Resources

_____

_____

_____

_____

_____

Organizing Your Day

Being a good student does not necessarily mean studying day and night and doing little else. Keep the following points in mind as you organize your day:

▶ Set realistic goals for your study time. Assess how long it takes to read a chapter in different types of textbooks and how long it takes you to review your notes from different instructors, and schedule your time accordingly. Give yourself adequate time to review and then test your knowledge when preparing for exams.

▶ Use waiting time (on the bus, before class, before appointments) to review.

▶ Prevent forgetting what you have learned by allowing time to review as soon as is reasonable after class. (Immediately after class might be possible, but not reasonable, if you are too burned out to concentrate!)

▶ Know your best times of day to study. Schedule other activities, such as laundry, e-mail, or spending time with friends, for times when it will be difficult to concentrate.

▶ Restrict repetitive, distracting, and time-consuming tasks like checking your e-mail, social-networking account, or cell phone to a certain time, not every hour.

▶ Avoid multitasking. Even though you might actually be quite good at it, or at least think that you are, the reality is that you will be able to study more effectively and retain more information if you concentrate on one task at a time.

▶ Be flexible. You cannot anticipate every disruption to your plans. Build extra time into your schedule so that unexpected interruptions do not prevent you from meeting your goals.

Making Sure Your Schedule Works for You

Consider what kind of class schedule will work best for you. If you live on campus, you might want to create a schedule that situates you near a dining hall at mealtimes or allows you to spend breaks between classes at the library. Or, you might need breaks in your schedule for relaxation, catching up with friends via e-mail or online social networking, or spending time in a student lounge, college union, or campus center. You might want to avoid returning to your residence hall room to take a nap between classes if the result might be feeling lethargic or oversleeping and missing later classes. Also, if you attend a large university, be sure that you allow adequate time to get from one class to another.

If you're a commuter student, or if you must carry a heavy workload in order to afford going to school, you might prefer to schedule your classes in blocks without breaks. However, while taking back-to-back classes allows you to cut travel time by attending school one or two days a week and might provide for more flexible scheduling of a job or family commitments, it can also have significant drawbacks. There is little time to process information or to study between classes.

When all your classes are scheduled in a block of time, you run several risks. If you become ill on a class day, you could fall behind in all of your classes. You might also become fatigued sitting in class after class. When one class immediately follows

◀ **Avoid multitasking so that your study time will be spent effectively.**

another, it will be difficult for you to have a last-minute study period immediately before a test because you will be attending another class and are likely to have no more than a 15-minute break. Finally, remember that for back-to-back classes, several exams might be held on the same day. Scheduling classes in blocks might work better if you have the option of attending lectures at alternative times in case you are absent, if you alternate classes with free periods, and if you seek out instructors who are flexible with due dates for assignments.

Don't Overextend Yourself

Being overextended is a primary source of stress for college students. Determine what a realistic workload is for you, but note that this can vary significantly from person to person. Although being involved in campus life is very important, don't allow your academic work to take a backseat to extracurricular activities or other time commitments. Do not take on more than you can handle. Learn to say "no." Do not feel obligated to provide a reason; you have the right to decline requests that will prevent you from getting your own work done.

Even with the best intentions, some students who use a time-management plan overextend themselves. If there is not enough time to carry your course load and meet your commitments, drop a course before the drop deadline so you won't have a low grade on your permanent record. If you receive financial aid, keep in mind that you must be registered for a minimum number of credit hours to be considered a full-time student and thereby maintain your current level of financial aid.

If dropping a course is not feasible, or if other activities are lower on your list of priorities, which is likely for most college students, assess your other time commitments and let go of one or more. Doing so can be very difficult, especially if you think that you are letting other people down. However, it is far preferable to excuse yourself from an activity in a way that is respectful to others than to fail to come through at the last minute because you have committed to more than you can possibly achieve.

Reducing Distractions

Where should you study? Some students find it's best not to study in places associated with leisure, such as the kitchen table, the living room, or in front of the TV, because these places lend themselves to interruptions and other distractions. Similarly, it might be unwise to study on your bed because you might drift off when you need to study or learn to associate your bed with studying and not be able to go to sleep when you need to. Instead, find quiet places, both on campus and at home, where you can concentrate and develop a study mind-set each time you sit down to do your work.

Try to stick to a routine as you study. The more firmly you have established a specific time and a quiet place to study, the more effective you will be in keeping up with your schedule. If you have larger blocks of time available on the weekend, for example, take advantage of that time to review or catch up on major projects, such as term papers, that can't be completed effectively in 50-minute blocks. Break down large tasks and take one thing at a time; you will make more progress toward your ultimate academic goals. Here are some more tips to help you deal with distractions:

▶ Turn off the TV, CD player, DVD, iPod, or radio, unless the background noise or music really helps you concentrate on your studies or drowns out more distracting noises (people laughing or talking in other rooms or hallways, for instance). Consider silencing your cell phone so you aren't distracted by incoming calls, or turn off your cell phone altogether so you aren't tempted to make calls or send text messages.

▶ Stay away from the computer if you're going to be tempted to check e-mail or a social networking site.

▶ Try not to let personal concerns interfere with studying. If necessary, call a friend or write in a journal before you start to study, and then put your worries away.

▶ Develop an agreement with your roommate(s) or family about quiet hours. If that's not possible, discover a quiet place where you can go to concentrate.

Respecting Others' Time

How does time management relate to respect? Think of the last time you made an appointment with someone who either forgot the appointment entirely or was very late. Were you upset or disappointed by the person for wasting your time? Most of us have experienced the frustration of having someone else disrespect our time. In college, if you repeatedly arrive late for class or leave before class periods have officially ended, you are breaking the basic rules of politeness, and you are intentionally or unintentionally showing a lack of respect for your instructors and your classmates.

At times, instructors might perceive certain behaviors to be inappropriate or disrespectful as a result of a cultural misunderstanding. All cultures view time differently. In American academic culture, punctuality is a virtue. This might be a difficult adjustment for someone raised in a culture that is more flexible in its approach to time, but it is important to recognize the values of the culture you have entered. Although you should not have to alter your cultural identity in order to be successful in college, you need to be aware of the expectations that faculty members typically place on students.

Be in class on time. Arrive early enough to shed your coat, shuffle through your backpack, and have your assignments, notebooks, and writing utensils ready to go. Likewise, be on time for scheduled appointments. Avoid behaviors that show a lack of respect for both the instructor and other students, such as leaving class to plug a parking meter or answer your cell phone, returning 5 or 10 minutes later, thus disrupting class twice. Similarly, doing homework for another class, falling asleep, or talking (even whispering) disrupt the class. Make adequate transportation plans in advance, get enough sleep at night, wake up early enough to be on time for class, and complete assignments prior to class.

Time management is a lifelong skill. Securing a better job after college will likely mean managing your own time and possibly that of other people you supervise. It is critical to understand the importance of demonstrating respect for others through your approach to managing your own time.

Managing Your Money

Just as the way you manage time is a reflection of what you most value, so is the way you manage money. Almost all college students have a fixed amount of money available to spend during any given month or term, but sticking to a fixed budget can be tough. So many students overspend their budgets by using credit cards. Some students get so overextended that they have to drop out of college and work to pay back their debts. In any case, overspending can cause significant stress and distract you from your academic work.

National surveys have found that most college students are worried about paying for college. But as you look at your classmates, you can assume that their financial situations vary. Some students have scholarships and financial aid, while others must work to pay their tuition; some have parents paying for their education. Many students work to pay bills and have spending money. Some might have student loans, car

Confessions of a College Student

Name: Drew Trimble

Age: 19

University: University of Kentucky

Hometown: Van Lear, KY

Major: Political Science and Communication

Favorite book(s): *Brave New World, The Fred Factor, Angels and Demons*

Favorite college course: Communication 101, Introduction to Communication

The person who inspires me the most or who I would most like to meet: Job of the Bible, a virtuous and kind man, who was subjected to a life of misery—everything the devil could throw at him—and emerged victorious.

Favorite way to relax: Sitting on front porches and running.

Your proudest moment or biggest accomplishment: My proudest moment occurred when a wrestler I trained and who has become like a brother to me won the Kentucky Middle School State Wrestling Championship.

Favorite food: Jolly Rancher Jelly Beans

Money management confession: I learned how to manage money from the mistakes of a friend, who was a compulsive shopper. When we ate lunch together, I noticed that she always put the bill on her credit card. At the mall she would put her numerous purchases on her card without even thinking. When I finally asked her where she got the money to pay for the food, clothes, and trips that she indulged in, she told me that she was thousands of dollars in debt and hoped someday to have a job that would allow her to pay it off. When I heard this, I convinced her to allow me to take her credit card and keep it in a safe place, and I promised myself never to let my credit get out of control. The good news is that she received some help from a family member, never asked me to return her card, and changed her spending habits. She is now a spokesperson for a major credit card company. It's funny how things work out.

payments, or credit card debt. For many students, graduating from college is a goal they can reach only with careful financial planning. It doesn't happen by chance or luck.

Write • DISCUSS • Compare • Ask • BLOG • Answer • *Journal*

> So far, how well or how poorly are you managing your money in college? Why is it difficult or easy?

Your Income and Expenses

Let's start by assessing your financial situation.

Earnings

▶ How much money is in your bank account?

▶ What is your approximate annual income?

▶ What other sources of support do you have?

Debt

▶ How much money do you owe, and at what interest rate?

▶ How much did your books, tuition, and fees cost this term?

▶ How much money have you spent on entertainment so far this month?

The Future

▶ When do you plan to graduate?

▶ How much do you expect your first salary to be after college?

▶ How much debt will you have when you graduate?

▶ How long will it take you to pay off your debt?

These questions address important issues that affect your short-term and long-term financial decisions. A smart money manager would know the answer to all of these questions or have records that would reveal the answers.

Navigating Financial Aid

Financial aid to help you pay for college comes from a number of sources, including federal and state financial aid programs, institutional grants, scholarships, jobs, and private agency funds. Most of this aid is awarded to students on the basis of a demonstrated financial need and/or recognition of some identifiable talent (such as top grades for an academic scholarship).

You should become familiar with the language and terms used by financial aid professionals on your campus so that you really understand what you're hearing, signing, or agreeing to do. Remember that although the financial aid office is there to serve you, you must become your own advocate. The following tips should help:

▶ File for financial aid every year. Even if you don't think you will receive aid for a certain year, you must file annually in case you become eligible in the future.

▶ Meet all filing deadlines. Financial aid is awarded from funds that are fixed. When the money has been awarded, there is usually none left for those who file late. Students who do not meet filing deadlines risk losing aid from one year to the next.

▶ Talk with your financial aid officer immediately if you or your family experience a significant loss (such as loss of a job or death of a parent or spouse). Don't wait for the next filing period; you might be eligible for funds for the current year.

▶ Inquire every year about criteria-based aid. Many colleges and universities have grants and scholarships for students who meet specific criteria. These might include grants for minority students, grants for students in specific academic majors, and grants for students of single parents. Sometimes a donor will give money to the school's scholarship fund for students meeting certain other criteria, even county or state of residence. Determine if any of these fit your circumstances.

▶ Inquire about campus jobs throughout the year as these jobs are not just available at the beginning of the term. If you do not have a job and want or need to work, keep asking. And remember that students who work on campus are more likely to graduate than students who work off campus.

▶ Consider asking for a reassessment. If you have reviewed your financial aid package and think that your circumstances deserve additional consideration, you can ask the financial aid office to reassess your eligibility. The office is not always required to do so, but the request might be worth your effort.

Budgeting

College is a time of new experiences and new freedoms. If you're like most students, your income will be limited, but you'll suddenly have more reasons to spend. Even though you're almost certain to be confronted with unexpected expenses and money shortages, you can learn to handle these new responsibilities by learning how to manage your finances.

Although managing a budget might sound complicated, it doesn't have to be. To manage your budget, you need to know your spending tendencies and learn how to create a budget that keeps track of your income and expenses.

Developing a Budget

Before you can develop a budget, you will need to track and begin to understand your spending habits. In college, you'll have many expenses that recur at regular intervals, such as tuition, books, fees, and room and board. Other expenses do not occur regularly; for example, the costs of entertainment and clothes are difficult to track. It's easy to say at the end of the month, "I have no idea where all my money went." That's why it's important to create a system for tracking your expenses, so you can plan for major events like spring break or study abroad. And because a budget is only as good as the person who keeps it, you not only need to work hard to develop an accurate, honest budgeting method, you need to stick to it.

Credit Cards, Debit Cards, and College

Many college students almost never write checks or pay for anything in cash. Instead, they use either credit or debit cards. While using credit and debit cards can make money management easier, you'll need to use these cards wisely in order to avoid financial trouble.

If you have not already been inundated with credit card offers, expect them to start rolling in. Credit card companies have significantly increased their marketing to college students over the past decade so that almost all college students have a credit card and many have multiple cards.

Credit card companies will wow you with fantastic offers. Retail chain stores offer their own cards and entice potential cardholders with 10 percent (or more) off your next purchase. It can be difficult to make these decisions when you are just learning how to manage your money and trying to establish a credit history at the same time.

Using a credit card is often viewed as an effective way to establish a positive credit history. But if you don't use the card wisely, you might owe more than you can afford to pay, damage your credit history, and create credit problems that are difficult to fix. Don't hold more credit cards than you can afford. A good rule of thumb is to not have more credit available to you than you can pay off in two months. Also, consider having only one widely accepted card, rather than several cards from a variety of retailers. Keeping your debt in one place will help you consolidate your payments and watch your spending.

By using a debit card rather than credit cards, you will restrict your spending to the amount of money in your bank account. However, since a debit card provides ready access to your bank account, it's important for you to keep your card in a safe place away from your personal identification number (PIN). The safest way to protect your account is to commit your PIN to memory. If you're afraid you'll forget your PIN, write it down and put it in a secure location.

Write • DISCUSS • Compare • Ask • BLOG • Answer • *Journal*

> Do you have a credit card? If not, what prevents you from getting one? If you do have a card or cards, do you feel that you're in control of the way you use it? Why or why not?

Ways to Stay Out of Financial Trouble

Many students have problems with finances during college. It's important to be committed to resolving those problems.

Protect Your Financial Information Would you leave $50 in cash in plain sight in your residence hall room with the door wide open? Most people would not be that trusting. It is equally important that you protect your other financial resources and information as if they were cash. Other people can steal and use your credit cards, debit cards, ATM cards and their numbers, Social Security number, bank statement, and checkbook. Keep them in a safe place out of public view. A simple way to help protect your credit or debit card is to write "picture ID required" under your signature. When salespeople check the signature, they should ask for a photo ID. If you lose one of your cards, call your bank immediately. If you have many cards, you might want to pay a small fee and join a credit card registry. If your purse or wallet is misplaced or stolen, this service will notify all of your credit card companies and request replacements.

Be Careful When Using ATM Cards These cards come with a PIN for security and protection, so keep your PIN secret. Do not use a number like your address, birth date, or phone number. People who know you might be able to guess the number.

Deal with Creditors Sooner Rather Than Later Do not put financial problems on the back burner. Debt will only get larger if you don't deal with it head-on. As soon as you begin to experience difficulties, contact your creditors to discuss why it is difficult for you to make payments. Most creditors will help you develop a more reasonable repayment plan. Don't wait until your creditors have turned your account over to a collection agency.

If you don't know what else to do, talk with someone you trust who understands your financial problems. Parents and relatives can be sources of good advice. On-campus financial counselors also might be available to you, or your financial aid office might be able to point you toward reputable people who can assist you.

Where To Go For **Help**

On Campus

Your Institution's Financial Aid Office Professionals in this office will help you understand financial aid opportunities and how to apply for scholarships.

Local United Way Office Many communities have credit counseling agencies within the local United Way.

Campus Programs Be on the lookout for special campus programs on money management. These programs are often offered in residence halls or through the division of student affairs.

The Business School or College Faculty or staff within a school or college of business sometimes offer a course in personal finance. Check your college catalogue, website, or call the business school office.

Counseling Center If money problems are related to compulsive shopping or gambling, your institution's counseling center can provide help.

My Institution's Resources

_____

_____

_____

_____

_____

_____

_____

▶▶▶ BUILDING YOUR PORTFOLIO
Credit Cards...A Slippery Slope!

Life was a lot simpler when what we honored was father
and mother rather than all major credit cards.

-Robert Orben (b. 1927), U.S. magician and comedy writer

To complete this portfolio activity electronically, please visit
academic.cengage.com/collsucc/Gardner/YCE8e.

Remember the saying "there is no free lunch"? That is a good maxim to keep in mind as you consider adding credit cards to your financial picture. Credit card companies often target college students with offers for a free T-shirt or discounts if they sign up for a new card. While it might seem harmless at the time, signing up for multiple credit cards can have you in financial trouble... and fast!

Let's take a look at one credit card offer available to college students and see just what the fine print has to say. Google "Student Visa Credit Card." You'll find many such cards offered. Pick one for your review.

1. Read all about it

   View the terms, conditions, and fees associated with a student Visa credit card offered to college students.

2. What does it all mean?

   a. What is the Annual Percentage Rate (APR) for purchases for this card?
   APR: _____%

   b. What is the APR or Transaction Fee for a bank or ATM cash advance for this card?
   Cash Advance: _____

   c. How long is the grace period for this card (the number of days between the statement closing date and the payment due date)?
   Grace Period: _____

   d. What would happen to the APR if you made a late payment, went over your credit limit, or made a payment that was not honored on this card?

   _____

Quick Reference

A big factor in effectively managing your credit card debt is being aware of the terms and fees that apply to each account you have. If you have credit cards (including gas cards and store credit cards such as a Gap or Sears Credit Card), find your last billing statement and make yourself a quick reference guide in your portfolio. Create a new entry in your portfolio for this activity with the title "Quick Reference." Record your work for this assignment there.

Card Issuer & Card Type	APR	Default APR	Due on:
Example: Bank of America Student Visa	18.25% variable	32.25 %	28th day of each month
Card 1:			
Card 2:			
Card 3:			

How We Learn

In this chapter YOU WILL LEARN:

▶ Many approaches to understanding your learning styles or preferences

▶ How learning styles and teaching styles often differ

▶ How to optimize your learning style in any classroom setting

▶ How to understand and recognize a learning disability

There are many ways to learn. What strategies do you use?

© Sam Pellissier/SuperStock

Tom Carskadon of Mississippi State University contributed his valuable and considerable expertise to the writing of this chapter.

How Do You LEARN?

A?B?C?A?B?C?A?B?C?

Read the following questions and choose the answer that most fits you.

1 *Do you know whether you learn better by seeing, hearing, reading, or working with your hands?*

(A) I haven't ever thought about this.

(B) Yes, I learned about my preferred learning style in another class.

(C) I think I know how I learn best, but I'm not really sure.

2 *Have you ever heard of the Myers-Briggs Type Indicator (MBTI)?*

(A) No, never. What does that do?

(B) Yes, I've completed the Myers-Briggs survey before and I know my MBTI type.

(C) Is it the same as the MBTI instrument that tells you about your personality? Then, maybe I do.

3 *Do you know how to utilize your learning style to do well in any class you take?*

(A) I really don't know what you're talking about.

(B) I know my own preferred learning style, but so far I've been able to adapt to any instructor and classroom situation.

(C) I know I don't learn well in big lecture classes. I'd much rather be in small classes where there is a lot of discussion. I really don't know exactly how I can learn in a big class where all I do is listen and take notes.

4 *If you were having trouble in your courses, especially with reading and taking exams, where would you go for help?*

(A) I'm too stubborn to get help—I'd probably fail first.

(B) I would visit the learning center on my campus to see if experts who work there could help me.

(C) I might go see my advisor or just tell my parents about it, but I'm not sure what else I would do.

5 *Do some of your courses require you to learn in different ways?*

(A) I never thought about it—I just go to class and take notes. I never do anything differently.

(B) Yes, definitely. Science and education courses use more hands-on learning. English and history courses are usually discussion or lecture style.

(C) I guess so—for some classes I only take notes, for others I participate in discussion.

Review your responses. (A) responses indicate that you haven't really thought about how you learn. This chapter will help you discover how to think about your learning strengths and preferences. (B) responses indicate that you have already thought clearly about how you learn best. You'll be able to increase your knowledge as you look at learning in different ways. (C) responses indicate that you are somewhat familiar with the idea of learning styles, but you can definitely benefit from more information so that you'll have a better idea of how you learn most effectively.

Have you ever thought about how you learn? People learn differently. This is hardly a novel idea, but in order for you to do well in college it is important that you become aware of your preferred way, or style, of learning. Experts agree that there is no one best way to learn.

Maybe you have trouble paying attention to a long lecture, or listening might be the way you learn best. You might love classroom discussion, or you might consider hearing what other students have to say in class a big waste of time.

Perhaps you have not thought about how college instructors, and even courses, have their own inherent styles, which can be different from your preferred style of learning. Many instructors rely almost solely on lecturing, and others use lots of visual aids such as PowerPoint outlines, charts, graphs, and pictures. In science courses, you will conduct experiments or go on field trips where you can observe or touch what you are studying; in dance, theater, or physical education, learning takes place in both your body and your mind. And in almost all courses, you'll learn by reading both textbooks and other materials. Some instructors are friendly and warm; others seem to want little interaction with students. It's safe to say that in at least some of your college courses, you won't find a close match between the way you learn most effectively and the way you're being taught. This chapter will help you first to understand how you learn best, and then to think of ways you can create a link between your style of learning and the expectations of each course and instructor.

There are many ways of thinking about and describing **learning styles**. Some of these will make a lot of sense to you; others might initially seem confusing or counterintuitive. Some learning style theories are very simple and others are far more complex. You will notice some overlap between the different theories, but using several of them might help you do a more precise job of discovering your learning style. If you are interested in reading more about learning styles, your library and your learning center will have many resources available to you.

Write • DISCUSS • Compare • Ask • BLOG • Answer • *Journal*

> Which of your current classes would you describe as your favorite?
> Do you think that your choice has anything to do with the
> instructor's teaching style? Why or why not?

In addition to its focus on learning styles, this chapter will also explore **learning disabilities**, which are very common among college students. You might know someone who has been diagnosed with a learning disability, such as dyslexia or attention deficit disorder. It is also possible that you have a special learning need and are not aware of it. This chapter seeks to increase your self-awareness and your knowledge about such challenges to learning. By reading this chapter, you will learn more about common types of learning disabilities, how to recognize them, and what to do if you or someone you know has a learning disability.

The VARK Learning Styles Inventory

The VARK focuses on how learners prefer to use their senses (hearing, seeing, writing, reading, or experiencing) to learn. The acronym VARK stands for "Visual," "Aural," "Read/Write," and "Kinesthetic." Visual learners prefer to learn information through charts, graphs, symbols, and other visual means. Aural learners prefer to hear information. Read/Write learners prefer to learn information that is displayed as words, and kinesthetic learners prefer to learn through experience and practice, whether simulated or real. To determine your learning style according to the VARK Inventory, respond to the questionnaire below.

The VARK Questionnaire
Version 7.0

This questionnaire is designed to tell you something about your preferences for the way you work with information. Choose the answer that best explains your preference. Check the box next to that item. Please select as many boxes as apply to you. If none of the response options apply to you, leave the item blank.

1. You are helping someone who wants to go to your airport, town center or railway station. You would:
   - ☐ a. go with her.
   - ☐ b. tell her the directions.
   - ☐ c. write down the directions (without a map).
   - ☐ d. draw, or give her a map.

2. You are not sure whether a word should be spelled 'dependent' or 'dependant'. You would:
   - ☐ a. see the words in your mind and choose by the way they look.
   - ☐ b. think about how each word sounds and choose one.
   - ☐ c. find it in a dictionary.
   - ☐ d. write both words on paper and choose one.

3. You are planning a holiday for a group. You want some feedback from them about the plan. You would:
   - ☐ a. describe some of the highlights.
   - ☐ b. use a map or website to show them the places.
   - ☐ c. give them a copy of the printed itinerary.
   - ☐ d. phone, text, or email them.

4. You are going to cook something as a special treat for your family. You would:
   - ☐ a. cook something you know without the need for instructions.
   - ☐ b. ask friends for suggestions.
   - ☐ c. look through the cookbook for ideas from the pictures.
   - ☐ d. use a cookbook where you know there is a good recipe.

5. A group of tourists want to learn about the parks or wildlife reserves in your area. You would:
   - ☐ a. talk about, or arrange a talk for them about parks or wildlife reserves.
   - ☐ b. show them Internet pictures, photographs or picture books.
   - ☐ c. take them to a park or wildlife reserve and walk with them.
   - ☐ d. give them a book or pamphlets about the parks or wildlife reserves.

6. You are about to purchase a digital camera or mobile phone. Other than price, what would most influence your decision?
   - ☐ a. Trying or testing it.
   - ☐ b. Reading the details about its features.
   - ☐ c. It is a modern design and looks good.
   - ☐ d. The salesperson telling me about its features.

7. Remember a time when you learned how to do something new. Try to avoid choosing a physical skill, (e.g., riding a bike). You learned best by:
   - ☐ a. watching a demonstration.
   - ☐ b. listening to somebody explaining it and asking questions.
   - ☐ c. diagrams and charts—visual clues.
   - ☐ d. written instructions—e.g., a manual or textbook.

8. You have a problem with your knee. You would prefer that the doctor:
   - ☐ a. gave you a web address or something to read about it.
   - ☐ b. used a plastic model of a knee to show what was wrong.
   - ☐ c. described what was wrong.
   - ☐ d. showed you a diagram of what was wrong.

9. You want to learn a new program, skill, or game on a computer. You would:
   - ☐ a. read the written instructions that came with the program.
   - ☐ b. talk with people who know about the program.
   - ☐ c. use the controls or keyboard.
   - ☐ d. follow the diagrams in the book that came with it.

10. I like websites that have:
    - ☐ a. things I can click on, shift, or try.
    - ☐ b. interesting design and visual features.
    - ☐ c. interesting written descriptions, lists, and explanations.
    - ☐ d. audio channels where I can hear music, radio programs, or interviews.

11. Other than price, what would most influence your decision to buy a new non-fiction book?
    - ☐ a. The way it looks is appealing.
    - ☐ b. Quickly reading parts of it.
    - ☐ c. A friend talks about it and recommends it.
    - ☐ d. It has real-life stories, experiences, and examples.

12. You are using a book, CD, or website to learn how to take photos with your new digital camera. You would like to have:
    - ☐ a. a chance to ask questions and talk about the camera and its features.
    - ☐ b. clear written instructions with lists and bullet points about what to do.

☐ c. diagrams showing the camera and what each part does.

☐ d. many examples of good and poor photos and how to improve them.

13. You prefer a teacher or a presenter who uses:

☐ a. demonstrations, models, or practical sessions.

☐ b. question and answer, talk, group discussion, or guest speakers.

☐ c. handouts, books, or readings.

☐ d. diagrams, charts, or graphs.

14. You have finished a competition or test and would like some feedback. You would like to have feedback:

☐ a. using examples from what you have done.

☐ b. using a written description of your results.

☐ c. from somebody who talks it through with you.

☐ d. using graphs showing what you had achieved.

15. You are going to choose food at a restaurant or cafe. You would:

☐ a. choose something that you have had there before.

☐ b. listen to the waiter or ask friends to recommend choices.

☐ c. choose from the descriptions in the menu.

☐ d. look at what others are eating or look at pictures of each dish.

16. You have to make an important speech at a conference or special occasion. You would:

☐ a. make diagrams or get graphs to help explain things.

☐ b. write a few key words and practice saying your speech over and over.

☐ c. write out your speech and learn from reading it over several times.

☐ d. gather many examples and stories to make the talk real and practical.

Source: www.vark-learn.com/english/index.asp

Scoring the VARK

Use the following scoring chart to find the VARK category that each of your answers corresponds to. Circle the letters that correspond to your answers. For example, if you answered b and c for question 3, circle V and R in the question 3 row.

Question	A category	B category	C category	D category
3	K	V	R	A

Scoring Chart

Question	A category	B category	C category	D category
1	K	A	R	V
2	V	A	R	K
3	K	V	R	A
4	K	A	V	R
5	A	V	K	R
6	K	R	V	A
7	K	A	V	R
8	R	K	A	V
9	R	A	K	V

Question	A category	B category	C category	D category
10	K	V	R	A
11	V	R	A	K
12	A	R	V	K
13	K	A	R	V
14	K	R	A	V
15	K	A	R	V
16	V	A	R	K

Count the number of each of the VARK letters you have circled to get your score for each VARK category.

Total number of **V**s circled =_____

Total number of **A**s circled =_____

Total number of **R**s circled =_____

Total number of **K**s circled =_____

Scoring VARK

Because you could choose more than one answer for each question, the scoring is not just a simple matter of counting. It is like four stepping stones across some water. Enter your scores **from highest to lowest** on the stones below, with their V, A, R, and K labels.

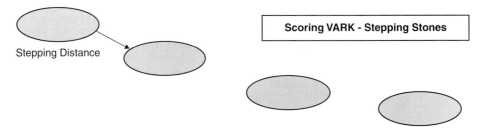

Stepping Distance

Scoring VARK - Stepping Stones

Your stepping distance comes from this table.

The total of my four VARK scores is -	My stepping distance is
16–21	1
22–27	2
28–32	3
More than 32	4

Follow these steps to establish your preferences.

1. Your first preference is always your highest score. Check that first stone as one of your preferences.

2. Now subtract your second highest score from your first. If that figure is larger than your stepping distance you have a *single preference*. Otherwise check this stone as another preference and continue with Step 3 below.

3. Subtract your third score from your second one. If that figure is larger than your stepping distance you have a *bi-modal preference*. If not, check your third stone as a preference and continue with Step 4 below.

4. Lastly, subtract your fourth score from your third one. If that figure is larger than your stepping distance you have a *tri-modal preference*. Otherwise, check your fourth stone as a preference and you have *all four modes as your preferences!*

Note: If you are bi-modal, tri-modal, or have checked all four modes as your preferences you can be described as *multi-modal* in your VARK preferences.

Write • DISCUSS • Compare • Ask • BLOG • Answer • *Journal*

> Did your VARK score surprise you at all? Did you know what type of learner you were before taking the test? If so, when did you discover this? How do you use your modality to your benefit?

Using VARK Results to Study More Effectively

How can knowing your VARK score help you do better in your college classes? Here are ways of using learning styles to develop your own study strategies:

▶ If you have a visual learning preference, underline or highlight your notes, use symbols, charts, or graphs to display your notes, use different arrangements of words on the page, and redraw your pages from memory.

▶ If you are an aural learner, talk with others to verify the accuracy of your lecture notes. Put your notes on tape and listen or tape class lectures. Read your notes out loud; ask yourself questions and speak your answers.

▶ If you have a read/write learning preference, write and rewrite your notes, and read your notes silently. Organize diagrams or flow charts into statements, and write imaginary exam questions and respond in writing.

▶ If you are a kinesthetic learner, you will need to use all your senses in learning—sight, touch, taste, smell, and hearing. Supplement your notes with real-world examples; move and gesture while you are reading or speaking your notes.

Kolb Inventory of Learning Styles

A learning model that is more complex than the VARK is the widely used and referenced Kolb Inventory of Learning Styles. While the VARK investigates how learners prefer to use their senses in learning, the Kolb Inventory focuses on abilities we need to develop in order to learn. This inventory, developed in the 1980s by David Kolb, is based on a four-stage cycle of learning (see Figure 3.1).

Confessions of a College Student

Name: Cristina B. Jimenez

Age: 27

College: Pima Community College

Hometown: Nogales Sonora, Mexico

Major: Education

Favorite books(s): *The Wretched of the Earth, Since Predator Came, Fantasies of the Master Race*

Favorite college course: American Heritage

The person who inspires me the most or who I would most like to meet: Ward Churchill; he is an inspiration to all of us who share Native American heritage.

Heroes: My heroes are all of those people who struggle every day to survive, those in a reservation living in extreme poverty and yet are happy and accomplish their goals.

Favorite way to relax: Running and playing with my dog.

Are you the first to go to college in your family? If so, what impact has that had on your experience? I am the first person to go to college in my family and am a great and positive influence to my nephews and nieces.

Favorite food: I am a vegan, which means I do not eat animals or animal derivate products.

My learning styles confession: I have two types of learning styles; I am a visual learner and a kinesthetic, according to the situation. I learn more when information is provided on graphics, PowerPoint presentations, or any other visual aids. This system works better for me in class. However, I also find myself a kinesthetic learner because when I study for a test I need to divide my time, 20 minutes studying and 10 minutes either watching television or listening to music. This helps me retain more information.

According to Kolb, effective learners need four kinds of abilities: *concrete experience* abilities, which allow them to immerse themselves in new experiences; *reflective observation* abilities, which help them to reflect on their experiences from many perspectives; *abstract conceptualization* abilities, which help them integrate observations into logically sound theories; and *active experimentation* abilities, which enable them to make decisions, solve problems, and test what they have learned in new situations.

Kolb's inventory of learning styles measures differences along the two basic dimensions of *abstract-concrete* and *active-reflective* and divides learners into four discrete groups: *divergers, assimilators, convergers,* and *accommodators* (see Figure 3.1). Doing well in college will require that you adopt some behaviors characteristic of each of these four styles. Some of them might be uncomfortable for you, but that discomfort will indicate that you're growing, stretching, and not relying on the learning style that might be easiest or most natural (Kolb, 1981).

If you are a diverger, you are adept at reflecting on situations from many viewpoints. You excel at brainstorming, and you're imaginative, people oriented, and

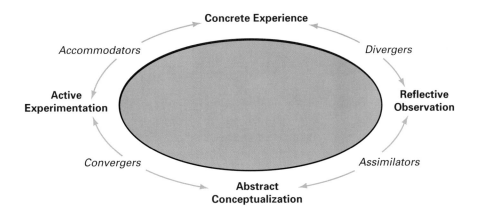

◀ **Figure 3.1**
The Experiential Learning Model. Adapted from Kolb, 1981.

sometimes emotional. On the downside, you sometimes have difficulty making decisions. Divergers tend to major in the humanities or social sciences.

If you are an assimilator, you like to think about abstract concepts. You are comfortable in classes where the instructor lectures about theoretical ideas without relating the lectures to real-world situations. Assimilators often major in math, physics, or chemistry.

If you are a converger, you like the world of ideas and theories, but you also are good at thinking about how to apply those theories to real-world, practical situations. You differ from divergers by your preference for tasks and problems rather than social and interpersonal issues. Convergers tend to choose health-related and engineering majors.

If you are an accommodator, you prefer hands-on learning. You are skilled at making things happen, and you rely on your intuition. You like people, but you can be pushy and impatient at times, and you might use trial and error, rather than logic, to solve problems. Accommodators often major in business, especially in marketing or sales.[1]

Write • DISCUSS • Compare • Ask • BLOG • Answer • *Journal*

> Based on the descriptions we have provided here, where do you see yourself in the Kolb Inventory? Are you more like a diverger, assimilator, converger, or accommodator? How can you use this knowledge in your courses?

In all your classes, but especially in liberal arts and social science courses, you will need to develop the strengths of divergers—imagination, brainstorming, and listening with an open mind. The abilities that are characteristic of assimilators, developing theories and concepts, are valuable for all students, especially those in the sciences. If you major in the health sciences or in engineering, you'll routinely practice the skills of convergers—experimenting with new ideas and choosing the best solution. Finally, whatever your major and ultimate career, you'll need to get things done, take some risks, and become a leader—skills that are characteristic of accommodators.

---

[1] Adapted from David A. Kolb, "Learning Styles and Disciplinary Differences," in *The Modern American College*, ed. Arthur W. Chickering, 232–55 (San Francisco: Jossey Bass, 1981).

WIRED WINDOW

IF YOU SCORED as having an aural, visual, or read/write preference on the VARK, you can use technology to enhance how you learn course material. Students with an aural preference can use a digital recorder or micro cassette recorder to record lectures and then listen to them again later. If you have an iPod, you can purchase a microphone attachment that allows you to use it as a digital audio recorder. Make sure that you have your professors' permission to record their lectures. In addition to recording lectures, you can find supplemental course material through podcasts and via iTunes. A number of universities provide podcasts for many of their courses for free on iTunes. You can browse through course offerings in the iTunesU section or you can search for a term in the iTunes store

and limit it to iTunesU results. Try searching the web to find podcasts and audio files to help you enhance your knowledge of a certain topic. (Hint: try searching for a specific subject and the word "podcast." For instance, you might search "Introduction to Philosophy podcast.") Once you have found the podcasts, you can download them in the sequence arranged by the podcaster, or download the ones that will supplement material for your course. As with other digital files, create a filing system that allows you to find them easily on your iPod or your computer when you need to review the material again later. When searching the web for supplemental audio, review the nine Cs for evaluating Internet sources found in Chapter 10.

▶ **Lecture classes require that you develop your listening and note-taking skills.**

© Bill Aron/PhotoEdit

The Myers-Briggs Type Indicator

One of the best known and most widely used personality inventories that can also be used to describe learning styles is the Myers-Briggs Type Indicator or MBTI. While the VARK measures your preferences for using your senses to learn and the Kolb Inventory focuses on learning abilities, the MBTI investigates basic personality characteristics and how those relate to human interaction and learning. The MBTI was created by Isabel Briggs Myers and her mother, Katharine Cook Briggs. The inventory identifies and measures psychological type as developed in the personality theory of Carl Gustav Jung, the great twentieth-century psychoanalyst. The MBTI is given to several million people around the world each year. Employers often use this test to give employees insight into how they perceive the world, go about making decisions, and get along with other people. Many first-year seminar or college success courses also include a focus on the MBTI because it provides a good way to begin a dialogue about human interaction and how personality type affects learning. All the psychological types described by the MBTI are normal and healthy; there is no good or bad or right or wrong—people are simply different. When you complete the Myers-Briggs survey instrument, your score represents your "psychological type"—the combination of your preferences on four different scales. These scales measure how you take in information and how you then make decisions or come to conclusions about that information. Each preference has a one-letter abbreviation. The four letters together make up your type. Although this book doesn't include the actual survey instrument, you will find a description of the basic MBTI types below. Which one sounds most like you?

Extraversion (E) vs. Introversion (I): The Inner or Outer World

The E-I preference indicates whether you direct your energy and attention primarily toward the outer world of people, events, and things or the inner world of thoughts, feelings, and reflections.

Extraverts tend to be outgoing, gregarious, and talkative. They often think "with the volume on," saying out loud what is going through their minds. They are energized by people and activity, and they seek this in both work and play. They are people of action, who like to spend more time doing things than thinking about them. At their best, they are good communicators who are quick to act and lead. However, they might seem to talk too much and too loudly, drowning out others, or acting before they think. (Note that when using the term in the context of psychological type and the MBTI, "extravert" is spelled with an "a" and not an "o," even though the latter is the more common spelling.)

Introverts prefer to reflect carefully on things and think them through before taking action. They think a lot, but if you want to know what's on their minds, you might have to ask them. They are refreshed by quiet and privacy. At their best, introverts are good, careful listeners whose thoughts are deep and whose actions are well considered. On the other hand, they might seem too shy and not aware enough of the people and situations around them, or they can think about things so long that they neglect to actually start doing them.

Sensing (S) vs. Intuition (N): Facts or Ideas

The S-N preference indicates how you perceive the world and take in information: directly, through your five senses, versus indirectly, by using your intuition.

Sensing types are interested above all in the facts, what is known and what they can be sure of. Typically they are practical, factual, realistic, and down-to-earth. They can be very accurate, steady, precise, patient, and effective with routine and details. They are often relatively traditional and conventional. They dislike unnecessary complication, and they prefer to practice skills they already know. At their best, sensing types can be counted on to do things right, taking care of every last detail. However, they can plod along while missing the point of why they are doing what they do, not seeing the forest (the whole picture) for the trees (the details).

Intuitive types are fascinated by possibilities—not so much the facts themselves, but what those facts mean, what concepts might describe those facts, how those might relate to other concepts, and what the implications of the facts would be. Intuitive types are less tied to the here and now and tend to look further into the future and the past. They need inspiration and meaning for what they do, and they tend to work in bursts of energy and enthusiasm. Often they are original, creative, and nontraditional. They can have trouble with routine and details, however, and they would rather learn a new skill than keep practicing the one they have already mastered. They can exaggerate facts sometimes without realizing it. At their best, intuitive types are bright, innovative people who thrive in academic settings and the world of invention and ideas, although they can also be impractical dreamers whose visions fall short because of inattention to detail.

Thinking (T) vs. Feeling (F): Logic or Values

The T-F preference indicates how you prefer to make your decisions: through logical, rational analysis, or through your subjective values, likes, and dislikes.

Thinking types are usually logical, rational, analytical, and critical. They pride themselves on reasoning their way to the best possible decisions. They tend to decide things relatively impersonally and objectively, and they are less swayed by feelings and emotions—both their own and other people's. In fact, other people's feelings sometimes puzzle or surprise them. They can deal with interpersonal disharmony and can be firm and assertive when they need to be. In all of their dealings, they need and value fairness. At their best, thinking types are firm, fair, logical, and just.

© Lisa Peardon/Getty Images

◀ **Compatibility of personality types can bring people together in social settings.**

On the other hand, they can seem cold, insensitive to other people's feelings, and overly blunt and hurtful in their criticisms.

Feeling types are typically warm, empathic, sympathetic, and interested in the happiness of others as well as themselves. They need and value harmony, and they can become distressed and distracted by argument and conflict. They sometimes have trouble being assertive when it would be appropriate to do so. Above all, they need and value kindness. At their best, feeling types are warm, affirming, and facilitate cooperation and goodwill among those around them while pursuing the best human values. However, feeling types can be illogical, emotionally demanding, reluctant to tackle unpleasant tasks, and unaffected by objective reason and evidence.

Judging (J) vs. Perceiving (P): Organization or Adaptability

The J-P preference indicates how you characteristically approach the outside world: by making decisions and judgments or by observing and perceiving instead.

Judging types approach the world in a planned, orderly, organized way; they try to order and control their part of it as much as possible. They make their decisions relatively quickly and easily because they like to make and follow plans. They are usually punctual and tidy, and they appreciate those traits in others. At their best, judging types are natural organizers who get things done and done on time. However, judging types might jump to conclusions prematurely, be too judgmental of people, make decisions too hastily without enough information, and have trouble changing their plans even when those plans are not working.

Perceiving types don't try to control their world, as much as adapt to it. Theirs is a flexible, wait-and-see approach. They deal comfortably and well with changes, unexpected developments, and emergencies, adjusting their plans and behaviors as needed. They tend to delay decisions so that they can keep their options open and gather more information. They might procrastinate to a serious degree, however, and they can try to juggle too many things at once, without finishing any of them. At their best, perceiving types are spontaneous, flexible individuals who roll with the punches and find ways to take the proverbial lemons in life and turn them into lemonade. On the other hand, perceiving types can be messy, disorganized procrastinators.

How to Use Your Strongest—and Weakest—Preferences

Because there are two possible choices for each of four different preferences, there are 16 possible psychological types. No matter what your Myers-Briggs type, all components of personality have value in the learning process. The key to success in college, therefore, is to use all of the attitudes and functions (E, I, S, N, T, F, J, and P) in their most positive sense. As you go about your studies, here is a system we recommend:

1. Sensing: Get the facts. Use sensing to find and learn the facts. How do we know facts when we see them? What is the evidence for what is being said?

2. Intuition: Get the ideas. Now use intuition to consider what those facts mean. Why are those facts being presented? What concepts and ideas are being supported by those facts? What are the implications? What is the big picture?

3. Thinking: Critically analyze. Use thinking to analyze the pros and cons of what is being presented. Are there gaps in the evidence? What more do we need to know? Do the facts really support the conclusions? Are there alternative explanations? How well does what is presented hang together logically? How could our knowledge of it be improved?

4. Feeling: Make informed value judgments. Why is this material important? What does it contribute to people's good? Why might it be important to you personally? What is your personal opinion about it?

5. Introversion: Think it through. Before you take any action, carefully review everything you have encountered so far.

6. Judging: Organize and plan. Don't just dive in! Now is the time to organize and plan your studying so you will learn and remember everything you need to. Don't just plan in your head, either; write your plan down, in detail.

7. Extraversion: Take action. Now that you have a plan, act on it. Do whatever it takes. Create note cards, study outlines, study groups, and so on. If you are working on a paper, now is the time to start writing.

8. Perceiving: Change your plan as needed. Be flexible enough to change your plan if it isn't working. Expect the unexpected and deal with the unforeseen. Don't give up the whole effort the minute your original plan stops working. Figure out what's wrong, and come up with another, better plan and start following that.[2]

[2] Isabel Briggs Myers, *Introduction to Type, 6th ed.* (Palo Alto, CA: CPP, Inc., 1998).

◄ College can introduce you to many different MBTI types and can teach you how to work alongside all of them.

Multiple Intelligences

Another way of measuring how we learn is the theory of *multiple intelligences*, developed in 1983 by Dr. Howard Gardner, a professor of education at Harvard University. Gardner's theory is based on the premise that the traditional notion of human intelligence is very limited. He proposes eight different intelligences to describe how humans learn.

As you might imagine, Gardner's work is controversial because it questions our longstanding definitions of intelligence. Gardner argues that students should be encouraged to develop the abilities they have and that evaluation should measure all forms of intelligence, not just linguistic and logical-mathematical.

As you think of yourself and your friends, what kinds of intelligences do you have? Do college courses measure all the ways that you are intelligent? Here is a short inventory that will help you recognize your multiple intelligences.

Multiple Intelligences Inventory

According to Gardner, all human beings have at least eight different types of intelligence. Depending on your background and age, some intelligences are likely to be more developed than others. This activity will help you find out what your intelligences are. Knowing this, you can work to strengthen the other intelligences that you do not use as often.

Put a check mark next to the items that apply to you.

Verbal/Linguistic Intelligence

_____ I enjoy telling stories and jokes.
_____ I have a good memory for trivia.
_____ I enjoy word games (for example, _Scrabble_ and puzzles),
_____ I read books just for fun.
_____ I am a good speller (most of the time).
_____ In an argument, I tend to use put-downs or sarcasm.
_____ I like talking and writing about my ideas.
_____ If I have to memorize something, I create a rhyme or saying to help me remember.
_____ If something breaks and won't work, I read the instruction book before I try to fix it.
_____ When I work with others in a group presentation, I prefer to do the writing and library research.

Visual/Spatial Intelligence

_____ I prefer a map to written directions.
_____ I daydream a lot.
_____ I enjoy hobbies such as photography.
_____ I like to draw and create.
_____ If I have to memorize something, I draw a diagram to help me remember.
_____ I like to doodle on paper whenever I can.
_____ In a magazine, I prefer looking at the pictures rather than reading the text.
_____ In an argument, I try to keep my distance, keep silent, or visualize some solution.
_____ If something breaks and won't work, I tend to study the diagram of how it works.
_____ When I work with others in a group presentation, I prefer to draw all the pictures.

Musical/Rhythmic Intelligence

_____ I enjoy listening to CDs and the radio.
_____ I tend to hum to myself when working.
_____ I like to sing.
_____ I play a musical instrument quite well.
_____ I like to have music playing when doing homework or studying.
_____ If I have to memorize something, I try to create a rhyme about the event.
_____ In an argument, I tend to shout or punch, or move in some sort of rhythm.
_____ I can remember the melodies of many songs.
_____ If something breaks and won't work, I tend to tap my fingers to a beat while I figure it out.
_____ When I work with others in a group presentation, I prefer to put new words to a popular tune or use music.

Logical/Mathematical Intelligence

_____ I really enjoy my math class.
_____ I like logical math puzzles or brain teasers.
_____ I find solving math problems to be fun.
_____ If I have to memorize something, I tend to place events in a logical order.
_____ I like to find out how things work.
_____ I enjoy computer and math games.
_____ I love playing chess, checkers, or Monopoly.
_____ In an argument, I try to find a fair and logical solution.
_____ If something breaks and won't work, I look at the pieces and try to figure out how it works.
_____ When I work with others in a group presentation, I prefer to create the charts and graphs.

Bodily/Kinesthetic Intelligence

_____ My favorite class is gym because I like sports.
_____ I enjoy activities such as woodworking, sewing, and building models.
_____ When looking at things, I like touching them.
_____ I have trouble sitting still for any length of time.
_____ I use a lot of body movements when talking.
_____ If I have to memorize something, I write it out a number of times until I know it.
_____ I tend to tap my fingers or play with my pencil during class.
_____ In an argument, I tend to strike out and hit or run away.
_____ If something breaks and won't work, I tend to play with the pieces to try to fit them together.
_____ When I work with others in a group presentation, I prefer to move the props around, hold things up, or build a model.

Interpersonal Intelligence

_____ I get along well with others.
_____ I like to belong to clubs and organizations.
_____ I have several very close friends.
_____ I like to teach other students.
_____ I like working with others in groups.
_____ Friends ask my advice because I seem to be a natural leader.
_____ If I have to memorize something, I ask someone to quiz me to see if I know it.
_____ In an argument, I tend to ask a friend or some person in authority for help.
_____ If something breaks and won't work, I try to find someone who can help me.
_____ When I work with others, I like to help organize the group's efforts.

(From www.ldrc.ca/projects/miinventory/mitest.html)

Intrapersonal Intelligence

_____ I like to work alone without anyone bothering me.

_____ I like to keep a diary.

_____ I like myself (most of the time).

_____ I don't like crowds.

_____ I know my own strengths and weaknesses.

_____ I find that I am strong willed, independent, and don't follow the crowd.

_____ If I have to memorize something, I tend to close my eyes and feel the situation.

_____ In an argument, I will usually walk away until I calm down.

_____ If something breaks and won't work, I wonder if it's worth fixing.

_____ When I work with others in a group presentation, I like to contribute something that is uniquely mine, often based on how I feel.

Naturalist Intelligence

_____ I am keenly aware of my surroundings and of what goes on around me.

_____ I love to go walking in the woods and looking at the trees and flowers.

_____ I enjoy gardening.

_____ I like to collect things like rocks, sports cards, and stamps.

_____ I like to get away from the city and enjoy nature.

_____ If I have to memorize something, I tend to organize it into categories.

_____ I enjoy learning the names of living things in our environment, such as flowers and trees.

_____ In an argument, I tend to compare my opponent to someone or something I have read or heard about and react accordingly.

_____ If something breaks down, I look around me to try and see what I can find to fix the problem.

_____ When I work with others in a group presentation, I prefer to organize and classify the information into categories so it makes sense.

A verbal/linguistic learner likes to read, write, and tell stories, and is good at memorizing information. A logical/mathematical learner likes to work with numbers, and is good at problem solving and logical processes. A visual/spatial learner likes to draw and play with machines and is good at puzzles and reading maps and charts. A bodily/kinesthetic learner likes to move around and is good at sports, dance, and acting. A musical/rhythmic learner likes to sing and play an instrument, and is good at remembering melodies and noticing pitches and rhythms. An interpersonal learner likes to have many friends and is good at understanding people, leading others, and mediating conflicts. Intrapersonal learners like to work alone, understand themselves well, and are original thinkers. A naturalistic learner likes to be outside and is good at preservation, conservation, and organizing a living area.

You can use your intelligences to help you make decisions about a major, choose activities, and investigate career options. Which of these eight intelligences best describes you?

TOTAL SCORE

_____ Verbal/Linguistic

_____ Logical/Mathematical

_____ Visual/Spatial

_____ Bodily/Kinesthetic

_____ Musical/Rhythmic

_____ Interpersonal

_____ Intrapersonal

_____ Naturalist

Add the number of check marks you made in each section. Your score for each intelligence will be a number between 1 and 10. Note your high scores of 7 or more in order to get a sense of your own multiple intelligences.

Write • DISCUSS • Compare • Ask • BLOG • Answer • _Journal_

Do you agree with Howard Gardner that there are eight styles of learning? Why or why not?

When Learning Styles and Teaching Styles Conflict

Educators who study learning styles maintain that instructors tend to teach in ways that conform to their own particular styles of learning. So, an introverted instructor who prefers abstract concepts and reflection (an assimilator, according to Kolb) and learns best in a read/write mode or aural mode, will probably structure the course in a lecture format with little opportunity for either interaction or visual and kinesthetic learning. Conversely, an instructor who needs a more interactive, hands-on environment will likely involve students in discussion and learning through experience.

Do you enjoy listening to lectures or do you find yourself gazing out the window or dozing? When your instructor assigns a group discussion, what is your immediate reaction? Do you dread talking with other students, or is that the way you learn best? How do you react to lab sessions when you have to conduct an actual experiment? Is this an activity you look forward to or one that you dread? Each of these learning situations appeals to some students more than others, but each is inevitably going to be part of your college classes. Your college or university has intentionally designed courses for you to have the opportunity to listen to professors who are experts in their field, interact with other students in structured groups, and learn through doing. Because these are all important components of your college education, it's important for you to make the most of each situation.

When you recognize a mismatch between how you best learn and how you are being taught, it is important that you take control of your learning process. Don't depend on the instructor or the classroom environment to give you everything you need to maximize your learning. Employ your own unique preferences, talents, and abilities to develop many different ways to study and retain information. Look back through this chapter to remind yourself of the ways that you can use your own learning styles to be more successful in any class you take.

Learning with a Disability

While everyone has a learning style, a portion of the population has what is characterized as a learning disability. Learning disabilities are usually recognized and diagnosed in grade school, but occasionally students can successfully compensate for a learning problem and reach college without having been properly diagnosed or assisted.

Learning disabilities affect people's ability to interpret what they see and hear or to link information across different parts of the brain. These limitations can show up as specific difficulties with spoken and written language, coordination, self-control, or attention. Such difficulties can impede learning to read, write, or do math. The term *learning disability* broadly covers a pool of possible causes, symptoms, treatments, and outcomes. Because of this, it is difficult to diagnose or pinpoint the causes. The types of learning disability that most commonly affect college students are attention disorders and those that affect the development of academic skills, including developmental reading, writing, and mathematics disorders.

Attention Disorders

Attention disorders are common in children, adolescents, and adults. Some students who have attention disorders appear to daydream excessively, and once you get their attention, they can be easily distracted. Individuals with either attention deficit disorder (ADD) or attention deficit hyperactivity disorder (ADHD) often have trouble organizing tasks or completing their work. They don't seem to listen to or follow directions, and their work might be messy or appear careless. Attention disorders, with or without hyperactivity, are not considered learning disabilities in themselves. However, because attention problems can seriously interfere with academic performance, they often accompany academic skills disorders.

If you have trouble paying attention or getting organized, you won't really know if you have ADD or ADHD until you are evaluated. Check out resources on campus or in the community. After you have been evaluated, follow the advice you get, which might or might not mean taking medication. If you do receive a prescription for medication, be sure to take it according to the physician's directions. In the meantime, if you're having trouble getting and staying organized, whether or not you have an attention disorder, you can improve your focus through your own behavioral choices. The National Institutes of Mental Health offer the following suggestions for adults with attention disorders (found on their website):

> ADHD adults can learn how to organize their lives by using "props"—a large calendar posted where it will be seen in the morning, date books, lists, reminder notes. They can have a special place for keys, bills, and the paperwork of everyday life. Tasks can be organized into sections, so that completion of each part can give a sense of accomplishment. Above all, ADHD adults should learn as much as they can about their disorder. (**www.nimh.nih.gov/publicat/adhd.cfm#simple.** Updated 10/26/06)

Cognitive Learning Disabilities

Other learning disabilities are related to cognitive skills. Dyslexia, for example, is a widespread developmental reading disorder. A person can have problems with any of the tasks involved in reading. However, scientists have found that a significant number of people with dyslexia share an inability to distinguish or separate the sounds in spoken words. For instance, dyslexic individuals sometimes have difficulty assigning the appropriate sounds to letters, either individually or when letters combine to form words. However, there is more to reading than recognizing words. If the brain is unable to form images or relate new ideas to those stored in memory, the reader can't understand or remember the new concepts. So other types of reading disabilities can appear when the focus of reading shifts from word identification to comprehension.

Writing, too, involves several brain areas and functions. The brain networks for vocabulary, grammar, hand movement, and memory must all be in good working order. So a developmental writing disorder might result from problems in any of these areas. Someone who can't distinguish the sequence of sounds in a word will often have problems with spelling. Persons with writing disabilities, particularly expressive language disorders (the inability to express oneself using accurate language or sentence structure), are often unable to compose complete, grammatical sentences.

▶ **Anyone can have a learning disability.**

A student with a developmental arithmetic disorder will have difficulty recognizing numbers and symbols, memorizing facts such as the multiplication table, aligning numbers, and understanding abstract concepts such as place value and fractions.

You can ask yourself some additional questions to help you determine whether you or someone you know has a learning disability. Do you perform poorly on tests even when you feel you have studied and are capable of performing better? Do you have trouble spelling words? Do you work harder than your fellow classmates at basic reading and writing? Do your instructors tell you that your performance in class is inconsistent, such as answering questions correctly in class but incorrectly on a written test? Do you have a really short attention span, or do your parents or instructors say that you do things without thinking? While responding "yes" to any of these questions does not mean that you have a disability, the resources of your campus learning center, office of special needs, or the student disabilities office can help you address any potential problems and devise ways to learn more effectively.

Most importantly, anyone who is diagnosed with a learning disability is in very good company. Magic Johnson, Jay Leno, Whoopi Goldberg, Tom Cruise, Cher, and Danny Glover are just a few of the famous and successful people who have diagnosed learning disabilities. A final important message: A learning disability is a learning difference, but is in no way related to intelligence. Having a learning disability is not a sign that you are dumb. In fact, some of the most intelligent individuals in human history have had a learning disability.

WHERE TO GO FOR HELP

On Campus

To learn more about learning styles and learning disabilities, talk to your first-year seminar instructor about campus resources. Most campuses will have a learning center or a center for students with disabilities. You might also find that instructors in the areas of education or psychology have a strong interest in the processes of learning. Finally, don't forget your library or the Internet. A great deal of published information is available to describe how we learn.

Books

Learning Outside the Lines *Two Ivy League Students with Learning Disabilities and ADHD Give You the Tools for Academic Success and Educational Revolution*, by Edward M. Hallowell (Foreword), Jonathan Mooney, and David Cole. New York: Fireside, 2000.

Survival Guide for College Students with ADD or LD, by Kathleen G. Nadeau. Washington, DC: Magination Press, 1994.

ADD and the College Student *A Guide for High School and College Students with Attention Deficit Disorder*, by Patricia O. Quinn, MD, ed. Washington, DC: Magination Press, 2001.

Online

LD Pride www.ldpride.net/learningstyles.MI.htm. This site was developed in 1998 by Liz Bogod, an adult with learning disabilities. It provides general information about learning styles and learning disabilities and offers an interactive diagnostic tool to determine your learning style.

Support 4 Learning www.support4learning.org.uk/education/learning_styles.cfm. This site is supported by HERO, Higher Education and Research Opportunities, which is the official online gateway to UK universities, colleges, and research organizations. The site provides learning style inventories and helpful hints about how to use your learning style to do well in college courses.

National Center for Learning Disabilities www.ncld.org. This is the official website for the National Center for Learning Disabilities. The site provides a variety of resources on diagnosing and understanding learning disabilities.

My Institution's Resources

_____

_____

_____

_____

_____

_____

_____

_____

_____

_____

_____

_____

▶▶▶ BUILDING YOUR PORTFOLIO
Are We on the Same Page?

It is what we think we know already that often prevents us from learning.

-Claude Bernard (1813-1878), French physiologist

To complete this portfolio activity electronically, please visit
academic.cengage.com/collsucc/Gardner/YCE8e.

Option 1: Complete the VARK (Visual, Aural, Read/Write, and Kinesthetic) Learning Styles Questionnaire in Chapter 3 and record your scores here.

My VARK Scores

Responses marked letter a = _____ (Visual)   Responses marked letter c = _____ (Read/Write)

Responses marked letter b = _____ (Aural)   Responses marked letter d = _____ (Kinesthetic)

Total Responses = _____

Using the guidelines in the textbook, do you have a strong or a weak learning preference, or are you multi-modal?

Now that you know more about your learning preferences, create a new entry in your portfolio with the title "My VARK Scores." For this entry, write yourself a brief letter to revisit as you begin your second term of college. In this letter, reflect on what you recognize to be your learning preferences and areas that you would like to improve. Be specific in noting the goals you have for using or adapting your learning styles to make the most of your academic experience. Encourage yourself to begin the new term with an open mind and confidence that you can adapt to many different types of learning environments.

Option 2: After reading about the Myers-Briggs Type Indicator in Chapter 3, do you have a guess as to what type you are? Place a check mark beside each type that you think best fits your personality.

E or I I think I am an Extravert _____ Introvert _____	**T or F** I think I am Thinking _____ Feeling _____
S or N I think I am Sensing _____ Intuition _____	**J or P** I think I am Judging _____ Perceiving _____

What do you think your four MBTI letters would be? _____ (e.g., ESTP)

Create a new entry in your portfolio with the title "MBTI." For this entry, use your favorite Internet search engine and search for suggested careers for MBTI types. You will find several websites that suggest specific careers based on specific personality types. Choose one site and list at least two careers that are recommended for the MBTI type that you identify with. Have you thought about these careers before? Do you think they would be a good fit for you? Why or why not?

Example: Careers recommended for ESTP: Sales representative, marketer, police, detective, paramedic, medical technician, computer technician, computer technical support, entrepreneur. Suggestions found at www.geocities.com/lifexplore/mbcareer.htm

Critical Thinking

In this chapter YOU WILL LEARN

▶ Why there are no "absolutely right" or "positively wrong" answers to many important questions

▶ Four key aspects of critical thinking

▶ How critical arguments differ from emotional arguments

▶ How college encourages critical thinking

▶ Why critical thinking is the basis of a liberal education

▶ The importance of critical thinking throughout your life

Critical thinking will help you solve life's difficult puzzles.

© Andrew Douglas/Masterfile

How Do Your CRITICAL THINKING SKILLS Measure Up?

A?B?C?A?B?C?A?B?C?

Read the following questions and choose the answer that most fits you.

1 *When you hear other people arguing strongly for a particular idea, how do you decide if the argument is valid?*

(A) I want to know something about them, such as what church they attend or whether they're members of my favorite political party.

(B) I can tell by the way they look and their tone of voice.

(C) I really listen to them carefully, then I seek other evidence to support or reject their arguments.

2 *When you make a decision, do you let your emotions get in the way?*

(A) Sometimes I am able to repress my anger or disappointment and think logically, but other times, my emotions just take over.

(B) Aren't your emotions what should guide your actions? I always think with my heart.

(C) I am pretty successful at thinking with my head first and can separate out my emotions.

3 *When you find a person irritating, can you still listen to what he or she has to say?*

(A) It depends on how irritating the person is—sometimes I can, but other times people can be so annoying that I just can't listen.

(B) Never—you just can't reason or talk with people like that.

(C) I think everyone deserves to be heard and can add to a discussion in some way.

4 *Do textbooks give you all the answers you need?*

(A) It depends on the course; some books have the answers to everything you need to know.

(B) Of course they do! Why else would the book be made, sold, and required for me to read?

(C) I don't think so. If I'm looking for answers, I like to read lots of different sources to learn other points of view, including the textbook.

5 *Do you believe that critical thinking is a desirable skill for prospective employers?*

(A) Some jobs require more critical thinking than others; some jobs might just need a robot to do the work.

(B) No—as long as you can get the work done for them, why does it matter?

(C) I think so. An employer will see that you are willing to problem solve and come up with alternatives that no one else might have considered.

Review your responses. (A) responses indicate that you have some understanding about critical thinking. But you'll need more practice applying thinking skills. (B) responses indicate that you haven't really thought much about what it means to think critically. (C) responses indicate that you have a good conceptual understanding of what critical thinking is all about. Whatever your responses, this chapter will help you learn more about this important skill, which you will use in college and beyond.

Imagine that one of your instructors tells you on the first day of class: I'm going to fill your minds with lots of important facts, and I expect you to take extensive notes and know those facts when you take your quizzes. The important thing in my class is how well you learn the details and how frequently you choose the right answers. And remember, while there are lots of wrong answers, there is only one correct answer.

In another class, the instructor introduces the course quite differently: Although I've taught this course many times, it's never quite the same. Each time a new group of students begins the course, they bring their own values, ideas, and past knowledge to the material. The important thing in my class is that you use your heads. You certainly will need to read the assignments and take notes on the lectures and discussions in class. But what's most important is that you learn to analyze facts, decide which facts are supportable by evidence, and know how to convince others of your beliefs. And remember, while there are lots of wrong conclusions, there also might be more than one right conclusion.

Write • DISCUSS • Compare • Ask • BLOG • Answer • *Journal*

> **Which of these two classes would you enjoy the most? Which would be the liveliest? Explain your answer.**

When you earn your college degree and land a job, chances are your employer is going to be more interested in how well you think than in how well you can memorize minute bits of information. The second instructor seems to be moving in that direction. She admits that many possibilities exist. She realizes that the class might come up with a better answer—or answers—if the students gather their information on the topic, discuss it in small groups, and share what they have learned with the teacher, who will then react to what she hears.

The first instructor will tell you what you should know; the second instructor wants you—through class discussion, small group sessions, problem solving, research, and other methods—to discover the truths yourself. So if you have this type of teacher, consider yourself fortunate: your critical thinking might actually begin with your first class discussion or assigned paper. Actually, every paper you write and every discussion you join will not only cultivate your critical thinking, it will prepare you for life after college.

College has been described as an investment in your future. College can not only prepare you for a career, it also can broaden your horizons in other ways. A main ingredient in a college education, and in life, is learning how to think critically. If you don't learn this skill, you might not be making the wisest decisions for your education and future. Far too often, people don't think critically (logically) and instead let their emotions govern their actions. In college and in life, that can lead to trouble.

From history classes, you might develop an interest in the French Revolution and other aspects of French culture instead of just memorizing your notes for an exam and forgetting them later. From music appreciation, you might become a regular concertgoer. A literature course can help you discover the authors you will be reading long after you've said goodbye to your campus. From other courses, you might develop interests in world travel, native crafts, or theater.

And if you believe that college is a path to a high-paying job, remember that a good critical thinker is a good job candidate. Our rapidly changing economy demands abilities and traits that are characteristic of critical thinking and essential to the new management structures of successful businesses. In such organizations, employers want workers to use judgment and make decisions rather than to merely follow directions as clones. Management layers disappear as workers take over many of the tasks that others used to do.[1]

---

[1] "Critical Thinking: Identifying the Targets." Copyright © 2004 Foundation for Critical Thinking.

▶ **Critical thinking is easier when you work and study with someone else.**

© David Fischer/Getty Images

Four Aspects of Critical Thinking

Critical thinking cannot be learned overnight. As William T. Daly, political science professor at The Richard Stockton College of New Jersey, explains, the critical thinking process can be divided into four basic steps. Practicing these basic ideas can help you become a more effective thinker.

1. Abstract Thinking: Moving from Details to Abstractions

Details are easy. Understanding what they all mean takes work. Seek the bigger ideas or abstractions behind the large numbers of facts you encounter. What are the key ideas? Even fields like medicine, which involve countless facts, culminate in general ideas, such as the principles of circulation or the basic mechanisms of cell division.

> If you already have "the facts," what's the point of working backwards to understand the basic principles?

Ask yourself to generalize from the details to larger concepts. For example, you read an article that describes how many people currently use the Internet, how much consumer information it provides, and the kinds of goods you can buy cheaply online. The article also reports that many low-income families still do not own computers. Think carefully about these facts, and you might arrive at several different important generalizations.

2. Creative Thinking: Seeking Connections, Finding New Possibilities, Rejecting Nothing

Use the abstraction you have found to see what further ideas it suggests. At this stage, you should not reject any of your ideas. Write them down. You'll narrow this list in the next step.

The creative phase of thinking might involve searching for ways to make the Internet more available to low-income households. Or it might involve searching out more detailed information on the interest that big companies have in marketing various goods to low-income families. In essence, the creative thinking stage involves extending the general idea, finding new ways to apply it, or identifying other ideas it might suggest. It's creative because it lets you brainstorm without fear of rejection.

The goal of **brainstorming** is to get everyone's creative juices flowing and to come up with as many related ideas as possible, saving judgment for the refinement stage. During a brainstorming exercise, everyone's ideas get written down, and no one is allowed to comment on them, either positively or negatively. The idea is to create a fertile environment in which each team member builds on the thoughts of others without getting sidetracked.

> Do you think brainstorming and being free to say what you think brings you closer to the solution, or is this process just a waste of time?

Some famous writers and artists say their ideas come to them while they're taking a shower or a long walk. Others get ideas while driving or talking about a topic with a friend. In "Stalking the Big Idea," advertising professional Terrence Poltrack

▶ **"Brainstorming[2] on Paper"**

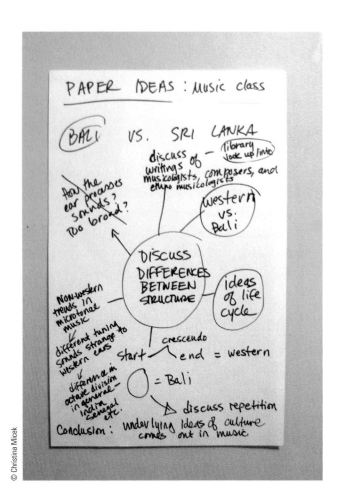

© Christina Micek

claimed "the process is one part reason, one part heart, and big part pure, simple intuition."[3]

In fact, the process for generating ideas practically parallels the critical thinking process:

1. *Immersion.* Totally immerse yourself in background research.

2. *Digestion.* Play with the information. Look at it from different perspectives. Jot down phrases. Exercise your mind.

3. *Incubation.* Put your notes aside. Go for a walk. Catch a movie. Shoot some hoops. Do whatever will relax your mind, and let your mind review the material while you have fun.

4. *Illumination.* Chances are, your mind will spurt out an idea or two. Be ready to write the idea down, because ideas won't stay in the mind very long.

5. *Reality Testing.* Is the idea really good? Does it solve the problem?

3. Systematic Thinking: Organizing the Possibilities, Tossing Out the Rubbish

If brainstorming is about quantity and options, the emphasis in the systematic stage is on making decisions. This process isn't necessarily a matter of figuring out the best idea. Depending on the goals of the activity, it might simply be the one that the group

[2] Jewler, A. Jerome and Drewniany, Bonnie. *Creative Strategy in Advertising,* 8th ed. (Belmont, CA: Wadsworth, 2005).
[3] Terrence Poltrack, "Stalking the Big Idea," Agency, May/June 1991.

thinks is most fun or practical. For a business decision, it might involve a cost/benefit analysis to decide which computer equipment to purchase for your lab. With kids in a learning center, it might be a matter of helping them decide on a plot for a video or on a topic for an inquiry-based learning project.

Systematic thinking involves looking at the outcome of the second phase in a more demanding, critical way. If you are looking for solutions to a problem, which ones really seem most promising after you have conducted an exhaustive search for materials? Do some answers conflict with others? Which ones can be achieved? If you have found new evidence, what does that new evidence show? Does your original generalization still hold up? Does it need to be modified? Which notions should be abandoned?

Write • DISCUSS • Compare • Ask • BLOG • Answer • *Journal*

> What is the difference between creative thinking and systematic thinking? Can you do one without the other? Why? Why not?

4. Precise Communication: Presenting Your Ideas Convincingly to Others

Thoughtful conclusions aren't very useful if you cannot share them with others. Consider what your audience will need to know to follow your reasoning and be persuaded. Remember to have your facts in hand as you attempt to convince others of the truth of your argument. Don't be defensive; instead, just be logical. To sharpen your writing and speaking skills even more, see chapter 9.

Employers hiring college graduates often say they want an individual who can find information, analyze it, organize it, draw conclusions from it, and present it convincingly to others. These skills are the basic ingredients of critical thinking, which includes the ability to:

▶ Manage and interpret information in a reliable way

▶ Examine existing ideas and develop new ones

▶ Pose logical arguments that further the absorption of knowledge. Here, "argument" refers not to an emotional confrontation but to reasons and information brought together in logical support of some idea.

▶ Recognize reliable evidence and form well-reasoned conclusions.

College Helps You Develop Critical Thinking Skills

A liberal education provides the foundation to define and pursue goals. In a liberal education, students learn to investigate all sides of a question and all possible solutions to a problem before reaching a conclusion or planning a course of action.

The word *liberal* as used here has no political connotation, but is a direct reference to the ability of education to free your mind. The word itself comes from the

WIRED WINDOW

BLOGS ALLOW ANYONE, even those with limited web-publishing experience, to post online journals that look professional. Blogs emerged in 2003 and their popularity has only increased, with Internet users creating over 100,000 new blogs every day. Because there are so many blogs, they cover just about any topic you can think of—from politics to purchasing, movies to money, sex to Silicone Valley. If you want to know a blogger's opinion about anything, you can find it in the blogosphere. Because there are so many blogs, opinions about an issue can range widely amongst bloggers, with some supporting a certain viewpoint, some being against it, and many others being somewhere in between. To sharpen your critical thinking skills, Google a current event that you find interesting. Next, search for blogs with commentary on the topic. (Hint: search for the topic keywords plus the word "blog.") Find two blogs with different viewpoints on the same topic. To help you, review the four aspects of critical thinking and answer the following questions: What is each blogger's viewpoint? Do the people who leave comments generally agree or disagree with the blogger's point of view? Why does the blogger hold that point of view? Is there any evidence on the blog that supports the blogger's view? Do you have an opinion on the topic? Which blogger do you most agree with? Why?

Latin *libero*, a verb meaning "to free." The goal of a liberal education is to free you from the biases, superstitions, prejudices, and lack of knowledge that might have characterized you before you came to college. Next time you wonder why you are required to take courses outside your major, remember how important they can be in terms of helping you develop critical thinking skills.

When you decided to come to college, did you consider other alternatives? Did you allow yourself to think critically about whether college is worth the time and money? Believe it or not, not everyone sees college the same way.

Theodora Kalikow, president of the University of Maine at Farmington, describes the benefits of a good college education. Almost all of these relate to critical thinking:

▶ A lithe mind, able to move rapidly in new directions

▶ The ability to analyze a problem

▶ The ability to imagine solutions, weigh them by rational criteria (or standards), and commit to one of them

▶ An understanding of the investigative approaches of various disciplines, or subject areas, to acquire the ability to become one's own best lifelong teacher

▶ A skepticism of superficial arguments and easy solutions and a distrust of simplistic analysis

▶ A tolerance for ambiguity and complexity

▶ An ability to imagine and share the perceptions of different individuals, cultures, and times

▶ An appreciation of the community and one's place in it—the need to contribute to society through public and private service [4]

[4] Theodora J. Kalikow, "Misconceptions about the Word 'Liberal' in Liberal Arts Education," *Higher Education and National Affairs*, June 8, 1998.

On the flip side, Pulitzer prizewinning author John Updike told a group of college students that he isn't particularly fond of higher education. "I'm not a great romantic of the college experience," he said. "I enjoyed my four years of college. But I didn't feel the need to extend them. I always kind of resented being educated. It takes away the self you brought to college," he concluded. Updike's views obviously conflict with many people's beliefs about the value of college. What do you suppose this successful writer (who enjoyed and completed college) could be thinking? Can you provide arguments for and against his statement?

Write • DISCUSS • Compare • Ask • BLOG • Answer • *Journal*

> Think critically about Updike's statement: "I always kind of resented being educated. It takes away the self you brought to college." What does he mean by this? Can you find arguments both for and against this statement? Remember, John Updike is a highly successful writer.

Updike and Kalikow are at opposite poles. Or are they? Unfortunately, most important questions do not have simple answers, and you will need to discover numerous ways to look at important issues. In any event, you must be willing to challenge assumptions and conclusions, even those presented by experts.

That is why your teacher might insist that more than one valid point of view exists: "So, for some types of students, you agree that bilingual education might be best? What other types of students should we consider?" Your instructor might require you to explain the reason for any point you reject in concrete terms: "You think this essay is flawed. Well, what are your reasons?" Or he or she might challenge the authority of experts: "Dr. Fleming's theory sounds impressive. But here are some facts he doesn't account for . . ." You might discover that your instructor often reinforces the legitimacy of your personal views and experiences: "So something like this happened to you once, and you felt exactly the same way. Can you tell us why?" And you also will discover that you can change your mind.

It is natural for new college students to find this mode of thinking difficult and to discover that answers are seldom entirely wrong or right, but more often somewhere in between. Yet, the questions that suggest complex answers usually are the ones most worthy of study.

If you hang on to these rules, we can't promise your classes will be easier, but we can promise that they certainly will be more interesting, for now you know how to use logic to figure things out instead of depending purely on how you feel or what you've heard about something.

A good class becomes a critical thinking experience. As you listen to the instructor, try to predict where the lecture is heading and why. When other students raise issues, ask yourself whether they have enough information to justify what they have said. And when you raise your hand to participate, remember that asking a sensible question might be more important than trying to find the elusive—and often nonexistent—"right" answer.

▶ How true can this claim be? What is the definition of "better"? Does the headline mean that other brands are just as good—but not better—than the one this ad promotes?

Better than any other Diet pill you may have tried.
The new and improved **SlimTab** is now available in stores near you!

Eat what you want! Stop watching every bite you take. With new SlimTab, all you have to do is take one tablet before each meal, and just watch the pounds fall off!! Feel at ease attending those holiday parties. Finally, something that really works and is better than the rest!

No more diet food!

Weight Loss-
Instant and Lasting!

Guaranteed

© ThinkStock/SuperStock

If you take demanding college courses with many opportunities to think aloud, engage in class discussions, and especially do research and write, you will learn, practice, and develop outstanding critical thinking skills. Take courses that use essay exams as opposed to multiple choice, true/false, short answer; the latter three are much less likely to develop your critical thinking skills.

From Certainty to Healthy Uncertainty

If you have just completed high school, you might be experiencing an awakening as you enter college. Even if you're an older returning student, discovering that your instructor trusts you to find valid answers might be both surprising and stressful. If your high school teacher asked, "What are the three branches of the U.S. government?"

you had only one choice: "legislative, executive, and judicial." You might have learned the names of the three branches, but you needed no critical thinking.

Instead of the question posed by a high school teacher, a college instructor might ask, "Under what circumstances might conflicts arise among the three branches of government, and what does this reveal about the democratic process?" Certainly, there is no simple—or single—answer. Most likely, your instructor is attempting not to embarrass you for giving a wrong answer but to engage you in the process of critical thinking.

Consider this situation: Citing environmental and seismic concerns, a judge blocked construction of a $125 million sports center at the University of California, Berkeley, because it would mean felling an oak grove. The plan to renovate Memorial Stadium and build a new training center and parking garage was challenged by neighbors and city officials as environmentally flawed and seismically treacherous because the site straddles the Hayward Fault, and a fault is a likely place for earthquakes. Plans to cut down about three dozen oaks to make way for the center prompted the most visible protest. Judge Barbara J. Miller of Alameda County Superior Court said opponents' arguments were strong enough to justify a preliminary injunction until a trial could be held.[5]

Explore this situation. We'll state the obvious: college officials want the stadium because sports make money and lure new students to campus, while city officials and neighbors don't want the risk of a future earthquake. Form two groups. If you're for sports, try to discover why the environmentalists are right. If you're for the environment, take the sports argument and run with it. Then, reconvene as a class with your findings. Allow no one to become emotional; that's not how you convince anyone. Use your library, the Internet, and other sources to learn more about the situation. Consult someone in the geology department and someone in the athletics office to get their views.

▲ **Uncertainty can be healthy; it makes you try harder.**

[5] The Associated Press. January 30, 2007.

While making the right decisions about a sports center is a good class exercise, you can also use your critical thinking skills in many everyday situations, such as these:

▶ You try to reach a classmate on the phone to ask a question about tomorrow's quiz. When you can't reach him, you become so anxious that you can't study or sleep.

▶ On the day an important paper is due, a heavy snowstorm rolls in. You brave the cold to get to class. When you arrive, no one—including the teacher—is there. You take a seat and wait.

Now let's transform you into a critical thinker and examine the possible outcomes:

▶ When you can't reach a classmate on the phone to ask a question about tomorrow's quiz, you review the material once more, then call one or more other classmates. Then you consider their views against your textbook and class. Instead of deciding on one point of view for each important topic, you decide to keep in mind all of those that make sense, leaving your final decision until you have the quiz in your hand.

▶ Before heading out to class amidst the snowstorm, you check the college website first thing that morning and discover that classes have been canceled. You stay at home.

Collaboration Fosters Critical Thinking

A 1995 study by Professor Anuradha A. Gokhale at Western Illinois University, published in the *Journal of Technology Education*, found that students who participated in collaborative learning performed significantly better on a test requiring critical thinking than students who studied individually. The study also found that both groups did equally well on a test requiring only memorization.[6]

Having more than one student involved in the learning process will generate a greater number of ideas. As a group learns to agree on the most reliable thoughts, it moves closer to a surer solution.

Collaboration occurs not only face to face, but also over the Internet. Christopher P. Sessums, creator of an award-winning blog, wrote:

> Weblogs offer several key features that I believe can support a constructive, collaborative, reflective environment. For one, it's convenient. The medium supports self-expression and 'voice.' Collaboration and connectivity can be conducted efficiently, especially in terms of participants' time or place. Publishing your thoughts online forces you to concretize your thoughts.
>
> Collaborative weblogs promote the idea of learners as creators of knowledge, not merely consumers of information. A collaborative environment like the one I'm suggesting can allow peers to be seen as valuable sources of knowledge and ideas; a connection that participants can rely on beyond any formal classroom structure, i.e., collaboration leading to a community of interest.

Without a clear intention or purpose for collaborative inquiry or reflective thinking, you cannot really expect any results.[7]

---

[6] Anuradha Gokhale, "Collaborative Learning Enhances Critical Thinking," *Journal of Technology Education* 7.1 (1995).
[7] Sessums, Christopher. Weblog, November 9, 2005.

Confessions of a College Student

Name: Taylor McFadden

Age: 18

College: Purchase College

Hometown: West Nyack, NY

Major: Dance

Favorite book(s): *The DaVinci Code*

Favorite college course: Culture and Society in the West

The person who inspires me the most or who I would most like to meet: Condoleezza Rice

Heroes: My parents

Favorite way to relax: A dance class or swimming

Your proudest moment or biggest accomplishment: Being accepted into a ballet company after many years of training.

Favorite food: Pretty much anything except fast food.

Critical thinking confession: Using critical thinking, I can evaluate the pros and cons of each topic and evaluate them logically. As a dancer, I tend to be a perfectionist, yet my critical thinking skills help me understand that nothing and nobody are perfect. Faced with making a decision I now can sort my priorities and come up with the better decision. Unfortunately, image is very important in our society and is fueled by advertising depicting people that are deemed by society as "perfect." I am grateful that critical thinking helps me look beyond those stereotypes and appreciate who I am.

Whether in person or through electronic communication, collaboration improves your ability to think critically. As you leave college and enter the world of work, you will find that collaboration is essential in almost any career you pursue, not only with those in your work setting, but also with others around the globe.

Examples of Sound Arguments

The complexity of the previous "trees versus earthquakes" situation practically demands that each person weigh all the options, think through consequences, and reach a decision, as opposed to groping for an answer. When thinking about an argument, a good critical thinker considers questions such as the following:

▶ Is the information given in support of the argument valid? For example, could it be possible that both the stadium backers and the environmentalists have a good case for their positions?

▶ Does the information really support the conclusion? If you determine that each side has its merits, what facts can you muster as proof?

▶ Do you need to withhold judgment until better evidence is available? Maybe you can't determine which way to go because you've never encountered such a situation.

▶ Is the argument really based on good reasoning, or does it appeal mainly to your emotions?

You might side with the stadium advocates because you love football or with the environmentalists because you want to do something about global warming. You see benefits on either side. But you need to come to terms with your emotions and ask if they, not the relevant information that supports the argument, are guiding you to this conclusion. Based on the available evidence, are other conclusions likely? Is there more than one right or possible answer? Perhaps there is a third or fourth way to settle the argument. What might those ways be?

What more needs to be done to reach a good conclusion? You might need to do more reading about the encroachment of society on the environment. Since you are probably far from an expert on this, perhaps you should hold a forum with local experts to gain more views on the pros and cons of the situation.

Good critical thinking also involves thinking creatively about the assumptions that might have been left out or the alternative conclusions that might not have been considered. When communicating an argument or idea to others, a good critical thinker knows how to organize it in an understandable, convincing way, either in speech or in writing.

Avoiding Logical Fallacies

Although logic is essential to solving any problem, whether simple or complex, you need to go one step further to make sure that your logical argument hasn't been compromised by **faulty reasoning**. Here are some guidelines:

▶ **Attack the Argument, Not the Person.** When you argue against other people's positions, make sure it's their arguments you're attacking and not their personalities.

▶ **Don't Make Threats to Win an Argument.** Your parents might make you admit they were right on some issue by suggesting that, unless you did what they asked, you might not receive your allowance for the month. Students use such arguments against instructors when they threaten to give them a poor evaluation.

▶ **Don't Beg.** "Please, officer, don't give me a ticket because if you do I'll lose my license, and I have five little children to feed and won't be able to feed them if I can't drive my truck." None of the driver's statements offer any evidence, in any legal sense, as to why he or she shouldn't be given a ticket. The truth is, the driver forgot to feed the meter. What should he or she say to the police officer?

▶ **Avoid Appeal to Authority.** If you base your claim on the authority of someone who might or might not be an authority on the topic, you're relying on the appearance of authority rather than real evidence to make your argument. We see this all the time in advertising. Sports stars who are not doctors, dieticians, or nutritionists urge us to eat a certain brand of fast food.

▶ **It's Not a Popularity Contest.** Sometimes we are more likely to listen to popular or famous people than to others. In other words, we believe more what we're told by successful and attractive people than what we're told by those who aren't so successful or attractive. Students frequently choose their classes on the basis of such irrelevant things as an instructor's looks or popularity.

▶ **It Isn't True Simply Because** It Hasn't Been Proven False. Go to a bookstore and you'll find dozens of books detailing close encounters with flying saucers and extraterrestrial beings. All of these books describe the person who had the close encounter as beyond reproach in integrity and sanity. Because critics could not disprove the claims of the witnesses, the events are said to have really occurred. Even in science, few things are ever proved completely false, but evidence can be discredited.

▶ **Don't Fall Victim to False Cause.** Frequently, we think that just because one event followed another, the first event must have caused the second. This reasoning is the basis for many superstitions. The ancient Chinese once believed that they could make the sun reappear after an eclipse by striking a large gong. They knew that the sun reappeared after a large gong had been struck on one such occasion. Along similar lines, students tend to blame their failure on the teacher all too often, yet students often cause their own failures by not reading assignments, not studying for tests, and so forth.

▶ **Avoid Hasty Generalizations.** If someone selected one green marble from a barrel containing 100 marbles, you wouldn't assume that the next marble would be green. After all, there are still 99 marbles in the barrel, and you know nothing about the colors of those marbles. However, given 50 draws from the barrel, each of which produced a green marble after the barrel had been shaken thoroughly, you would be more willing to conclude that the next marble drawn would be green, too. Likewise, reaching a conclusion in a research paper based on the opinion of one source is like figuring all the marbles in the barrel are green after pulling out only one.

To test your reasoning, ask the following of your arguments: If the conclusion I inferred from my premises is false, isn't it likely that one or more of my premises is also false? If you're convinced the answer is yes, you probably have a proper argument. If your answer is no, try another argument; chances are, you've committed a fallacy in your reasoning. Above all, never forget that correct reasoning is a key factor for success in college and in life.

Write • DISCUSS • Compare • Ask • BLOG • Answer • *Journal*

> Name all of the logical **fallacies** you have engaged in and why you employed each of them. How has this chapter changed your views about logical fallacies?

Critical Thinking in Everyday Life

Once you practice the skills of critical thinking in college, they will become a natural part of your life. Suppose you're shopping for a surround sound system. One good friend urges you to buy the top of the line. Another well-meaning friend steers you to one brand and warns you not to choose another brand. "They break down fast," he says. Now all you know is that two of your good friends offered information that might or might not be true. How would you critically think your way out of this one?

Alternatively, a close friend offers you a ticket to a concert that night. You'd love to go, but you need to study. What factors would you consider in making your decision? What would be the consequences of each decision?

A newspaper reports that the governor of your state, who is running for reelection, should not win. It offers a number of negatives, but no real positives. Should you accept this at face value or not? If not, where would you go for balanced information?

Even children can be taught to use critical thinking, as the following book excerpt points out:

> Questions you can ask about implications:
>
> ▶ If I decide to do X, what things might happen?
>
> ▶ If I decide not to do X, what things might happen?
>
> ▶ When the main character in the story made an important decision, what happened as a result?
>
> ▶ What were the consequences?
>
> ▶ What are the possible implications of riding your bike too fast down the hill?
>
> ▶ What are the implications of touching that hot pot on the stove?[8]

Questioning the Internet

Anyone can put anything on the Internet. An academic researcher found a movie review on the Internet, printed it, and discussed it in his seminar, only to realize later that it was written by an adoring fan, not an authoritative critic.

It is often difficult to tell where something on the Internet comes from, how it got there, or who wrote it. In other words, the lack of a proper citation makes it difficult to judge the credibility of the information. So the first thing to do is to look for a citation. Then, using the citation, do a search for the original source and evaluate its authenticity. If there is no citation, chances are you should avoid the site. Ask yourself other questions, too.

1. Is it credible? Is it the original? Is it quoted out of context? Plagiarized? Altered—intentionally or unintentionally—from the original? Has the material been reviewed by experts?

2. Who is the author? What can you find out about her or him? Is the author qualified to write this article? If you can't find information on the author, think twice before using the information. Beware of sites that have no date on the document, make sweeping generalizations, and use information that is biased and does not acknowledge opposing views.

3. Does it reflect mainstream opinions? Whether you're looking for a fact, an opinion, or some advice, it is a good idea to find at least three sources that agree.

---

[8] *The Miniature Guide to Critical Thinking for Children.* CA: Dillon Beach. © 2005 Foundation for Critical Thinking.

If the sources do not agree, do further research to find out the range of opinion or disagreement before you draw your conclusions. If the site is sponsored by an advocacy group, be aware of the group's agenda or cause; it will affect the reliability of the information.[9]

How and Where to Check

Check online directory sources for affiliations and biographical information. Look for other works by the author. Read a few of them. How accurate and unbiased do they sound?

An editorial board reviews most print matter (books, articles, and so forth). Frequently it's difficult to confirm that the same is true for information on an Internet source, with some exceptions. If you are searching through a database, such as the Human Genome Database, the Civil War Database, or Eldis: the Gateway to Development Information (a poverty database), it is highly likely that sources from these collections have been reviewed.

Of course, you might use the search engines, too; but you should compare the information you find with information from print sources or at least two other critically examined electronic databases.

▶ WHERE TO GO FOR HELP

On Campus

Logic Courses Check out your philosophy department's introductory course in logic. This might be the single best course designed to teach you critical thinking skills. Virtually every college offers such a course.

Argument Courses and Critical Thinking Courses These are usually offered in the English department. They will help you develop the ability to formulate logical arguments and avoid such pitfalls as **logical fallacies.**

Debating Skills Some of the very best critical thinkers developed debating skills during college. Go to either your student activities office or your department of speech/drama and find out if your campus has a debate club or team. Debating can be fun and chances are you would meet some interesting student thinkers.

Online

Check the following website for a critical review of *The Encyclopedia of Stupidity*: http://arts. independent.co.uk/books/reviews/article112328.ece

My Institution's Resources

_____

_____

_____

_____

_____

_____

_____

---

[9] Excerpt from *VirtualSalt.com*, **www.virtualsalt.com.** Reprinted by permission.

▸▸▸ BUILDING YOUR PORTFOLIO
My Influences

We all take different paths in life, but no matter where we go,
we take a little of each other everywhere.

–Tim McGraw (b. 1967), American country music singer

To complete this portfolio activity electronically, please visit
academic.cengage.com/collsucc/Gardner/YCE8e.

Our past experiences shape the way we think and perceive the world around us. Sometimes it is easy to interpret things without stopping to think about why we feel the way we do. How have people or events shaped the way you see the world today?

For this activity, you will create a new entry in your portfolio with the title "My Influences." You will insert photos of people (family, friends, celebrities, national leaders) and events (a personal experience or local/national/international event) that have affected your worldview. Beneath each photo, write a description and a reflection based on the questions/model below.

1. Describe how the people you select have influenced you.

Upload photo here.

_____

_____

_____

_____

_____

_____

Upload photo here.

_____

_____

_____

_____

_____

Upload photo here.

_____

_____

_____

_____

_____

Listening, Taking Notes, and Being Engaged in Class

In this chapter YOU WILL LEARN

▶ How to assess and improve your note-taking skills

▶ Why it's important to review your notes soon after class

▶ How your five senses can assist in learning and remembering

▶ How to prepare before class

▶ How to listen critically and take good notes in class

▶ Why you should speak up in class

▶ How to review class and textbook materials after class

▶ How being engaged in the classroom improves your learning

This reporter needs to listen, ask the right questions, and be engaged in the task at hand.

© AFP/Getty Images

Jeanne L. Higbee of the University of Minnesota Twin Cities contributed her valuable and considerable expertise to the writing of this chapter.

How Do You LISTEN, TAKE NOTES, and Become ENGAGED in Class?

A?B?C?A?B?C?A?B?C?

Read the following questions and choose the answer that most fits you.

1 *How would you prepare for a class beforehand?*

(A) I sometimes glance at the syllabus to see what we're covering, but that's usually all I do.

(B) I read the assigned materials and go over my notes from the previous class; it helps me get focused for the class.

(C) I eat my breakfast or lunch and show up to class.

2 *If you arrive to class early, how would you spend your time there?*

(A) Depending on where my seat is, I'll either chat with some friends if they're nearby or take a peek at the chapter I should have read.

(B) I try to go over my notes before class starts so that I refresh my memory and get geared up for the class.

(C) I text message some friends to see what we'll be doing after classes.

3 *If the instructor puts an outline on the board or overhead projector, how would you take notes?*

(A) I listen the first time and then try to write everything down afterwards, but I usually have trouble remembering and I then miss what the instructor talks about next.

(B) I write down the main points and stop to listen, then put what the instructor said into my own words.

(C) I think I have a photographic memory, so I don't need to write anything down.

4 *If you realized that you missed something important in your notes, what would you do?*

(A) Maybe I'd ask my friend in the class, if I remembered before the exam.

(B) I make sure I have someone reliable in my class who I can exchange notes with in case I miss something. If we both missed it, I'd go to my instructor during office hours to get what I missed.

(C) I don't usually realize I missed something until late the night before an exam, so there wouldn't be anything I could do about it.

5 *If you do not understand something in class, what would you do?*

(A) In smaller classes, I'd probably ask a question, but never in a large lecture—that's too embarrassing.

(B) I would ask a question if it's something I don't understand, or wait until after class to ask the instructor for clarification.

(C) I'd just assume it's not important.

Review your responses. (A) responses indicate that you have some idea of how to listen, take notes, and become engaged in the classroom, but in order to do your best, you'll need to improve. (B) responses indicate that you have a good idea of important learning strategies to use in the classroom. (C) responses indicate that you need to develop a better understanding of what it takes to do well in college classes. Wherever you are in your current understanding, this chapter will help you learn more about the basics of success in the classroom.

In virtually every college class you take, you'll need to master certain skills to earn high grades, such as listening, taking notes, and being engaged in learning. Engagement in learning means that you take an active role in your classes by listening carefully, asking questions, contributing to discussions, and providing answers. Those active learning behaviors will enhance your ability to understand abstract ideas, find new possibilities, organize those ideas, and recall the material once the class is over. How much you learn also results from how much energy and attention you invest in really concentrating and working hard to listen, taking notes, and thinking about what the professor and the other students say.

Your academic success relies on engaged listening and taking notes in class because your college instructors will likely introduce new material that your texts don't cover, and chances are, much of this material will resurface on quizzes and

> What kind of notes did you take in high school? Do you think you
> learned how to take good notes? Is the same method working
> for you now? Why or why not?

exams. You might consider tape-recording the lecture if you have the instructor's permission. Also, take notes on the discussion. If there are points you don't understand, consider asking your instructor to speak slower or repeat key points. You can also meet with the instructor after class or during office hours and with a study group to compare notes on the lecture content.

Choose the note-taking system that works for you. This chapter reviews several methods to consider. Since writing down everything the instructor says is probably not possible and you might not be sure what's most important, ask questions in class. This will ensure that you clearly understand your notes. Reviewing your notes with a tutor or someone from your campus learning center or comparing your notes to a friend's might also help you get an idea of the most important points.

What the instructor says in class may not always be in the textbook, and vice versa. And instructors often think that what they say in class is more important than the material in the text; therefore you are more likely to see information from a lecture on a test.

And be sure to speak up! When you have question to ask or a comment to share, don't let embarrassment or shyness stop you. You will be more likely to remember what happens in class if you are an active participant.

Why We Forget

Have you ever noticed how easy it is to learn the words of a song? We remember songs more easily than other kinds of information because they follow a tune and have a beat, because we might repeat them (sometimes unconsciously) over and over in our heads, and because they often have a personal meaning for us: we relate them to something in our everyday lives. We remember prose less easily—unless we make an effort to relate it to what we already know.

Most forgetting takes place within the first 24 hours of encountering the information. So, if you do not review almost immediately after class, it can be difficult to retrieve the material later. In two weeks, you will have forgotten up to 70 percent of it! Forgetting can be a serious problem when you are expected to learn and remember a mass of different facts, figures, concepts, and relationships. Once you understand how to improve your ability to remember, you will retain information more easily and completely. Retaining information will help your overall understanding as well as your ability to recall important details during exams.

David Young-Wolff/PhotoEdit

Using Your Senses in the Learning Process

You can enhance memory by using as many of your senses as possible while learning. How do you believe you learn most effectively?

▶ Do you learn best by listening to other people talk, or does your mind begin to wander when listening passively for more than a few minutes?

▶ Do you like reading? Do you learn best when you can see the words on the printed page? During a test, can you actually visualize where the information appears in your text? Can you remember data best when it's presented in the form of a picture, graph, chart, map, or video?

▶ Do you enjoy discussing course work with friends, classmates, or the teacher? Does interacting with others about information from the lecture or the text help you remember it?

▶ Do you learn through your sense of touch? Does typing or writing your notes help you remember them?

▶ Can you learn better when your body is in motion? When participating in sports, dancing, or working out, do you know immediately if a movement feels right? Do you learn more effectively by doing than by listening or reading about it?

▶ Does your sense of taste or smell contribute to your learning process? Do you cook using a recipe or by tasting and adding ingredients? Are you sensitive to odors?

Two or three of these modes probably describe your preferred ways of learning better than the others. At the college level, many faculty members share information primarily via lecture and the textbook. However, many students like to learn through visual and interactive means, creating a mismatch between learning and teaching styles. Is this a problem? Not necessarily. It is only a problem if you do not learn how to adapt lecture material and the text to your preferred modes of learning.

Before Class: Prepare to Remember

Because you might have difficulty understanding many lectures, you need to be prepared before class begins. You would not want to be unprepared to start a speech, interview for a job, plead a case in court, or compete in sports. For each of these situations, you would want to prepare in some way. For the same reasons, you should begin listening, learning, and remembering before the lecture.

Even if lectures don't allow for active participation, you can take a number of steps to become more engaged and to make your listening and note-taking more efficient. By following these steps you will learn and remember more, understand what the instructor considers important, and ultimately earn better grades.

1. Do the assigned reading. Otherwise, you might find the lecturer's comments disjointed, and you might not understand some terms used. Some instructors refer to assigned readings for each class session; others might distribute a **syllabus** and assume you are keeping up with the assigned readings. Completing them on time will help you listen better and pick out the most important information when taking notes in class. Read carefully and take good notes. In books that you own, **annotate** (add critical or explanatory margin notes), highlight, or underline the text. In books that you do not own, such as library books, make a photocopy of the pages and then annotate or highlight.

2. Pay careful attention to your course syllabus. Syllabi are formal statements of course expectations, requirements, and procedures. Instructors assume students will understand and follow course requirements with few or no reminders once they have received a syllabus.

3. Make use of auxiliary materials provided by the instructors. Many post lecture outlines or notes to a website prior to class. Download and print these materials for easy reference during class. These materials often provide hints regarding the material that the instructor considers most important; they also can create an organizational structure for taking notes.

4. Warm up for class by reviewing chapter introductions and summaries, referring to related sections in your text, and scanning your notes from the previous class period. This prepares you to pay attention, understand, and remember.

5. Get organized. Decide what type of notebook will work best for you. Many study skills experts suggest using three-ring binders because you can punch holes in syllabi and other course handouts and keep them with class notes. You might want to buy notebook paper with a larger left-hand margin (sometimes called "legal-ruled") to easily annotate your lecture notes. And don't forget your pencils and pens.

During Class: Listen Critically and with an Open Mind

Listening in class is not like listening to a TV show, listening to a friend, or even listening to a speaker at a meeting. Knowing how to listen in class can help you get more out of what you hear, understand better what you have heard, and save time. Here are some suggestions:

1. Be ready for the message. Prepare yourself to hear, to listen, and to receive the message. If you have done the assigned reading, you will already know details from the text so that you can focus your notes on key concepts during the lecture. You will also be able to notice information that the text does not cover, and you will be prepared to pay closer attention when the instructor is presenting unfamiliar material.

2. Listen to the main concepts and central ideas, not just to fragmented facts and figures. Although facts are important, they will be easier to remember and will make more sense when you can place them in a context of concepts, themes, and ideas.

3. Listen for new ideas. Even if you are an expert on a topic, you can still learn something new. Do not assume that college instructors will present the same information you learned in a similar course in high school. As a critical thinker, make a note of questions that arise in your mind as you listen, but save the judgments for later.

4. Repeat mentally. Words can go in one ear and out the other unless you make an effort to retain them. Think about what you hear and restate it silently in your own words. If you cannot translate the information into your own words, ask for further clarification.

5. Decide if what you have heard is not important, somewhat important, or very important. If it's really not important, let it go. If it's very important, make it a major point in your notes by highlighting or underscoring it, or use it as a major topic in your outline if that is the method you use for taking notes. If it's somewhat important, try to relate it to a very important topic by writing it down as a subset of that topic.

6. Keep an open mind. Every class holds the promise of discovering new ideas and uncovering different perspectives. Some teachers might intentionally present information that challenges your value system. One of the purposes of college is to teach you to think in new and different ways and to learn to provide support for your own beliefs. Instructors want you to think for yourself, and do not necessarily expect you to agree with everything they or your classmates say. However, if you want people to respect your values and ideas, you must show respect for them as well by listening to what they have to say with an open mind.

7. Ask questions. Early in the term, determine whether the instructor is open to responding to questions during lecture. Some teachers prefer to save questions for the end or want students to ask questions during separate discussion sections or

office hours. To some extent, this might depend on the nature and size of the class, such as a large lecture versus a small seminar. If your teacher is open to answering questions as they arise, do not hesitate to ask if you did not hear or understand what was said. It is best to clarify things immediately, if possible, and other students are likely to have the same questions. If you can't hear another student's question or response, ask that it be repeated.

Write • DISCUSS • Compare • Ask • BLOG • Answer • *Journal*

> Is it hard or easy for you to raise your hand and ask questions in most of your classes? Why? What kind of improvements can you make in your current classes to be more involved?

8. Sort, organize, and categorize. When you listen, try to match what you are hearing with what you already know. Take an active role in deciding how best to recall what you are learning.

During Class: Take Effective Notes

You can make class time more productive by using your listening skills to take effective notes, but first you have to decide on a system. Any system can work as long as you use it in every class.

Cornell Format

One of the best known methods for organizing notes is called the **Cornell format**, in which you create a "recall" column on each page of your notebook by drawing a vertical line about 2 to 3 inches from the left border. (See Figure 5.1.) As you take notes during lecture—whether writing down ideas, making lists, or using an outline or paragraph format—write only in the wider column on the right and leave the recall column on the left blank. (If you have large handwriting and this method seems unwieldy, consider using the back of the previous notebook page for your recall column.) The recall column is essentially the place where you write down the main ideas and important details for tests and examinations as you sift through your notes as soon after class as is feasible, preferably within an hour or two. Many students have found the recall column to be a critical part of effective note-taking that becomes an important study device for tests and examinations.

Outline Format

Some students find that an outline is the best way for them to organize their notes. You are probably already acquainted with what a formal outline looks like, with key ideas represented by Roman numerals, and other ideas relating to each key idea represented in order by uppercase letters, numbers, and lowercase letters. If you use this approach, try to determine the instructor's outline and recreate it in your notes. Add details, definitions, examples, applications, and explanations. (See Figure 5.2.)

Paragraph Format

You might decide to write summary paragraphs when you are taking notes on what you are reading. This method doesn't work as well for class notes because it might be difficult to summarize the topic until your teacher has covered it completely. By the end of the lecture, you might have forgotten critical information. (See Figure 5.3.)

List Format

This format can be effective when taking notes on lists of terms and definitions, facts, or sequences, such as the body's pulmonary system. It is easy to use lists in combination with the Cornell format, with key terms on the left and their definitions and explanations on the right. (See Figure 5.4.)

	Psychology 101, 1/31/05
	Theories of Personality
Personality trait: define	Personality trait = "durable disposition to behave in a particular way in a variety of situations"
Big 5: Name + describe them	Big 5-McCrae + Costa- (1)extroversion, (or positive emotionality)=outgoing, sociable, friendly, upbeat, assertive,; (2) neuroticism=anxious, hostile, self-conscious, insecure, vulnerable; (3)openness to experience=curiosity, flexibility, imaginative,; (4) agreeableness=sympathetic, trusting, cooperative, modest; (5)conscientiousness=diligent, disciplined, well organized, punctual, dependable
Psychodynamic Theories: Who?	Psychodynamic Theories-focus on unconscious forces Freud-psychoanalysis-3 components of personality-(1)id=primitive, instinctive,
3 components of personality: name and describe	operates according to pleasure principle (immediate gratification); (2)ego=decision-making component, operates according to reality principle (delay gratification until appropriate); (3)superego=moral component, social standards, right + wrong
3 levels of awareness: name and describe	3 levels of awareness-(1) conscious=what one is aware of at a particular moment; (2)preconscious=material just below surface, easily retrieved; (3)unconscious=thoughts, memories, + desires well below surface, but have great influence on behavior

▲ **Figure 5.1** Note-taking in the Cornell Format

Once you have decided on a format for taking notes, you might also want to develop your own system of abbreviations. For example, you might write "inst" instead of "institution" or "eval" instead of "evaluation." Just make sure you will be able to understand your abbreviations when it's time to review.

Write • DISCUSS • Compare • Ask • BLOG • Answer • *Journal*

Which of these four note-taking methods (Cornell, outline, paragraph, list) is most like the one you use? Does your current system work well for you? Why or why not? What changes will you make in how you take notes now that you've read this portion of the chapter?

Psychology 101, 1/31/05: Theories of Personality

I. Personality trait = "durable disposition to behave in a particular way in a variety of situations"

II. Big 5-McCrae + Costa

   A. Extroversion, (or positive emotionality)=outgoing, sociable, friendly, upbeat, assertive

   B. Neuroticism=anxious, hostile, self-conscious, insecure, vulnerable

   C. Openness to experience=curiosity, flexibility, imaginative

   D. Agreeableness=sympathetic, trusting, cooperative, modest

   E. Conscientiousness=diligent, disciplined, well organized, punctual, dependable

III. Psychodynamic Theories-focus on unconscious forces-- Freud—psychoanalysis

   A. 3 components of personality

      1. Id=primitive, instinctive, operates according to pleasure principle (immediate gratification)

      2. Ego=decision-making component, operates according to reality principle (delay gratification until appropriate)

      3. Superego=moral component, social standards, right + wrong

   B. 3 levels of awareness

      1. Conscious=what one is aware of at a particular moment

      2. Preconscious=material just below surface, easily retrieved

      3. Unconscious=thoughts, memories, + desires well below surface, but have great influence on behavior

▲ **Figure 5.2** Note-taking in the Outline Format

Psychology 101, 1/31/05: Theories of Personality

A personality trait is a "durable disposition to behave in a particular way in a variety of situations"

Big 5: According to McCrae + Costa most personality traits derive from just 5 higher-order traits: extroversion (or positive emotionality), which is outgoing, sociable, friendly, upbeat, assertive,; neuroticism, which means anxious, hostile, self-conscious, insecure, vulnerable; openness to experience characterized by curiosity, flexibility, imaginative,; agreeableness, which is sympathetic, trusting, cooperative, modest; and conscientiousness, means diligent, disciplined, well organized, punctual, dependable

Psychodynamic Theories: Focus on unconscious forces

Freud, father of psychoanalysis, believed in 3 components of personality: id, the primitive, instinctive, operates according to pleasure principle (immediate gratification); ego, the decision-making component, operates according to reality principle (delay gratification until appropriate); and superego, the moral component, social standards, right + wrong

Freud also thought there are 3 levels of awareness: conscious, what one is aware of at a particular moment; preconscious, the material just below surface, easily retrieved; and unconscious, the thoughts, memories, + desires well below surface, but have great influence on behavior

▲ **Figure 5.3** Note-taking in the Paragraph Format

Note-Taking Techniques

Whatever note-taking system you choose, follow these important steps:

1. Identify the main ideas. Well-organized lectures always contain key points. The first principle of effective note-taking is to identify and write down the most important ideas around which the lecture is built. Although supporting details are important as well, focus your note-taking on the main ideas. Such ideas can be buried in details, statistics, anecdotes, or problems, but you will need to identify and record them for further study.

Psychology 101, 1/31/05: Theories of Personality

- A personality trait is a "durable disposition to behave in a particular way in a variety of situations"
- Big 5: According to McCrae + Costa most personality traits derive from just 5 higher-order traits
    - extroversion, (or positive emotionality)=outgoing, sociable, friendly, upbeat, assertive
    - neuroticism=anxious, hostile, self-conscious, insecure, vulnerable
    - openness to experience=curiosity, flexibility, imaginative
    - agreeableness=sympathetic, trusting, cooperative, modest
    - conscientiousness=diligent, disciplined, well organized, punctual, dependable
- Psychodynamic Theories: Focus on unconscious forces
- Freud, father of psychoanalysis, believed in 3 components of personality
    - id=primitive, instinctive, operates according to pleasure principle (immediate gratification)
    - ego=decision-making component, operates according to reality principle (delay gratification until appropriate)
    - superego=moral component, social standards, right + wrong
- Freud also thought there are 3 levels of awareness
    - conscious=what one is aware of at a particular moment
    - preconscious=material just below surface, easily retrieved
    - unconscious=thoughts, memories, + desires well below surface, but have great influence on behavior

▲ **Figure 5.4** Note-taking in the List Format

Some instructors announce the purpose of a lecture or offer an outline, thus providing you with the skeleton of main ideas, followed by the details. Others develop overhead transparencies or PowerPoint presentations, and might make these materials available on a class website before the lecture. If so, you can enlarge them, print them out, and take notes on the teacher's outline or next to the PowerPoint slides.

Some lecturers change their tone of voice or repeat themselves for each key idea. Some ask questions or promote discussion. If a lecturer says something more than once, chances are it is important. Ask yourself, "What does my instructor want me to know at the end of today's class?"

Personality trait	I. Personality trait = "durable disposition to behave in a particular way in a variety of situations"
	II. Big 5-McCrae + Costa
Big 5: Who? Name + describe them	A. Extroversion, (or positive emotionality) = outgoing, sociable, friendly, upbeat, assertive
	B. Neuroticism = anxious, hostile, self-conscious, insecure, vulnerable
	C. Openness to experience = curiosity, flexibility, imaginative
	D. Agreeableness = sympathetic, trusting, cooperative, modest
	E. conscientiousness = diligent, disciplined, well organized, punctual, dependable
	III. Psychodynamic Theories-focus on unconscious forces-- Freud-psychoanalysis
Psychodynamic Theories: Who? 3 components. Name, define, relate each to a principle	A. 3 components of personality
	1. Id = primitive, instinctive, operates according to pleasure principle (immediate gratification)
	2. Ego = decision-making component, operates according to reality principle (delay gratification until appropriate)
	3. Superego = moral component, social standards, right + wrong
	B. 3 levels of awareness
3 levels of awareness: name and describe	1. conscious = what one is aware of at a particular moment
	2. preconscious = material just below surface, easily retrieved
	3. unconscious = thoughts, memories, + desires well below surface, but have great influence on behavior

▲ **Figure 5.5** Cornell Format combined with Outline Format

2. Don't try to write down everything. Some first-year students try to do just that. They stop being thinkers and become stenographers. (See an exception in the section on taking notes in math and science courses on pages 97-98. As you take notes, leave spaces so that you can fill in additional details that you might have missed during class but remember later. But remember to do it as soon after class as possible; remember the "forgetting curve": how quickly you forget what you didn't write down.

3. Don't be thrown by a disorganized lecturer. When a lecture is disorganized, it's your job to try to organize what is said into general and specific frameworks.

Confessions of a College Student

Name: Ivan D. Buenrostro

Age: 23

University: Arizona State University

Hometown: Phoenix, AZ

Major: Aeronautical Management Technology

Favorite book(s): *The Da Vinci Code, The House on Mango Street, Nickel and Dimed, Esperanza's Box of Saints*

Favorite college course: U.S. History, Ethnic Relations

The person who inspires me the most: That would have to be my mom for her determination and motivation.

Favorite way to relax: Going to the beach, playing the guitar/piano, listening to music, swimming, and hiking

Are you the first to go to college in your family? If so, what impact has that had on your experience? Because I am the first in my family to go to college, I hold myself to high standards because I feel I am setting an example for my two younger siblings. Although I have accomplished many things, I also have enjoyed my college experience. Being the first in my family to attend college has had a positive effect on me. In a way, being the first to go to college has served as additional motivation to achieve what I once viewed as unattainable.

Your proudest moment or biggest accomplishment: My first solo flight

Note-taking confession: To be honest, I used to hate taking notes or going over them to retain more of the material. I figured I could organize thoughts in my head faster than I could by writing them down on paper. You could say I wrote "in between the lines." Rewriting my notes? Why do more work? Although I took plenty of notes in class, they turned out to be virtually useless.

Reading my notes became tedious, so I hardly ever bothered with it, reviewing only a day or two before the exam. Wow, did my grades suffer! What I finally realized was that the material covered in class was only a portion of what I needed to review.

To improve my note-taking, I attended college-sponsored workshops designed to help students take better notes and improve other study skills. All of a sudden, it was the end of the term, with final exam week on top of me. I hadn't studied for a few of my classes and realized that my old note-taking habits really took more of my time than if I had taken neat, organized, and relevant notes in the first place. The class syllabus became a bible for studying. I constantly reviewed the requirements and asked my professors if they had further suggestions. Slowly I learned to understand their style of teaching. Most importantly, I learned how to take effective notes. In the end, I was able to reduce my study time, and my grades improved dramatically. The only thing I regret is not having discovered note-taking techniques sooner.

When the order is not apparent, you'll need to indicate in your notes where the gaps lie. After the lecture, consult the reading material or classmates to fill in these gaps, or ask your instructor. Most instructors have regular office hours for student appointments, yet it is amazing how few students use these opportunities for one-on-one instruction. Asking questions during class also might help your instructor discover which parts of the lecture need more attention and clarification.

WIRED WINDOW

YOU WILL DISCOVER many options for using technology to enhance your note-taking skills and your engagement with learning. Some students prefer to bring their laptops to class and either type their notes or use the tablet feature to handwrite their notes into digital files. We think it's important to strike a balance between taking notes on your computer and paying attention to class discussion. Most students can't type as quickly as they can write and will need to be much more selective about the information they choose to enter, so you might face a greater challenge extracting the most important points of the lecture or discussion while it is happening. QipIt, a free service, allows you to take pictures of documents including PowerPoint presentations, whiteboard notes, and overheads, and have them converted to digital documents. If you choose to use such a service, make sure you have obtained permission from your professor to reproduce their notes. Whether you use QipIt or type your own notes in a word processor, it's helpful to organize them so you can find what you are looking for. Just assign file names that reflect the content of the notes and the date you took them.

4. Keep your notes and supplementary materials (such as handouts) for each course in a separate three-ring binder labeled with the course number and name. If the binders are too bulky to carry around all day in your backpack, create a separate folder for each class, stocked with loose-leaf notebook paper. Before class, label and date the paper you will be using for taking notes. Then, as soon after class as possible, move your notes from the folder to the binder.

5. Download any notes, outlines, or diagrams, charts, graphs, and other visual representations of the material that are provided on the instructor's website prior to class and bring them with you. You might be able to save yourself considerable time during the lecture if you do not have to try to copy complicated graphs and diagrams while the instructor is talking; instead you can focus on the ideas being presented, meanwhile adding your own labels and notes to the visual image.

6. Organize your notes chronologically in your binder. Then create separate tabbed sections for homework, lab assignments, returned tests, and other materials.

7. If handouts are distributed in class, label them and place them in your binder either immediately before or immediately after the notes for that day. Purchase a portable three-ring hole-punch that can be kept in your binder. Do not let handouts accumulate in your folders; add any handouts to your binders as you review your notes each day.

Taking Notes in Non-lecture Courses

Always be ready to adapt your note-taking methods to match the situation. Group discussion is becoming a popular way to teach in college because it engages students in active participation. On your campus you might also have **Supplemental Instruction** (SI) classes that provide further opportunity to discuss the information presented in lectures.

How do you keep a record of what's happening in such classes? Assume you are taking notes in a problem-solving group assignment. You would begin your notes by asking yourself "What is the problem?" and writing down the answer. As the discussion progresses, you would list the solutions offered. These would be your main ideas. The important details might include the positive and negative aspects of each view or solution. The important thing to remember when taking notes in non-lecture courses is that you need to record the information presented by your classmates as well as by the instructor, and to consider all reasonable ideas, even though they might differ from your own.

When a course has separate lecture and discussion sessions, you will need to understand how the discussion sessions relate to and augment the lectures. If different material is covered in lecture or discussion, you might need to ask for guidance in organizing your notes. When similar topics are covered, you can combine your notes so that you have comprehensive, unified coverage of each topic.

How to organize the notes you take in a class discussion depends on the purpose or form of the discussion. But it usually makes good sense to begin with the list of issues or topics that the discussion leader announces. Another approach is to list the questions that the participants raise for discussion. If the discussion explores reasons for and against a particular argument, it makes sense to divide your notes into columns or sections for pros and cons. When conflicting views are presented in discussion, it is important to record different perspectives and the rationales behind them. Your teacher might ask you to defend your own opinions in light of those of others.

Taking Notes in Science and Mathematics Courses

Many mathematics and science courses build on each other from term to term and year to year. When you take notes in these courses, you will likely need to refer to them in future terms. For example, when taking organic chemistry, you might need to refer to notes taken in earlier chemistry courses. This can be particularly important when time has elapsed since your last course, like after a summer break. Also, taking notes in math and science courses can be different from other types of classes, where it is not a good idea to try to write down every word the instructor says. Here are some tips to keep in mind specifically when taking quantitative and scientific classes:

▶ Write down any equations, formulas, diagrams, charts, graphs, and definitions that the instructor puts on the board or screen.

▶ Quote the instructor's words precisely, to the extent possible. Technical terms often have exact meanings and cannot be paraphrased.

▶ Use standard symbols, abbreviations, and scientific notation.

▶ Write down all worked problems and examples, step-by-step. They often provide the template for exam questions. Actively engage in solving the problem yourself as it is solved at the front of the class. Be sure that you can follow the logic and understand the sequence of steps. If you have questions that you cannot ask during lecture, write them down in your notes so that you can ask them in discussion, lab, or during the instructor's office hours.

▶ Consider taking your notes in pencil or erasable pen. You will probably need to use an eraser or make changes in your notes when copying long equations while also trying to pay attention to the instructor or when copying problems that other students are solving at the board. You want to keep your notes as neat as possible. You can then use colored ink to add other details later.

▶ Listen carefully to other students' questions and the instructor's answers. Take notes on the discussion and during question-and-answer periods.

▶ Use asterisks, exclamation points, question marks, or symbols of your own to highlight important points in your notes or questions that you need to come back to when you review.

▶ Refer back to the textbook after class; the text might contain more accurate diagrams and other visual representations than you are able to draw while taking notes in class. If they are not provided in handouts or on the instructor's website, you might even want to photocopy diagrams from the text and include them with your notes in your binder.

▶ Keep your binders for math and science courses until you graduate (or even longer if there is any chance that you will attend graduate school at some point in the future). They will serve as beneficial review materials for later classes in math and science sequences and for preparing for standardized tests like the Graduate Record Exam (GRE) or Medical College Admission Test (MCAT). In some cases, these notes can also prove helpful in the workplace.

Using Technology to Take Notes

While some students use laptops for note-taking, others find they prefer taking notes by hand so they can easily circle important items or copy complex equations or diagrams while they are being presented in class. If you handwrite your notes, entering them on a computer after class for review purposes might be helpful, especially if you are a kinesthetic learner. After class you can also cut and paste diagrams and other visual representations into your notes and print a copy that might be easier to read than notes you wrote by hand.

Some students, especially aural learners, find it is advantageous to tape lectures. But if you tape, resist the temptation to become passive in class rather than actively listening. Students with specific types of disabilities might be urged to tape lectures or have note-takers who type at a laptop while the student views the notes on a separate screen.

After Class: Write, Recite, Review

Don't let the forgetting curve take its toll on you. As soon after class as possible, review your notes and fill in the details you still remember but missed writing down. At this point, it might be a good idea to relate new information to other things you already know. That will provide another way for you to organize your information.

One way to remember is to recite important data to yourself every few minutes. If you are an aural learner, you might want to repeat your notes out loud. Another idea is to tie one idea to another idea, concept, or name, so that thinking of one will prompt recall of the other. Or you might want to create your own poem, song, or slogan using the information.

For interactive learners, the best way to learn something might be to teach it to someone else. You will understand something better and remember it longer if you try to explain it. This helps you discover your own reactions and uncover gaps in your comprehension of the material. (Asking and answering questions in class also provides you with the feedback you need to make certain your understanding is accurate.) Now you're ready to embed the major points from your notes in your memory. Use these three important steps for remembering the key points from the lecture:

1. Write down the main ideas. For 5 or 10 minutes, quickly review your notes and select key words or phrases that will act as labels or tags for main ideas and key information in the notes.

2. Recite your ideas out loud. Recite a brief version of what you understand from the class in which you have just participated. If you don't have a few minutes after class when you can concentrate on reviewing your notes, find some other time during that same day to review what you have written. You might also want to ask your teacher to glance at your notes to determine whether you have identified the major ideas.

3. Review the previous day's notes just before the next class session. As you sit in class the next day waiting for the lecture to begin, use the time to quickly review the notes from the previous day. This will put you in tune with the lecture that is about to begin and also prompt you to ask questions about material from the previous lecture that might not have been clear to you.

These three ways to engage with the material will pay off later, when you begin to study for your exams.

What if you have three classes in a row and no time for studying between them? Recall and recite as soon after class as possible. Review the most recent class first. Never delay recall and recitation longer than one day; if you do, it will take you longer to review, select main ideas, and recite. With practice, you can complete the review of your main ideas from your notes quickly, perhaps between classes, during lunch, or while riding the bus.

Comparing and Recopying Notes

You might be able to improve your notes by comparing notes with another student or in a study group, Supplemental Instruction session, or a learning community, if one is available to you. Knowing that your notes will be seen by someone else will prompt you to make your notes well organized, clear, and accurate. Compare your notes: Are they as clear and concise as other students'? Do you agree on the most important points? Share with each other how you take and organize your notes. You might get new ideas for using abbreviations. Take turns testing each other on what you have learned. By doing this, you are predicting exam questions and determining whether you can answer them. Incidentally, comparing notes is not the same as copying somebody else's notes. You simply cannot learn as well from someone else's notes, no matter how good they are, if you have not attended class.

If your campus has a note-taking service, check with your instructor about making use of this for-pay service, but keep in mind that such notes are intended to supplement the ones you take, not to substitute for them. Some students choose to copy their own notes as a means of review, or because they think their notes are messy and that they will not be able to understand them later. Unless you are a tactile learner, copying or typing your notes might not help you learn the material. A more profitable approach might be to summarize your notes in your own words.

Finally, have a backup plan in case you do need to be absent due to illness or a family emergency. Exchange phone numbers and e-mail addresses with other students so that you can contact one of them to learn what you missed and get a copy of their notes. Also contact your instructor to explain your absence and set up an appointment during office hours to make sure you understand the work you missed.

Class Notes and Homework

Good class notes can help you complete homework assignments. Follow these steps:

1. Review the homework assignment so that you will know what to look for in your notes.

2. Skim the notes and put a question mark next to anything you do not understand at first reading. Draw stars next to topics that warrant special emphasis. Try to place the material in context: What has been going on in the course for the past few weeks? How does today's class fit in?

3. Do any assigned problems and answer any assigned questions. When you start doing your homework, read each question or problem and ask, "What am I supposed to find or find out?" If you work the problem or answer the question without referring to your notes or text, you will test your knowledge and know when you are prepared for exams.

4. Persevere. Don't give up too soon. When you encounter a problem or question that you cannot readily handle, consult your textbook or notes. If you can't find the answer, move on only after a reasonable effort. After you have completed the entire assignment, come back to those items that stumped you. Try once more, then take a break. You might need to mull over a particularly difficult problem for several days. Let your unconscious mind have a chance. Inspiration can come when you are waiting for a stoplight or just before you fall asleep.

You might be thinking, "That all sounds good, but who has the time to do all that extra work?" But all that work actually saves you time and can improve your grades. Try it for a few weeks to see if it works for you.

Write • DISCUSS • Compare • Ask • BLOG • Answer • *Journal*

> What is your reaction to these suggestions about taking notes and studying for class? Which ideas will you implement in your note-taking strategies? Why? Do you think they have the potential to help you earn better grades? Why?

Participating in Class: Speak Up!

Learning is not a spectator sport. To really learn, you must talk about what you are learning, write about it, relate it to past experiences, and make what you learn part of yourself. Participation is the heart of **active learning**. When we say something in class, we are more likely to remember it than when someone else does. So when a teacher tosses a question your way, or when you have a question to ask, you're actually making it easier to remember the day's lesson.

Naturally, you will be more likely to participate in a class where the teacher emphasizes discussion, calls on students by name, shows students signs of approval and interest, and avoids criticizing you for an incorrect answer. Often, answers you and others offer that are not quite correct can lead to new perspectives on a topic.

Unfortunately, large classes often cause instructors to use the lecture method, and large classes can be intimidating. If you speak up in a class of 100 and think you've made a fool of yourself, you also think that 99 other people will know it. Of course, that's somewhat unrealistic, since you've probably asked a question that they were too timid to ask, and they'll silently thank you for doing so. If you're lucky, you might even find that the instructor of such a class takes time out to ask or answer questions. To take full advantage of these opportunities, try using these techniques:

1. Take a seat as close to the front as possible. If you're seated by name and your name is Zitch, plead bad eyesight or hearing—anything to get moved up front.

2. Keep your eyes trained on the teacher. Sitting up front will make this easier for you to do.

3. Focus on the lecture. Do not let yourself be distracted. It might be wise not to sit near friends who can be distracting without meaning to be.

4. Raise your hand when you don't understand something. The instructor might answer you immediately, ask you to wait until later in the class, or throw your question to the rest of the class. In each case, you benefit in several ways. The instructor gets to know you, other students get to know you, and you learn from both the instructor and your classmates. But don't overdo it. Both the instructor and your peers will tire of too many questions that disrupt the flow of the class.

5. Speak up in class. Ask a question or volunteer to answer a question or make a comment. It becomes easier every time you do this.

6. Never feel that you're asking a stupid question. If you don't understand something, you have a right to ask for an explanation.

7. When the instructor calls on you to answer a question, don't bluff. If you know the answer, give it. If you're not certain, begin with, "I think . . . , but I'm not sure I have it all correct." If you don't know, just say so.

8. If you've recently read a book or article that is relevant to the class topic, bring it in. Use it either to ask questions about the piece or to provide information from it that was not covered in class. Next time you have the opportunity, speak up. Class will go by faster, you and your fellow students will get to know one another, your instructor will get to know you, and he or she will, in all likelihood, be grateful to have your participation.

Becoming Engaged in Learning

No matter how good your listening and note-taking techniques are, you will not get the most out of college unless you become an engaged learner. Engaged students devote the time and the energy necessary to develop a real love of learning, both in and out of class.

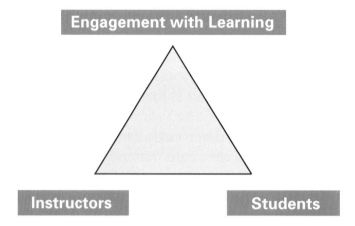

▶ **Figure 5.6**
When all three of these parts work in harmony, learning tends to improve.

Although you might acquire knowledge listening to a lecture, you might not be motivated to think about what that knowledge means to you. By being actively engaged in learning, you will learn not only the material in your notes and textbooks, but also how to:

▶ Work with others

▶ Improve your critical thinking, listening, writing, and speaking skills

▶ Function independently and teach yourself

▶ Manage your time

▶ Gain sensitivity to cultural differences

Engagement in learning requires that you be a full and active participant in the learning process. While your instructors will set the stage and provide valuable information, it's up to you to do the rest. Your college experience will be more rewarding if you take advantage of the resources your college offers, including the library, cultural events, the faculty, and other students. This approach to learning has the potential to make you well rounded in all aspects of life. The hexagon in Figure 5.7 depicts seven aspects of development, with intellectual development at its center. Optimal development depends on each area supporting every other area.

The One-Minute Paper and Other Tips for Engagement

Another simple way to become engaged in learning is through a process called the "one-minute paper." In a major study of teaching at Harvard University, a simple feedback exercise constituted one of many suggestions for improving learning. At the end of each class, students wrote down their understanding of the main issue of that class and what their unanswered questions were for the next class. Using the one-minute paper helps instructors to determine if they provided a clear presentation and to use your unanswered questions for the next class. Even if your instructors don't require it, try writing a one-minute paper each day at the end of class. Use it to think about the main issues discussed that day, and save it so that you will be prepared to

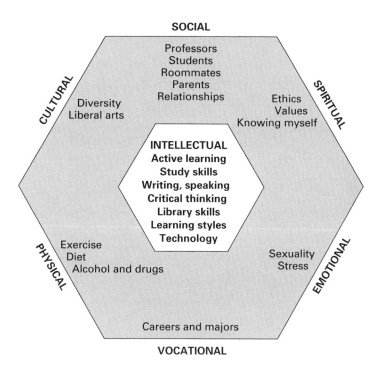

◀ **Figure 5.7**
Aspects of Student
Development

ask good questions at the next class meeting. If you're in a study group, compare answers and questions; you might learn something!

Here are some additional things you can do to become engaged in learning:

▶ Ask friends which teachers employ active learning before you choose a class.

▶ Go beyond the required reading. Investigate other information sources in the library or on the Internet.

▶ If you disagree with what your instructor says, politely offer your opinion. Instructors will listen and might still disagree with you, but they might also think more of you for showing you can think.

▶ Interact with professors, staff members, and other students. One easy way is through e-mail. Some professors offer first-year students the opportunity to collaborate in research projects and service activities. You'll also find many opportunities to become involved in campus organizations. Becoming involved in out-of-class opportunities will help you develop relationships with others on campus.

Collaborative Learning Teams

More than likely, you'll be working with others after college, so now is a good time to learn how to **collaborate**. Collaboration with other students in learning groups will increase your engagement, and will help you learn more effectively.

Joseph Cuseo of Marymount College, an expert on collaborative learning, points to these advantages of learning groups:

▶ Students learn from one another as well as from the instructor.

▶ "Two heads are better than one. Collaboration can lead to more ideas, alternative approaches, new perspectives, and better solutions.

▶ If you're not comfortable speaking out in larger classes, you will tend to be more comfortable speaking in smaller groups, resulting in better communication and better ideas.

▶ You will develop stronger bonds with other students in the class, which can increase everyone's interest in attending.

▶ "Positive competition" among groups happens when several groups are asked to solve the same problem, as long as the instructor clarifies that the purpose is for the good of all.

▶ Working in groups can help you develop leadership skills.

Write • DISCUSS • Compare • Ask • BLOG • Answer • *Journal*

How do you respond when an instructor assigns group work? What is your initial reaction? Why do you think you react that way? How might group work be beneficial for you outside of college?

Making Learning Teams Productive

Not all learning groups are equally effective. Sometimes teamwork is unsuccessful or fails to reach its potential because no thought was given to how the group was formed or how it should function. Use the following strategies to develop high-quality learning teams that maximize the power of peer collaboration:

1. Remember that learning teams are more than study groups. Effective student learning teams collaborate regularly for academic tasks other than test review sessions.

2. In forming teams, seek students who will contribute quality and diversity to the group. Resist the urge to include people just like you. Look for students who are motivated, attend class regularly, are attentive and participate actively while in class, and complete assignments. Include teammates of different genders; ethnic, racial, or cultural backgrounds; different age groups; and different personality types and learning styles.

3. Keep the group small (four to six teammates). Smaller groups allow for more face-to-face interaction and eye contact and less opportunity for any one individual to shirk responsibility to the team.

4. Hold individual team members personally accountable for contributing to the learning of their teammates. One way to ensure accountability is to have each member come to group meetings with specific information or answers to share with teammates as well as questions to ask the group.

The Many Uses of Learning Teams

The following lists various types of learning teams:

▶ Note-taking teams. Team up with other students immediately after class to share and compare notes so that your group can consult with the instructor about any missing or confusing information.

▶ Reading teams. After completing reading assignments, team with other students to compare highlighting and margin notes. See if all agree.

▶ Library research teams. This is an effective way to develop a support group for reducing "library anxiety" and for locating and sharing sources of information. This does not constitute cheating or plagiarizing as long as the final product you turn in represents your own work.

▶ Team/instructor conferences. Have your learning team visit the instructor during office hours to seek additional assistance, as needed.

▶ Team test results review. After receiving test results, members of a learning team can review their individual tests together to help one another identify the sources of their mistakes and to review any answers that received high scores.

If you are a returning student, you and other returnees might form your own group and discuss the differences between your lives before college and now; or, you might prefer to join a group of recent high school graduates to hear and provide a different point of view.

▶ WHERE TO GO FOR HELP

On Campus

Learning Assistance Center Almost every campus has one of these, and this chapter's topic is one of their specialties. More and more, the best students, and good students who want to be the best students, use learning centers as much as students who are having academic difficulties. These services are offered by both full-time professionals and highly skilled student tutors, all of whom are available at times convenient for you.

Fellow College Students Often the best help we can get is the closest to us: fellow students. Keep an eye out in your classes, residence hall, co-curricular groups, and other places for the most serious, purposeful, and directed students. Those are the ones to seek out. Find a tutor. Join a study group. Students who do these things are much more likely to stay in college and be successful. It does not diminish you in any way to seek assistance from your peers.

Online

Toastmasters International offers public speaking tips at http://www.toastmasters.org/pdfs/top10.pdf
See guidelines for speaking in class at:
http://www.school-for-champions.com/grades/speaking.htm

My Institution's Resources

_____

_____

_____

_____

_____

_____

▶▶▶ BUILDING YOUR PORTFOLIO
Making Meaning

It is important that students bring a certain ragamuffin, barefoot irreverence to their studies; they are not here to worship what is known, but to question it.

—Jacob Bronowski (1908–1974), English-Polish mathematician

To complete this portfolio activity electronically, please visit
academic.cengage.com/collsucc/Gardner/YCE8e.

Chapter 5 includes several examples of note-taking strategies, but did you catch the emphasis on what you do with your notes after class? Sometimes it is helpful to associate a concept with something of interest for you. And often, preparing to teach someone else how to do something or explaining a complex idea to others can help you to fully understand the information.

1. Create a new entry in your portfolio with the title "Making Meaning." Record your work for this activity there.

2. Choose a set of current class notes (it doesn't matter which class) and specifically look for connections between the subject matter and your personal interests and goals (future career, social issue, sports, hobbies, etc.)

   a. Next, develop a five-minute presentation using PowerPoint to present to your classmates; your presentation should outline your class notes and show the connection to your interests.

      i. Introduction slide
      Tip: Be sure to include your name and the date of the presentation.

      ii. Content slides (A good rule of thumb is one slide per minute)
      Tip: Keep your slides simple by focusing on key words and concepts. Use short phrases rather than complete sentences so you won't be tempted to read directly from the slide.

      iii. Closing slides
      Tip: Anticipate questions your audience might have by reviewing the questions at the end of the textbook chapter or by recalling questions that were asked during your class session.

3. Write a brief introduction/description and then attach your PowerPoint presentation to your description. You probably won't be creating PowerPoint presentations for all of your class notes, but making a habit of connecting class content to your life is an easy way of remembering information. When it is time to prepare for a test, try pulling your notes into a presentation that you would feel comfortable presenting to your classmates—after that, the exam should be a breeze!

CHAPTER 6

Reading Strategies

In this chapter YOU WILL LEARN

▶ How to prepare to read

▶ How to preview reading material

▶ How to read your textbooks efficiently

▶ How to mark your textbooks

▶ How to review your reading

▶ How to adjust your reading style to the material

▶ How to develop a more extensive vocabulary

Reading effectively will help you find the road to college success.

© Rhoda Sidney/PhotoEdit

Jeanne L. Higbee of the University of Minnesota Twin Cities and Mary Ellen O'Leary of the University of South Carolina at Columbia contributed their valuable and considerable expertise to the writing of this chapter.

What Are Your READING Strategies?

A?B?C?A?B?C?A?B?C?

Choose the response that best applies to you:

1 **When you are assigned a reading for class, how do you usually begin your reading?**

(A) I sometimes flip through to see if there will be any interesting topics or pictures I can look forward to.

(B) I take a look at all of the headings and skim the chapter for material I'm familiar with.

(C) When I do the reading, I just read from beginning to end—I like to be surprised when I read for my courses.

2 **How do you take notes when you read for your courses?**

(A) I sometimes use a highlighter to mark words I should look up.

(B) I pencil my notes in the margin to summarize what I read and put it into my own words—that helps me remember it and proves to myself I understand what I read.

(C) I only skim the reading a few minutes before class and don't have time to make notes.

3 **When do you review your reading from class?**

(A) Right away, if it's something I'm interested in, but if I'm not interested, I just force myself to look at it again right before the exam.

(B) Once a week—I designate a day to go over readings to be sure they are fresh in my head.

(C) Never—I read it once, so there's nothing else to go over.

4 **Why do you think professors assign readings for your courses?**

(A) So we have something to talk about in class and they can test us on it.

(B) So that they can refer to readings during class and have students expand their knowledge on the subject.

(C) So that they can keep students busy.

5 **Do you set reading goals for yourself?**

(A) I try to, but I usually get distracted before I can meet my goal.

(B) I go to a place where I can concentrate, finish my reading, and then give myself a break to relax and start again.

(C) No, I usually don't do the reading.

Review your responses. (A) responses indicate that you have some idea of how to read effectively for class, but in order to do your best, you'll need to improve. (B) responses indicate that you have a good idea of how to read and comprehend course material. (C) responses indicate that you need to develop a better understanding of the reading strategies you will need to do well in college classes. Wherever you are in your current understanding, this chapter will help you learn more about why reading is a basic strategy for success in the classroom.

Why is reading college textbooks more challenging than reading high school texts or reading for pleasure? College texts are loaded with concepts, terms, and complex information that you are expected to learn on your own in a short period of time. To accomplish all this, it's best that you learn and use reading strategies such as the ones explained in this chapter. These strategies are intended to help you get the most out of your college reading.

The following plan for textbook reading can pay off. It is designed to increase your focus and concentration, promote greater understanding of what you read, and prepare you to study for tests and exams. This system is based on four steps:

1. Previewing
2. Reading
3. Marking
4. Reviewing

Write • DISCUSS • Compare • Ask • BLOG • Answer • *Journal*

> Which of these four steps do you always, sometimes, or never do?
> Do any seem unnecessary? Why? After you read this chapter,
> go back and see if you have changed your mind.

Previewing

The purpose of previewing is to get the big picture, to understand how what you are about to read connects with what you already know and to the material the instructor covers in class. Begin by reading the title of the chapter. Ask yourself, "What do I already know about this subject?" Next, quickly read through the introductory paragraphs, then read the summary at the beginning or end of the chapter (if there is one). Finally, take a few minutes to skim through the chapter headings and subheadings. Note any study exercises at the end of the chapter.

As part of your preview, note how many pages the chapter contains. It's a good idea to decide in advance how many pages you can reasonably expect to cover in your first 50-minute study period. This can help build your concentration as you work toward your goal of reading a specific number of pages. Before long, you'll know how many pages are practical for you.

Keep in mind that different types of textbooks might require more or less time to read. For example, depending on your interests and previous knowledge, you might be able to read a psychology text more quickly than a logic text that presents a whole new symbol system.

Mapping

Mapping the chapter as you preview it provides a visual guide for how different chapter ideas fit together. Because many students identify themselves as visual learners, visual mapping is an excellent learning tool for test preparation, as well as reading (see chapter 3: How We Learn). How do you map a chapter? While you preview the chapter, use either a wheel or a branching structure. In the wheel structure, place the central idea of the chapter in the circle. The central idea should be found in the introduction to the chapter and might also be apparent in the chapter title. Place secondary ideas on the spokes emanating from the circle, and place offshoots of those ideas on the lines attached to the spokes. In the branching map, the main idea goes at the top, followed by supporting ideas on the second tier, and so forth. Fill in the title first. Then, as you skim through the rest of the chapter, use the headings and subheadings to fill in the key ideas.

Alternatives to Mapping

Perhaps you prefer a more linear visual image. If so, consider making an outline of the headings and subheadings in the chapter. You can fill in the outline after you read. Or, make a list. Making a list can be particularly effective when dealing with a text that

Wheel Map

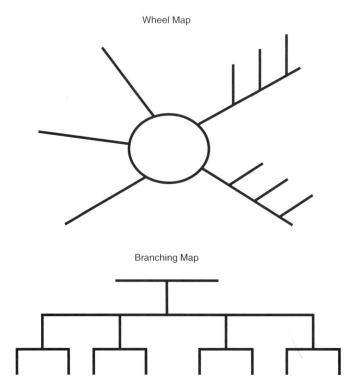

Branching Map

▶ **Figure 6.1**
Wheel and Branching Maps

introduces lots of new terms and their definitions. Set up the list with the terms in the left column and fill in definitions, descriptions, and examples on the right after you read. Divide the terms on your list into groups of five, seven, or nine, and leave white space between the clusters so that you can visualize each group in your mind. This practice is known as "**chunking.**" Research indicates that we learn material better in chunks of five, seven, or nine.

If you are an interactive learner, make lists or create a flash card for each heading and subheading. Then, fill in the back of each card after reading each section in the text. Use the lists or flash cards to review with a partner, or recite the material to yourself.

Previewing, combined with mapping, outlining, or flash cards, might require more time up front, but it will save you time later because you have created an excellent review tool for quizzes and tests. You will be using your visual learning skills as you create "advanced organizers" to help you associate details of the chapter with the larger ideas. Such associations will come in handy later. As you preview the text material, look for connections between the text and the related lecture material. Call to mind the related terms and concepts that you recorded in the lecture. Use these strategies to warm up. Ask yourself, "Why am I reading this? What do I want to know?"

Reading Your Textbook

Read Before You Highlight After completing your preview, you are ready to read the text actively. With your skeleton map or outline, you should be able to read more quickly and with greater comprehension. To avoid marking too much or marking the wrong information, first read without using your pencil or highlighter. When

◀ **Reading enriches your college experience**

you have read enough to understand what is important, you can then go back and highlight. When you have reached the end of a section, stop and ask yourself, "What are the key ideas in this section? What do I think I'll see on the test?" Then, and only then, decide what to underline or highlight.

Annotate You might want to try annotating the text, a strategy discussed in chapter 5. In your own words, write key ideas in the margins of the text. By using annotations, you can remind yourself what is most important or what you might want to reread before the test.

Learn to Concentrate Students commonly have trouble concentrating or understanding the content when they read textbooks. Many factors might affect your ability to concentrate and understand texts: the time of day, your energy level, your interest in the material, and your study location.

Consider these suggestions, and decide which would help you improve your reading ability:

▶ Find a study location that is removed from traffic and distracting noises, preferably in the campus library.

▶ Read in blocks of time, with short breaks in between. Some students can read for 50 minutes; others find that a 50-minute reading period is too long. By reading for small blocks of time frequently during the day instead of cramming in all your reading at the end of the day, you should be able to process material more easily.

▶ Set goals for your study period, such as "I will read 20 pages of my psychology text in the next 50 minutes." Reward yourself with a 10-minute break after each 50-minute study period.

▶ If you have trouble concentrating or staying awake, take a quick walk around the library or down the hall. Stretch or take some deep breaths and think positively about your study goals. Then resume studying.

▶ Jot study questions in the margins, take notes, or recite key ideas. Reread confusing parts of the text, and make a note to ask your instructor for clarification.

Write • DISCUSS • Compare • Ask • BLOG • Answer • *Journal*

Do you have trouble concentrating while you read your textbooks?
What strategies do you use to make sure
that your mind doesn't wander?

▶ Focus on the important portions of the text. Pay attention to the first and last sentences of paragraphs and to words in italics or bold print.

▶ Use the glossary in the text or a dictionary to define unfamiliar terms.

As you begin reading, be sure to learn more about the textbook and its author by reading the front matter in the book, such as the preface, foreword, introduction, and author's biographical sketch. The preface is usually written by the author (or authors) and will tell you why the book was written and what material it covers. Textbooks often have a preface written to the instructor and a separate preface for the students. The foreword is often an endorsement of the book written by someone other than the author. Some books will have an additional introduction that reviews the book's overall organization and its contents chapter by chapter. Books might also include biographical information about the authors that will give you important details about their background. Some textbooks will have questions at the end of each chapter that you can use as a study guide or as a quick check on your understanding of the chapter's main points. Take time to read and respond to these questions, whether or not your instructor requires you to do so.

Write • DISCUSS • Compare • Ask • BLOG • Answer • *Journal*

Look at the front material in this book. What does it tell you about
the authors? How do the authors' biographies change the way you
think about what's written in this book?

Textbooks by their very nature try to cover a lot of material in a fairly limited space. Although many of them seem detailed, they won't necessarily provide all the things you want to know about a topic—those things that can make your reading more interesting. If you find yourself fascinated by a particular topic, go to the **primary sources**—the original research or document. You'll find those referenced in many

Confessions of a College Student

Name: Marisa F. Rodriguez

Age: 30

College: Pima Community College

Hometown: Tucson, AZ

Major: Business, Finance

Favorite book(s): *My Sister's Keeper, The House of the Spirits*

Favorite college course: Writing

The person who inspires me the most or who I would most like to meet: My kids inspire me the most.

Heroes: My mom and my grandma

Favorite way to relax: Reading a good book

Your proudest moment or biggest accomplishment: I would have to say that having my children were my proudest moments as well as my biggest accomplishments to date. I plan to add graduating from college to this list.

Favorite food: Lasagna

Reading strategies confession: I find college texts difficult to read because the information they contain isn't always something that is particularly interesting to me, so I find myself procrastinating. Yet, I know the reading is important to my studies, so I have to get through it. To help myself through this difficulty, I first skim the material and only read the portions that interest me. Then I go through the material again later in more detail, this time taking notes. Writing down important details helps me remember things more solidly than if I just read the material and try to memorize it. I find that talking out loud to myself helps me work through particularly difficult areas of the reading. I put the text in my own words so that I can relate to the reading and therefore make it easier to remember.

Reading the text for each course is crucial to your college education. Each chapter of your text contains information your instructors might use in their lectures. By reading the text before the lectures, you will better understand what they say. You will also be able to ask informed questions.

textbooks, either at the end of the chapters or in the back of the book. You can read more information about primary sources on page 119.

You might also go to other related sources that are credible—whatever makes the text more interesting and informative for you. Remember, most texts are not designed to treat topics in depth. Your textbook reading will be much more interesting if you dig a bit further in related sources. Because some textbooks are sold with "test banks," your instructors might draw their examinations directly from the text, or they might use the textbook only to supplement the lectures. Ask your instructors, if they have not made it clear, what the tests will cover and the types of questions used. In addition, you might try to find a student who has taken a course with your instructor so that you can get a better idea of how tests are designed. Some instructors expect that you will learn the kinds of detail that you can only get through the textbook. Others are much more concerned that you be able to understand broad concepts that come from lectures, in addition to texts and other readings.

Finally, not all textbooks are equal. Some are simply better designed and written than others. If your textbook is exceptionally hard to understand or seems disorganized, let your instructor know your opinion. Based on what you say, your instructor might focus on explaining the text and how it's organized or use a different text for future classes.

Write • DISCUSS • Compare • Ask • BLOG • Answer • *Journal*

What is your favorite text in one of your current courses? Why? Which is your least favorite text? Why? How can you work to make this text more interesting?

Reading Math Texts

While the previous suggestions about textbook reading apply across the board, mathematics textbooks present some special challenges because they tend to have lots of symbols and very few words. Each statement and every line in the solution of a problem needs to be considered and digested slowly. Typically, the author presents the material through definitions, theorems, and sample problems. As you read, pay special attention to definitions. Learning all the terms in a new topic is the first step toward understanding.

Derivations of formulas and proofs of theorems are usually included to maintain mathematical rigor. You must understand and be able to apply the formulas and theorems, but unless your course has a particularly theoretical emphasis, you are less likely to be responsible for all the proofs. Thus, if you get lost in the proof of a theorem, go on to the next item in the section. When you come to a sample problem, it's time to get busy. Pick up pencil and paper and work through the problem with the author. Then, cover the solution and think through the problem on your own. Of course, the exercises that follow each text section form the heart of any math book. A large portion of the time you devote to the course will be spent completing assigned textbook exercises. It is absolutely vital that you do this homework in a timely manner, whether or not your instructor collects it. Success in mathematics requires regular practice, and students who keep up with math homework, either alone or in groups, perform better than those who don't.

After you complete the assignment, skim through the other exercises in the problem set. Reading the unassigned problems will deepen your understanding of the topic and its scope. Finally, talk it through to yourself, and be sure your focus is on understanding the problem and its solution, and not on memorization. Memorizing something might help you remember how to work through one problem, but it does not help you understand the steps involved so that you can employ them for other problems.

Reading Science Texts

Your approach to your science textbook will depend somewhat on whether you are studying a math-based science, such as physics, or a text-based science, such as biology. In either case, you need to become acquainted with the overall format of the book. Review the table of contents and the glossary and check the material in the appendices. There you will find lists of physical constants, unit conversions, and various charts and tables. Many physics and chemistry books also include a mini-review of the math you will need in science courses.

Notice the organization of each chapter and pay special attention to graphs, charts, and boxes. The amount of technical detail might seem overwhelming, but—believe it or not—the authors have sincerely tried to present the material in an easy-to-follow format. Each chapter might begin with chapter objectives and conclude with a short summary, sections you might wish to study both before and after reading the chapter. You will usually find answers to selected problems in the back of the book. Use the answer key or the student solutions manual in a responsible way to promote your mastery of each chapter.

As you begin an assigned section in a science text, skim the material quickly to gain a general idea of the topic. Begin to absorb the new vocabulary and technical symbols. Then skim the end-of-chapter problems so you'll know what to look for in your detailed reading of the chapter. State a specific goal: "I'm going to learn about recent developments in plate tectonics," or "I'm going to distinguish between mitosis and meiosis," or "Tonight I'm going to focus on the topics in this chapter that were stressed in class."

Should you underline and highlight, or should you outline the material in your science textbooks? You might decide to underline or highlight for a subject such as anatomy, which involves a lot of memorization. But use restraint with a highlighter; it should pull your eye only to important terms and facts. If highlighting is actually a form of procrastination for you (you are reading through the material but planning to learn it at a later date) or if you are highlighting nearly everything you read, your highlighting might be doing you more harm than good as you won't be able to quickly identify important concepts if they're lost in a sea of color.

In most sciences, it is best to outline the text chapters. You can usually identify main topics, subtopics, and specific terms under each subtopic in your text by the size of the print. For instance, in each chapter of this textbook, the main topics (or level-1 headings) are in large purple letters. Following each major topic heading, you will find subtopics, or level-2 headings, printed in blue letters. The level-3 headings, which tell more about the subtopics, are in bold, red letters.

To save time when you are outlining, you won't write full sentences, but you will include clear explanations of new technical terms and symbols. Pay special attention to topics that the instructor covered in class. If you aren't sure whether your outlines contain too much or too little detail, compare them with those of members of your study group. In preparing for a test, it's a good idea to make condensed versions of your chapter outlines so that you can see how everything fits together.

Reading Social Science and Humanities Texts

Many of the suggestions that apply to science textbooks also apply to reading in the social sciences (sociology, psychology, anthropology, economics, political science, and history). Social science texts are filled with special terms or "jargon" unique to the field of study. They also describe research and theory building and contain references to many primary sources. Your social science texts might also describe differences in opinions or perspectives. Not all social scientists agree on any one issue, and you

▶ **Careful highlighting will draw your eyes to important material**

© Don Smetzer/PhotoEdit

might be introduced to a number of ongoing debates about particular issues. In fact, your reading can become more interesting if you seek out different opinions about a common issue. You might have to go beyond your particular textbook, but your library will be a good source of various viewpoints about ongoing controversies.

Textbooks in the **humanities** (philosophy, religion, literature, music, and art) provide facts, examples, opinions, and original material, such as stories or essays. You will often be asked to react to your reading by identifying central themes or characters.

Some instructors believe that the way we structure courses and majors artificially divides human knowledge and experience. For instance, they argue that subjects such as history, political science, and philosophy are closely linked, and studying each subject separately results in only partial understanding. By stressing the linkages between courses, you are encouraged to think in an **interdisciplinary** manner. You might be asked to consider how the book or story you're reading or the music you're studying reflects the political atmosphere or the culture of the period. Your art instructor might direct you to think about how a particular painting gives you a window on the painter's psychological make-up or religious beliefs.

Write • DISCUSS • Compare • Ask • BLOG • Answer • *Journal*

Are you ever tempted not to buy a textbook? Why? What can you do as an alternative? How important do you think textbooks are in your courses? What other ways can you tell your instructor you are accessing the information they want you to learn?

Reading Primary Source Material

Whether or not your instructor requires you to read material in addition to the textbook, your reading will be enriched if you go to some of the primary sources that are referenced in each chapter of your text. These sources can take the form of journal articles, research papers, dissertations (the major research papers that students write to earn a doctoral degree), or original essays, and can be found in your library and on the Internet. Reading primary source material gives you a depth of detail that few textbooks accomplish.

Many primary sources were originally written for other instructors or researchers. Therefore they often use language and refer to concepts that are familiar to other scholars but not necessarily to first-year college students. If you are reading a journal article that describes a theory or research study, one technique for easier understanding is to read from the end to the beginning. Read the article's conclusion and discussion, then go back to see how the author performed the experiment or formulated the ideas. If you aren't concerned about the specific method used to collect the data, you can skip over the "methodology" section. In almost all scholarly journals, articles are introduced by an abstract, a paragraph-length summary of the methods and major findings. Reading the **abstract** is a quick way to get the gist of a research article before you dive in. As you're reading research articles, always ask yourself, "So what?" Was the research important to what we know about the topic, or, in your opinion, was it unnecessary?

Marking Your Textbook

Think a moment about your goals for making marks in your own texts. Some students report that **marking** is an active reading strategy that helps them to focus and concentrate on the material as they read. In addition, most students expect to use

▲ **Purchasing, as well as reading, course textbooks is essential for college success.**

their text notations when studying for tests. To meet these goals, some students like to underline, some prefer to highlight, and others use margin notes or annotations. Figure 6.2 provides an example of each method. No matter what method you prefer, remember these two important guidelines:

1. Read before you mark. Finish reading a section before you decide which are the most important ideas and concepts. Mark only those ideas, using your preferred methods (highlighting, underlining, circling key terms, annotating).

2. Think before you mark. When you read a text for the first time, everything can seem important. Only after you have completed a section and reflected on it will you be ready to identify the key ideas. Ask yourself, "What are the most important ideas? What will I see on the test?" This can help you avoid marking too much material.

Two other considerations might affect your decisions regarding textbook marking. First, if you just make notes or underline directly on the pages of your textbook, you are committing yourself to at least one more viewing of all the pages that you have already read—all 400 pages of your anatomy or art history textbook. A more productive use of your time might be taking notes, creating flash cards, making lists, or outlining textbook chapters. These methods are also more practical if you intend to review with a friend or study group.

Second, sometimes highlighting or underlining can provide you with a false sense of security. You might have determined what is most important, but you have not necessarily tested yourself on your understanding of the material. When you force yourself to put something in your own words while taking notes, you are not only predicting exam questions but assessing whether you can answer them. Although these active reading strategies take more time initially, they can save you time in the long run because they not only promote concentration as you read but also make it easy to review. So, you probably won't have to pull an all-nighter before an exam.

Reading to Question, Interpret, and Understand

Monitor Your Comprehension

An important step in textbook reading is to monitor your comprehension. As you read, ask yourself, "Do I understand this?" If not, stop and reread the material. Look up words that are not clear. Try to clarify the main points and how they relate to one another.

Another way to check comprehension is to try to recite the material aloud, either to yourself or your study partner. Using a study group to monitor your comprehension gives you immediate feedback and is highly motivating. One way that group members can work together is to divide up a chapter for previewing and studying and get together later to teach the material to one another.

Recycle Your Reading

After you have read and marked or taken notes on key ideas from the first section of the chapter, proceed to each subsequent section until you have finished the chapter.

CONCEPT CHECKS

7. Some students who read a chapter slowly get very good grades; others get poor grades. Why?

8. Most actors and public speakers who have to memorize lengthy passages spend little time simply repeating the words and more time thinking about them. Why? (Check your answers on page 288.)

People need to monitor their understanding of a text to decide whether to keep studying or whether they already understand it well enough. Most readers have trouble making that judgment correctly.

Self-Monitoring of Understanding

Whenever you are studying a text, you periodically have to decide, "Should I keep on studying this section, or do I already understand it well enough?" Most students have trouble monitoring their own understanding. In one study, psychology instructors asked their students before each test to guess whether they would do better or worse on that test than they usually do. Students also guessed after each test whether they had done better or worse than usual. Most students' guesses were no more accurate than chance (Sjostrom & Marks, 1994). Such inaccuracy represents a problem: Students who do not know how well they understand the material will make bad judgments about when to keep on studying and when to quit.

why

Even when you are reading a single sentence, you have to decide whether you understand the sentence or whether you should stop and reread it. Here is a sentence once published in the student newspaper at North Carolina State University:

> He said Harris told him she and Brothers told French that grades had been changed.

How

Ordinarily, when good readers come to such a confusing sentence, they notice their own confusion and reread the sentence or, if necessary, the whole paragraph. Poor readers tend to read at their same speed for both easy and difficult materials; they are less likely than good readers to slow down when they come to difficult sentences.

Although monitoring one's own understanding is difficult and often inaccurate, it is not impossible. For example, suppose I tell you that you are to read three chapters dealing with, say, thermodynamics, the history of volleyball, and the Japanese stock market. Later you will take tests on each chapter. Before you start reading, predict your approximate scores on the three tests. Most people make a guess based on how much they already know about the three topics. If we let them read the three chapters and again make a guess about their test performances, they do in fact make more accurate predictions than they did before reading (Maki & Serra, 1992). That improvement indicates some ability to monitor one's own understanding of a text.

A systematic way to monitor your own understanding of a text is the **SPAR method:** **S**urvey, **P**rocess meaningfully, **A**sk questions, and **R**eview and test yourself. Start with an overview of what a passage is about, read it carefully, and then see whether you can answer questions about the passage or explain it to others. If not, go back and reread.

SPAR
Survey
Process
Ask
Review

Also decide about larger units?

The Timing of Study

Other things being equal, people tend to remember recent experiences better than earlier experiences. For example, suppose someone reads you a list of 20 words and asks you to recall as many of them as possible. The list is far too long for you to recite from your phonological loop; however, you should be able to remember at least a few. Typically, people remember items at the beginning and end of the list better than they remember those in the middle.

That tendency, known as the **serial-order effect,** includes two aspects: The *primacy effect* is the tendency to remember the first items; the *recency effect* refers to the tendency to remember the last items. One explanation for the primacy effect is that the listener gets to rehearse the first few items for a few moments alone with no interference from the others. One explanation for the recency effect is that the last items are still in

Cause of primacy effect

Memory Improvement

283

▲ **Figure 6.2** Sample Marked Pages

Cause of recency effect

the listener's phonological loop at the time of the test.

The phonological loop cannot be the whole explanation for the recency effect, however. In one study, British rugby players were asked to name the teams they had played against in the current season. Players were most likely to remember the last couple of teams they had played against, thus showing a clear recency effect even though they were recalling events that occurred weeks apart (Baddeley & Hitch, 1977). (The phonological loop holds information only for a matter of seconds.)

So, studying material—or, rather, *reviewing* material—shortly before a test is likely to improve recall. Now let's consider the opposite: Suppose you studied something years ago and have not reviewed it since then. For example, suppose you studied a foreign language in high school several years ago. Now you are considering taking a college course in the language, but you are hesitant because you are sure you have forgotten it all. Have you?

Harry Bahrick (1984) tested people who had studied Spanish in school 1 to 50 years previously. Nearly all agreed that they had rarely used Spanish and had not refreshed their memories at all since their school days. (That is a disturbing comment, but beside the point.) Their retention of Spanish dropped noticeably in the first 3 to 6 years, but remained fairly stable from then on (Fig-

ure 7.18). In other words, we do not completely forget even very old memories that we seldom use.

In a later study, Bahrick and members of his family studied foreign-language vocabulary either on a moderately frequent basis (practicing once every 2 weeks) or on a less frequent basis (as seldom as once every 8 weeks), and tested their knowledge years later. The result: More frequent study led to faster learning; however, less frequent study led to better long-term retention, measured years later (Bahrick, Bahrick, Bahrick, & Bahrick, 1993).

The principle here is far more general than just the study of foreign languages. *If you want to remember something well for a test,* your best strategy is to study it as close as possible to the time of the test, in order to take advantage of the recency effect and decrease the effects of retroactive interference. Obviously, I do not mean that you should wait until the night before the test to start studying, but you might rely on an extensive review at that time. You should also, ideally, study under conditions similar to the conditions of the test. For example, you might study in the same room where the test will be given, or at the same time of day.

However, *if you want to remember something long after the test is over,* then the advice I have just given you is all wrong. To be able to remember something whenever you want, wherever you are, and whatever you are doing, you should study it under as varied circumstances as possible. Study and review at various times and places with long, irregular intervals between study sessions. Studying under such inconsistent conditions will slow down your original learning, but it will improve your ability to recall it long afterwards (Schmidt & Bjork, 1992).

Studying for test vs. studying for long term

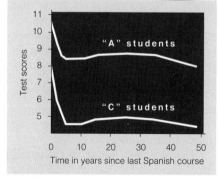

FIGURE 7.18
(Left) Spanish vocabulary as measured by a recognition test shows a rapid decline in the first few years but then long-term stability. (From Bahrick, 1984.) (Right) Within a few years after taking your last foreign-language course, you may think you have forgotten it all. You have not, and even the part you have forgotten will come back (through relearning) if you visit a country where you can practice the language.

CHAPTER 7
MEMORY
284

▶ **Figure 6.2** Sample Marked Pages (continued)

> How do you monitor your own reading comprehension? Based on the material in this chapter, what are some strategies you could use to ensure you understand what you are reading?

After you have completed each section—and before you move on to the next section—ask again, "What are the key ideas? What will I see on the test?" At the end of each section, try to guess what information the author will present in the next section.

Good reading should lead you from one section to the next, with each new section adding to your understanding.

Reviewing

The final step in effective textbook reading is reviewing. Many students expect the improbable—that they will read through their text material one time and be able to remember the ideas 4, 6, or even 12 weeks later at test time. More realistically, you will need to include regular reviews in your study process. Here is where your notes, study questions, annotations, flash cards, visual maps, or outlines will be most useful. Your study goal should be to review the material from each chapter every week.

Consider ways to use your many senses to review. Recite aloud. Tick off each item in a list on each of your fingertips. Post diagrams, maps, or outlines around your living space so that you will see them often and will likely be able to visualize them while taking the test.

Improving Your Reading

With effort, you can improve your reading dramatically, but remember to be flexible. How you read should depend on the material. Assess the relative importance and difficulty of the assigned readings, and adjust your reading style and the time you allot accordingly. Connect one important idea to another by asking yourself, "Why am I reading this? Where does this fit in?" When the textbook material is virtually identical to the lecture material, you can save time by concentrating mainly on one or the other. It takes a planned approach to read textbook materials and other assigned readings with good understanding and recall.

Developing Your Vocabulary

Textbooks are full of new terminology. In fact, one could argue that learning chemistry is largely a matter of learning the language of chemists and that mastering philosophy or history or sociology requires a mastery of the terminology of each particular **discipline.**

▶ WHERE TO GO FOR HELP

On Campus

Learning Assistance Center Most campuses have learning centers, and they specialize in reading assistance. Both the best students and struggling students use learning centers, where full-time professionals and skilled student tutors offer services.

Fellow college students Your best help can come from a fellow student. Look for the best students—those who appear to be the most serious and conscientious. Hire a tutor if you can, or join a study group. You are much more likely to be successful.

Online

Middle Tennessee State University: http://www.mtsu.edu/~studskl/Txtbook.html The "Study Skills Help" web page has a link to "Reading Your Textbooks."

Niagara University's Office for Academic Support: http://www.niagara.edu/oas/learning_center/study_reading_strategies/21_Tips_For_Better_Textbook_Reading.htm Read these "21 Tips for Better Textbook Reading."

My Institution's Resources

_____

_____

_____

_____

_____

_____

If words are such a basic and essential component of our knowledge, what is the best way to learn them? Follow these basic vocabulary-building strategies:

▶ During your overview of the chapter, notice and jot down unfamiliar terms. Consider making a flash card for each term, or making a list.

▶ When you encounter challenging words, consider the context. See if you can predict the meaning of an unfamiliar term using the surrounding words.

▶ If context by itself is not enough, try analyzing the term to discover the root, or base part, or other meaningful parts of the word. For example, emissary has the root "to emit" or "to send forth," so we can guess that an emissary is someone sent forth with a message. Similarly, note prefixes and suffixes. For example, "anti" means "against" and "pro" means "for."

▶ Use the glossary of the text, a dictionary, or the online **Merriam-Webster Dictionary** to locate the definition. Note any multiple definitions, and search for the meaning that fits this usage.

▶ Take every opportunity to use these new terms in your writing and speaking. If you use a new term, you'll soon know it. In addition, studying new terms on flash cards or study sheets can be handy at exam time.

Listening, note-taking, and reading are the essentials for success in each of your classes. You can perform these tasks without a plan, or you can practice some of the ideas presented in this chapter. If your notes are already working, great. If not, now you know what to do.

▶ **A dictionary is a college student's best friend.**

If English Is Not Your First Language

The English language is one of the most difficult languages to learn. Words are often spelled differently from the way they sound, and the language is full of **idioms**—phrases that are peculiar and cannot be understood from the individual meanings of the words. If you are a non-native English speaker and are having trouble reading your texts, don't give up. Reading slowly and reading more than once can help you improve your comprehension. Make sure that you have two good dictionaries—one in English and one that links English with your primary language—and look up every word that you don't know. Be sure to practice thinking, writing, and speaking in English, and take advantage of your college's helping services. Your campus might have ESL (English as a Second Language) tutoring and workshops. Ask your advisor or your first-year seminar instructor to help you locate those services.

▶▶▶ BUILDING YOUR PORTFOLIO
The Big Picture

The more that you read, the more things you will know.
The more that you learn, the more places you'll go.

–Theodor Seuss Geisel, a.k.a. Dr. Seuss (1904–1991), American writer and cartoonist

To complete this portfolio activity electronically, please visit
academic.cengage.com/collsucc/Gardner/YCE8e.

Chapter 6 of *Your College Experience* introduces a reading strategy called **mapping** as a visual tool for getting the big picture of what you are preparing to read. Mapping a textbook chapter can help you quickly recognize how different concepts and terms fit together and make connections to what you already know about the subject. There are a number of ways of mapping, including "wheel maps" and "branching maps," noted in chapter 6. You might also use other types of maps, such as *matrices* to compare and contrast ideas or show cause and effect; a *spider web* to connect themes; or *sketches* to illustrate images, relationships, or descriptions.

1. Create a new entry in your portfolio with the title "The Big Picture." Record your work for this assignment there.

2. Look through your course syllabi and identify a reading assignment that you need to complete in the next week.

   Which class are you preparing for? _____

3. Begin by previewing the first chapter of the reading assignment. Practice mapping the chapter by filling out the wheel map below or create your own version using the drawing toolbar in Microsoft Word. Attach it to your portfolio entry.

   Chapter title: _____

   a. Place the central idea of the chapter in the center of the wheel.

   b. Place supporting ideas on the "spokes" of the wheel.

   c. Place important details on the lines attached to the spokes.

   Tip: A good place to start is with chapter headings and subheadings, then move on to terms in bold, using graphics like charts, tables, and diagrams. Textbooks often have study questions at the end of the chapter; these can give you clues as to the most important concepts.

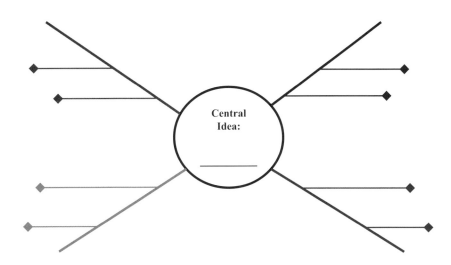

Optional: Create your own previewing map: map one chapter of your reading assignment, and include the document in your portfolio.

Reading a textbook efficiently and effectively requires that you develop reading strategies to make the most of your study time. Mapping can help you to organize and retain what you have read, making it a good reading and study tool. Writing, reciting, and organizing the main points, supporting ideas, and key details of the chapter will help you to recall the information on test day.

Learning to Study, Comprehend, and Remember

In this chapter YOU WILL LEARN

▶ How study groups can help you prepare

▶ How cheating hurts you, your friends, and your college or university

▶ How commonsense study methods can produce greater learning

▶ Common myths about memory

▶ How to improve your ability to memorize

▶ Why a good memory can be an asset, but isn't all you need to do well in college

Spend 5 seconds looking at this photo and then close the book. How many things can you remember from the photo?

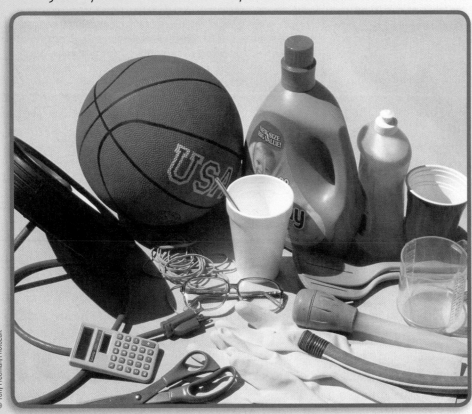

© Tony Freeman/PhotoEdit

Jeanne L. Higbee of the University of Minnesota Twin Cities contributed her valuable and considerable expertise to the writing of this chapter.

How Well Do You STUDY, COMPREHEND, and REMEMBER?

A?B?C?A?B?C?A?B?C?

Read the following questions and choose the answer that most fits you.

1   How do you remember information for a test?

A   I review my notes, make index cards of key points, and review each week prior to the exam.

B   Once I've heard it in class, I don't ever need to review. If it stuck in my memory, then it's important.

C   I sometimes review, but I find that I always forget a few things for every exam. If I had known them, I would have gotten an A.

2   How would you rate your attention span when instructors lecture and explain course material?

A   I can focus my attention on what is being presented by taking careful notes and making sure I understand everything that is being said.

B   I am always doodling on my page, text messaging friends, or snoozing.

C   No matter how hard I try to pay attention, my mind wanders and I have to make myself focus again, so I feel like I only get parts of the lecture.

3   Do you have a good idea of the kinds of study and memory techniques that work best for you?

A   Definitely. I use a variety of methods, but the best one is studying in a group.

B   I don't really have particular techniques for studying and remembering.

C   I've been trying different techniques but haven't found the right ones yet. I'm working on it.

4   Do you use strategies for organizing information that help you remember it better?

A   I organize my notes after each class so that I can connect and remember information that is presented.

B   However the instructor presents the material is how it's organized for me—they've already done the work, so why should I reorganize it?

C   Sometimes I'll put all the keywords, phrases, or dates together and review them, but that strategy doesn't work for all my classes.

5   Is memorizing the same as understanding something?

A   I don't think so—you can memorize anything if you try, but to understand something, you need to really think about it.

B   Sure it is—it's in my brain, right? So it must mean I understand it.

C   I'm not sure—it seems like it could sometimes be the same, but not always.

Review your responses. **A** responses indicate that you have a good idea of how to study and remember course material. **B** responses indicate that you don't currently understand how to study or prepare for exams. **C** responses indicate that you have some idea of how to study and remember, but you still need to improve. Wherever you are currently, this chapter will help you learn more about basic strategies of studying, understanding, and remembering course material.

Studying

Studying and remembering are essential to getting the most out of your college experience. While many students think that the only reason for studying is to do well on exams, a far more important reason is to learn and understand course information. If you study in order to increase your understanding, you are more likely to remember and apply what you learn not only to tests, but also to future courses and to life beyond college.

You might have learned to study effectively while you were in high school, or you might be finding that you need to learn more about how to study. In college you will need to spend time out of class reviewing course material, doing assigned reading, and keeping up with your homework. Occasionally you will also want to go the extra mile by doing additional (unassigned) reading and investigating particular topics that interest you.

This chapter offers you a number of strategies for making the best use of your study time and also addresses the important topic of memory. There's no getting around it: if you can't remember what you have read or heard, you won't do well on course exams.

Tips for Effective Studying

Whether you are completing class assignments or preparing for a test, these strategies will help you study more effectively.

1. Make studying a part of your daily routine. Don't allow days to go by when you don't crack a book or keep up with course assignments.

2. Manage your study time wisely. Create a schedule that will allow you to prepare for exams and complete course assignments on time. Be aware of "crunch times" when you might have several exams or papers due at once. Create some flexibility in your schedule to allow for unexpected distractions.

3. Collaborate with others. One of the most effective ways to study is in a group with other students. Gather a group of students who study together in your first year of college. Study groups can meet throughout the term, or they can review for midterms or final exams.

4. Look back at your VARK score from chapter 3 and make your learning style work for you as you study. If you are a visual learner, create diagrams, lists, flash cards, or other visual aids that will enhance memory. If you are an aural learner, be sure to attend discussions and tutorials. Use a tape recorder in class and replay the lecture. Aural learners often find that talking out loud is more effective than reciting in their heads. This might mean that you'll occasionally need to study alone so you won't bother others when you're talking to yourself. If you are a read/write learner, take notes on your notes and read them again. Turn diagrams and charts into words. If you are a kinesthetic learner, move around the room while you study. Gesture with your arms and hands. Try to convert your notes into real life examples.

5. Be alert for external distractions. Choose a place to study where you can concentrate. That might be in your residence hall or room at home, or you might have to go somewhere else. The campus library is often the best place to go for uninterrupted study.

Write • DISCUSS • Compare • Ask • BLOG • Answer • *Journal*

> Where do you usually study? Is this a good location for concentrating—why or why not?

6. Get enough sleep. Don't cut back on your sleep in order to cram in additional study hours. Remember that most tests will require you to be able to think clearly about the concepts that you have studied. Especially during final exam weeks, it is important to be well rested in order to remain alert for extended periods of time.

7. Follow a regular exercise program. Walking, jogging, swimming, or other aerobic activities might help you think more clearly and provide positive and needed study breaks.

8. Get a tutor. Tutoring is not just for students who are failing. Often the best students seek tutorial assistance to ensure that they understand course material. Many tutors are students, and many campus tutoring services are free. Ask your academic advisor, counselor, or campus learning center about the availability of tutoring or other kinds of academic support.

Studying to Understand and Remember

Studying will help you accomplish two goals: understanding and remembering. While memory is a necessary tool for learning, what's most important is that you study to develop a deep understanding of course information. When you truly comprehend what you are learning, you will be able to place names, dates, and specific facts in context and you will also be able to exercise your critical thinking abilities.

The human mind has discovered ingenious ways to understand and remember information. Here are some methods that might be useful to you as you're trying to nail down the causes of World War I, remember the steps in a chemistry problem, or absorb a mathematical formula:

1. Pay attention to what you're hearing or reading. This suggestion is perhaps the most basic and the most important. If you're sitting in class thinking about everything except what the professor is saying or if you're reading and you find that your mind is wandering, you're wasting your time. Force yourself to focus.

> *Write* • DISCUSS • Compare • Ask • BLOG • Answer • *Journal*
>
> When you're in class, how would you rate your level of concentration on what the instructor is saying? Is it good, fair, or poor? In which classes do you concentrate best and worst? Why do you think it's easier to concentrate more in some classes than in others?

2. "Overlearn" the material. After you know and think you understand the material you're studying, go over it again to make sure that you'll retain it for a long time. Test yourself or ask someone else to test you. Recite what you're trying to remember aloud in your own words.

3. Check the Internet. If you're having trouble remembering what you have learned, google a keyword and try to find interesting details that will engage you in learning more, not less, about the subject. Many first-year courses cover such a large amount of material that you'll miss the more interesting details—unless you seek them out for yourself. But as your interest increases, so will your memory.

4. Be sure you have the big picture. Whenever you begin a course, make sure that you're clear on what the course will cover. You can talk with someone who has already taken the course or you can take a brief look at all the reading assignments. Having the big picture will help you understand and remember the details of what you're learning.

◀ **Studying with others will improve your learning and your ability to do well on tests.**

5. Look for connections between your life and what's going on in your courses. College courses might seem irrelevant to you, but actually, if you look, you'll find many connections between course material and your daily life. Seeing those connections will make your course work more interesting and will help you remember what you're learning. For example, if you're taking a music theory course and studying chord patterns, listen for those patterns in contemporary music.

6. Get organized. If your desk or your computer is organized, you'll spend less time remembering a file name or where you put a particular document. And as you rewrite your notes, putting them in a logical order (either chronological or thematic) that makes sense to you will help you learn and remember them.

Write • DISCUSS • Compare • Ask • BLOG • Answer • *Journal*

> Look around your room and at your computer desktop. Is your living environment neat and organized? How about your "electronic environment"? Does a lack of organization ever cause you to waste time? What strategies could you use to become better organized?

7. Reduce stressors in your life. Although there's no way to determine how much worry or stress causes you to be unable to focus or to forget, most people will agree that stress can be a distraction. Healthy, stress-reducing behaviors, such as meditation, exercise, and sleep, are especially important for college students. Many campuses have counseling or health centers that can provide resources to help you deal with whatever might be causing stress in your daily life.

▶ **Both exercise and relaxation can help you relieve stress.**

© Sidney Shaffer/Getty Images

How Memory Connects to Deep Learning

It's easy for many of us to blame a poor memory on the way we live; multitasking has become the norm for college students and instructors. Admittedly, it's hard to focus on anything for very long if your life is full of daily distractions and competing responsibilities, or if you're not getting the sleep you need. Have you ever had the experience of walking into a room with a particular task in mind and immediately forgetting what that task was? You were probably interrupted either by your own thoughts or by someone or something else. Or have you ever felt the panic that comes from blanking on a test, even though you studied hard and thought you knew the material? It might have been that you pulled an all-nighter studying and that exhaustion raised your stress level and caused your mind to go blank. Such experiences are common and happen to everyone at one time or another. But obviously, to do well in college—and in life—it's important that you improve your ability to remember what you're reading, hearing, and experiencing. As one writer put it, "there is no learning without memory."[1] On the other hand, not all memory involves real learning.

Is a good memory all you need to do well in college? Most memory strategies tend to focus on helping you remember names, dates, numbers, vocabulary, graphic materials, formulas—the bits and pieces of knowledge. But if you know the date the Civil War began and the fort where the first shots were fired, but you don't really know why the Civil War was fought, you're missing the point of a college education. College is

[1] Harry Lorayne, *Super Memory, Super Student: How to Raise Your Grades in 30 Days* (Boston: Little, Brown and Company, 1990).

about deep learning, understanding the "why" and "how" behind the details. So don't forget that while recall of specific facts is certainly necessary, it isn't sufficient. In order to do well in college courses you will need to understand major themes and ideas, and you will also need to hone your ability to think critically about what you're learning—a topic discussed in depth in chapter 4 of this book.

How Memory Works

Kenneth Higbee describes two different processes involved in memory. The first is **short-term memory,** defined as how many items you are able to perceive at one time. Higbee found that information stored in short-term memory is forgotten in less than 30 seconds (and sometimes much faster), unless you take action to either keep that information in short-term memory or move it to long-term memory.

While short-term memory is significantly limited, it has a number of uses. It serves as an immediate but temporary holding tank for information. It helps you maintain a reasonable attention span so that you can keep track of topics mentioned in conversation, and it enables you to stay on task with the goals you are pursuing at any moment. But even these simple functions of short-term memory fail on occasion. If the telephone rings, if someone asks you a question, or if you're interrupted in any way, you might find that your attention suffers and that you essentially have to start over in reconstructing short-term memory.

The second memory process is **long-term memory,** and this is the type of memory that you will need to improve in order to remember what you're learning in college. Long-term memory can be described in three ways. "Procedural" remembering concerns knowing how to do something, such as solving a mathematical problem or playing a musical instrument. "Semantic" memory involves facts and meanings without remembering where and when you learned those things. And, "episodic" memory deals with particular events, their time, and place.[2]

You are using your procedural memory when you get on a bicycle you haven't ridden in years, when you can recall the first piece you learned to play on the piano, or when you effortlessly type a letter or class report. Your semantic memory is used continuously to recall word meanings or important dates, such as your mother's birthday. Episodic memory allows you to remember events in your life—a vacation, your first day in school, the moment you opened your college acceptance letter. Some people can recall not only the event but also the very date and time the event happened. For others, although the event stands out, the dates and times are harder to remember immediately.

Short-term memory	Long-term memory
Stores information for about 30 seconds	Procedural: remembering how to do something
Can contain from five to nine chunks of information at one time	Semantic: remembering facts and meanings Episodic: remembering the time and place of events
Information either forgotten or moved to long-term memory	

[2] W. F. Brewer & J. R. Pani, The Structure of Human Memory. In *The Psychology of Learning and Motivation: Advances in Research and Theory*, ed. G. H. Bower, vol. 17, 1–38 (New York: Academic Press, 1983).

Strategies for Improving Your Memory

Throughout history, human memory has been a topic of great interest and fascination for scientists and the general public. Although severe problems with memory are extremely rare, you're in good company if you find that occasionally your memory lets you down, especially if you're nervous or stressed or when grades depend on immediate recall of what you have read, heard, or written.

So how can you increase your ability to store information in your brain for future use? Psychologists and learning specialists have conducted research on memory and have developed a number of strategies that you can use as part of a study skills regimen. Some of them might be new to you, but others will be simple commonsense ways to maximize your learning—ideas that you've heard before, but perhaps not in the context of increasing your memory.

The benefits of having a good memory are obvious. In college, your memory will help you retain information and ace tests. After college, the ability to recall names, procedures, presentations, and appointments will save you energy, time, and a lot of embarrassment.

There are many ways to go about remembering. Have you ever had to memorize a speech or lines from a play? How you approach committing the lines to memory might depend on your learning style. If you're an aural learner, you might choose to record your lines as well as lines of other characters and listen to them on tape. If you're a visual learner, you might remember best by visualizing where your lines appear on the page in the script. If you learn best by reading, you might simply read and reread the script over and over, and if you're a kinesthetic learner, you might need to walk or move across an imaginary stage as you read the script.

Write • DISCUSS • Compare • Ask • BLOG • Answer • *Journal*

> How can you apply your learning style to remembering material for an exam? List some strategies that you already use or might want to try in the future.

Although knowing specific words will help, remembering concepts and ideas can be much more important. To embed such ideas in your mind, ask yourself these questions as you review your notes and books:

1. What is the essence of the idea?

2. Why does the idea make sense? What is the logic behind it?

3. How does this idea connect to other ideas in the material?

4. What are some possible arguments against the idea?

Confessions of a College Student

Name: Alyssa Cantu

Age: 19

University: Sam Houston State University

Hometown: Houston, TX

Major: Psychology

Favorite book: *Blue Like Jazz*

Favorite college course: Contemporary Biology

The person who inspires me the most or who I would most like to meet: My mother inspires me to do the best in everything I do, take nothing for granted, and reminds me constantly that nothing is impossible; she is the person who inspires me the most.

Favorite way to relax: Watching a good comedy movie

Are you the first to go to college in your family? If so, what impact has that had on your experience? Yes, I am the first person in my family to go to college. I feel like I am gaining a valuable experience my parents were not able to have, so I have worked hard to succeed because I *want* to learn and don't want to let them down. I have tried to be

involved in as many activities as I can and have kept my grades up so that I can make them proud.

Favorite food: Pepperoni pizza!

Memory confession: I have learned that writing good notes has helped me remember the material more easily. Taking notes by writing instead of keyboarding helps me pay attention and focus on the topic. After I write my notes, I type them later and organize them at the same time. So actually, I'm going over the material once again. If I need to master vocabulary for a class, I study with index cards. If the material is extensive, I might write down keywords highlighted in the text.

Mnemonics

Mnemonics (pronounced "ne MON iks") are various methods or tricks to aid the memory. Mnemonics tend to fall into four basic categories.

1. Acronyms. New words created from the first letters of several words can be helpful in remembering. The Great Lakes can be more easily recalled by remembering the word "HOMES" for Huron, Ontario, Michigan, Erie, and Superior.

2. Acrostics. An acrostic is a verse in which certain letters of each word or line form a message. Many piano students were taught the order of sharps by remembering the acrostic "Francis Can Go Down And Eat Bread" – F, C, D, A, E, B.

3. Rhymes or Songs. Do you remember learning "Thirty days hath September, April, June, and November. All the rest have 31, excepting February alone. It has 28 days time, but in leap years it has 29"? You were using a mnemonic rhyming technique to remember the days in each month.

4. Visualization. You use visualization to associate words, concepts, or stories with visual images. The more ridiculous the image, the more likely you are to remember it. So use your imagination to create mental images when you're studying important words or concepts. For example, as you're driving to campus, choose some landmarks along the way to help you remember material for your history test. The next day, as you pass those landmarks, relate them to something from your class notes or readings. A white picket fence might remind you of the British army's eighteenth-century approach to warfare, with its official uniforms and straight lines of infantry, while a stand of trees of various shapes and sizes might remind you of the Continental army's more rustic approach.

Mnemonics work because they make information meaningful through the use of rhymes, patterns, and associations. They impose meaning where meaning might be hard to recognize. Mnemonics provide a way of organizing material, a sort of mental filing system. That's why mnemonics probably aren't needed if what you are studying is very logical and organized.

Although mnemonics are a time-tested way of remembering, the method has some limitations. The first is time. Thinking up rhymes, associations, or visual images can take longer than simply learning the words themselves through repetition. Also, it is often difficult to convert abstract concepts into concrete words or images, and it's possible that you might be able to remember an image without recalling the underlying concept. Finally, memory specialists debate whether learning through mnemonics actually helps with long-term knowledge retention and whether this technique helps or interferes with deeper understanding.

Myths about Memory

Although scientific knowledge about how our brains function increases all the time, Kenneth Higbee suggests that you might have heard some myths about memory (or maybe even believe them). Here are five of these memory myths, and what experts say about them.

1. Myth: Some people are stuck with bad memories.

Reality: Although there are probably some differences among people in innate memory (the memory ability you are born with), what really gives you the edge are memory skills that you can learn and use. Virtually anyone can improve the ability to remember and recall.

2. Myth: Some people have photographic memories.

Reality: Although a few individuals have truly exceptional memories, most research has found that these abilities more often result from learned strategies, interest, and practice rather than some innate ability. Even though you might not have what psychologists would classify as an exceptional memory, applying the memory strategies presented later in this chapter can help you improve it.

3. Myth: Memory benefits from "exercise."

Reality: Practicing memorizing can help improve memory. If you have ever been a server in a restaurant, you might have been required to memorize the menu.

You might even have surprised yourself at your ability to memorize not only the main entrees, but sauces and side dishes. Experts acknowledge that practice often improves memory, but they argue that the way you practice, such as using special creative strategies, is more important than how long you practice.

4. Myth: Remembering too much can clutter your mind.

Reality: For all practical purposes, the storage capacity of your memory is unlimited. In fact, the more you learn about a particular topic, the easier it is to learn even more.

5. Myth: People only use 10 percent of their brain power.

Reality: No scientific research is available to accurately measure how much of our brain we actually use. However, most psychologists and learning specialists believe that we all have far more mental ability than we actually tap.

Using Your Memory to Study for Tests

Through the consistent use of proven study techniques, you will already have processed and learned most of what you need to know. As you prepare for a test or exam, you will be ready to focus your study efforts on the most challenging concepts and details.

Using Review Sheets, Mind Maps, and Other Tools

To prepare for an exam covering large amounts of material, you need to condense the volume of notes and text pages into manageable study units. Review your materials with these questions in mind: Is this one of the key ideas in the chapter or unit? Will I see this on the test? As indicated in chapter 6, you might prefer to highlight, underline, or annotate the most important ideas or create outlines, lists, or visual maps.

Use your notes to develop review sheets. Make lists of key terms and ideas (from the recall column, if you've used the Cornell method) that you need to remember. Also, do not underestimate the value of using your lecture notes to test yourself or others on information presented in class.

A **mind map** is essentially a review sheet with a visual element. Its word and visual patterns provide you with highly charged clues to jog your memory. Because they are visual, mind maps help many students recall information more easily.

Figure 7.1 shows what a mind map might look like for a chapter on listening and learning in the classroom. See if you can reconstruct the ideas in the chapter by following the connections in the map. Then make a visual mind map for this chapter, and see how much more you can remember after studying it a number of times.

In addition to review sheets and mind maps, you might want to create flash cards. One of the advantages of flash cards is that you can keep them in an outside pocket of your backpack and pull them out to study anywhere, even when you might not think that you have enough time to pull out your notebook to study. Also, you always know where you left off. Flash cards can assist you in making good use of time that otherwise might be wasted, like time spent on the bus or waiting for a friend.

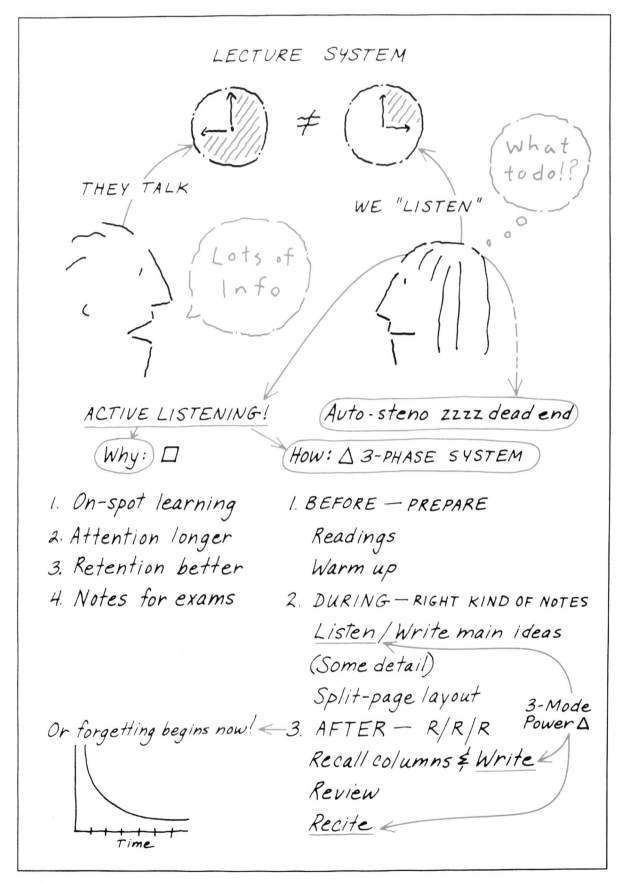

▲ **Figure 7.1** Sample Mind Map on Listening and Learning in the Classroom

Summaries

Writing summaries of class topics can be helpful in preparing for essay and short-answer exams. By condensing the main ideas into a concise written summary, you store information in your long-term memory so you can retrieve it to answer an essay question. Here's how:

1. Predict a test question from your lecture notes or other resources.

2. Read the chapter, supplemental articles, notes, or other resources. Underline or mark main ideas as you go, make notations, or outline on a separate sheet of paper.

3. Analyze and abstract. What is the purpose of the material? Does it compare two ideas, define a concept, or prove a theory? What are the main ideas? How would you explain the material to someone else?

4. Make connections between main points and key supporting details. Reread to identify each main point and supporting evidence. Create an outline to assist you in this process.

5. Select, condense, order. Review underlined material and begin putting the ideas into your own words. Number what you underlined or highlighted in a logical order.

6. Write your ideas precisely in a draft. In the first sentence, state the purpose of your summary. Follow this statement with each main point and its supporting ideas. See how much of the draft you can develop from memory without relying on your notes.

7. Review your draft. Read it over, adding missing transitions or insufficient information. Check the logic of your summary. Annotate with the material you used for later reference.

8. Test your memory. Put your draft away and try to recite the contents of the summary to yourself out loud, or explain it to a study partner who can provide feedback on the information you have omitted.

9. Schedule time to review summaries, and double-check your memory shortly before the test. You might want to do this with a partner, but some students prefer to review alone. Some faculty members will also be open to assisting you in this process and providing feedback on your summaries.

Technology–A Help or a Hindrance to Memory?

Do you have a PDA, a computer calendar, or a watch that beeps when you have an appointment? These are just a few of the devices that can help you remember names, dates, telephone numbers, addresses, and your daily schedule. But there can be a danger in becoming too dependent on technology and losing trust in your own memory. While technological devices are valuable as memory and time management aids, be careful not to rely on them exclusively. Work to move important numbers, names, dates, and information from your short-term to your long-term memory, and use that memory bank first. A PDA or some other computerized device can be a handy backup, but since any electronic device can crash, also be sure to keep backups of information that is critically important to you.

▶ Electronic devices can help you manage your time and remember important information.

© Jon Feingersh/CORBIS

The Temptation to Cheat

Occasionally when you haven't studied or prepared adequately for a test or assignment, you might be tempted to cheat. Are you clear about what constitutes cheating in your classes and what does not? Although some forms of cheating are widely recognized, other behaviors might be considered dishonest by some professors, but not by others. Be sure that you are clear on how your professors define cheating. Read the following five situations. Which ones do you think would be considered cheating?

1. Your professor assigns a take-home exam. You and your best friend decide to complete the exam questions together.

2. You have a paper due in two days. When surfing the net, you find a site that advertises term papers for sale with a guaranteed grade of A or B. You decide to purchase a term paper and submit it as your own work.

3. Your club or organization has a file of tests given by your psychology professor in previous years. You decide to look over the tests to prepare for the exam.

4. While you are taking an exam, you notice that a friend sitting next to you is looking at your answers. You move your exam so that your friend can see it more easily.

5. Your math exam requires that you remember several mathematical formulas. Just to be sure you won't forget, you write them on the palm of your hand.

WIRED WINDOW

EVER WISH THAT YOU could store memories like your computer does? Well, you can… sort of. Using online and handheld tools can help lift some of the burdens of remembering long to-do lists and important dates. You might already have your own PDA. Most cell phones and iPods have calendar software built in. Search your cell phone or iPod menus to see if you have a calendar function. (Hint: the calendar on the iPod is found under "Extras" in the main menu). Try using the calendar in your cell phone or iPod for a few weeks—input all of your assignment due dates and activities that you don't want to forget. Use reminders to alert you of upcoming dates. At the end of your trial period, ask yourself if it helped to use these features. If you don't have a cell phone, iPod, or one with a calendar function, you'll find plenty of free calendar services online. For instance, Google offers Google Calendar, which integrates with Gmail. Try using an online calendar for a few weeks. Some institutions offer access to an online calendar that is saved on a campus server (such as the calendar included in Microsoft Outlook). Campus-based calendars have the added feature of allowing you to directly schedule appointments and events with other students, faculty, and staff.

Although you can probably recognize that the second situation is clearly cheating, the other situations might seem more ambiguous. For instance, some professors will allow you to complete a take-home exam with someone else or with a group. Be sure that you understand the rules about collaborative work and how they apply to take-home exams in your classes. If you find yourself in the third situation and belong to an organization that maintains a test file, ask your professors whether you have their permission to use old tests for review. Some will say that's okay; others might use the same tests from year to year and will consider that to be cheating. In the fourth scenario, both parties are at fault. When you allow someone to use your work as their own, you are also participating in cheating and could receive the same punishment as the person copying your work. And unless your math professor tells you it's okay to bring formulas to class, you will need to commit them to memory, not bring them along with you to the test.

If you decide to cheat, however you accomplish it, you are doing something that is ethically wrong and unfair to yourself and to other students, that shortchanges your own ability to learn, and that can result in serious penalties, including course failure and expulsion. And cheating easily can become a habit, one that will likely catch up with you at some critical point in your life. So trust your ability to learn and devote the time and energy necessary to do your own work. In the long run, you'll be a wiser person.

Write • DISCUSS • Compare • Ask • BLOG • Answer • *Journal*

> Why do you think some students cheat? In your opinion, what can colleges and universities do to reduce the incidence of cheating?

▶ WHERE TO GO FOR **HELP**

On Campus

Your campus probably has a study skills center or learning center that can help you develop effective memory strategies. Other students and faculty can also give you tips on how they remember course material. And your college library will have many books on the topic of memory. Some are written by researchers for the research community, but others are written for people like you who are trying to improve their memory.

Check out these resources:

Books

Kenneth L. Higbee, Ph.D., *Your Memory: How It Works and How to Improve It*, 2nd rev. ed. New York: Marlowe & Co., 2001.

Tony Buzan, *Use Your Perfect Memory*, 3rd rev. ed. New York: Penguin Books, 1991.

Harry Lorayne, *Super Memory, Super Student: How to Raise Your Grades in 30 Days.* Boston: Little, Brown and Company, 1990.

Online

Review of the Research on Memory and College Student Learning: **http://www.ferris.edu/htmls/academics/center/Teaching_and_Learning_Tips/Memory/indexMemory.htm**. This website is designed for instructors, though it also includes lots of interesting information for students.

Memorization Techniques: **http://www.accd.edu/sac/history/keller/ACCDitg/SSMT.htm**. This excellent website is maintained by the Alamo Community College District.

My Institution's Resources

_____

_____

_____

_____

_____

▶▶▶ Building Your Portfolio
Takes Me Back

The sense of smell can be extraordinarily evocative, bringing back pictures as sharp as photographs of scenes that had left the conscious mind.

–Thalassa Cruso (1909–1997), from To Everything There is a Season (1973)

To complete this portfolio activity electronically, please visit
academic.cengage.com/collsucc/Gardner/YCE8e.

Is there a song that reminds you of a certain time in your life or even the exact moment that something happened every time you hear it? Or, maybe you have a photo that you take out every so often to take a trip down memory lane? As discussed in chapter 7, our senses often trigger our memories.

1. Create a new entry in your portfolio with the title "Takes Me Back." Record your work for this activity there.

2. Recall a photo, song, or object that prompts you to recall a life event or time period. If possible, attach your photo or song to your portfolio entry. Or, describe the photo, song, or object. Often it is possible to find song lyrics by doing a quick Internet search.

Upload a song that takes you back.

Insert a photo that brings back memories here.

Or, describe the photo, song, or object.

_____

_____

3. Describe this memory in as much detail as possible.

_____

_____

_____

4. How does that memory make you feel?

_____

_____

_____

5. How might you use photos (or drawings), songs, or mnemonics (methods or tricks to aid the memory) to remember ideas or concepts in your classes?

_____

_____

_____

CHAPTER 8

Taking Exams and Tests

In this chapter YOU WILL LEARN

▶ Ways to prepare yourself for exams

▶ How study groups can help you prepare

▶ How to devise a study plan for an exam

▶ How to reduce test anxiety

▶ What to do during the exam

▶ How to take different types of tests

▶ How cheating hurts you, your friends, and your college or university

How would you describe what is happening in this photo?

© Gabe Palmer/CORBIS

Jeanne L. Higbee of the University of Minnesota Twin Cities and Christel Taylor of University of Wisconsin at Waukesha contributed their valuable and considerable expertise to the writing of this chapter.

How Well Do YOU TAKE EXAMS and TESTS?

A?B?C?A?B?C?A?B?C?

Read the following questions and choose the answer that fits you best.

1 When do you begin studying for a test or examination?

(A) I try to study as I go along so that I don't have to cram before an exam. A few days before the exam, I review all my notes and reading.

(B) I think I learn best under pressure, so I wait until the night before the exam.

(C) I try to keep up with my reading and reviews, but I still do last-minute cram sessions.

2 Do you usually know what to expect on a test before you go into the exam?

(A) I make sure I know the test format and what exactly we'll be tested on so that I'm not surprised the day of the exam.

(B) No, I like to be surprised—I work well under the pressure.

(C) Sometimes—I assume math and science exams will be multiple choice and that English and history exams will be essay format, although I'm not always right.

3 When presented with an essay question on an exam, what do you do?

(A) I pinpoint keywords so that I am sure I know what the question is asking me and then formulate an outline of my answer to help organize my thoughts.

(B) I begin writing my answer immediately and ramble on until I've gotten everything down I know about the topic.

(C) If I don't know the answer, I might panic, but if I do, I can usually get through the question somewhat coherently.

4 What do you do when you finish an exam early?

(A) I like to look over my answers to be sure I didn't make any silly mistakes on multiple choice exams and to clean up any writing errors on essay exams.

(B) Hand it in and get out of there—I'm just glad it's over!

(C) I get a little nervous when I'm the first person in the class to finish, and I will look over my exam until someone else turns in theirs. Then I'll turn mine in.

5 How do you feel after you've taken an exam?

(A) Since I know I prepared well, I usually feel pretty confident.

(B) It's always up in the air for me—I never know how I did until I get it back. I'm usually surprised by my grade, whether it's good or bad.

(C) I'm somewhere between being confident and being panicky until I get the exam back.

Review your responses. (A) responses indicate that you are prepared to do well on exams and tests in college. (B) responses indicate that you haven't really thought much about how to prepare effectively. (C) responses indicate that you have some understanding of what you need to do to prepare, but you need to improve your skills in order to do your best on exams. Whatever your responses, this chapter will help you learn more about this important skill that you will use while you're in college and in life beyond.

You can prepare for exams in many ways, and certain methods are more effective depending on the subject matter, your preferred learning style, and the type of test you'll be taking. Sometimes you'll need to be able to recall names, dates, and other specific bits of information, especially if you are taking multiple-choice or short-answer exams. Many instructors, especially in humanities and social science courses, such as literature, history, and political science, will expect you to go beyond names and dates and have a good conceptual understanding of the subject matter. They often prefer essay exams that require you to use higher-level critical thinking skills, such as analysis, synthesis, and evaluation. They expect you to be able to provide the reasons, arguments, and assumptions on which a given position is based, and the evidence that confirms or discounts it. They want you to be able to support your opinions, to see how you think. They are not looking for answers that merely prove that you can memorize the material presented in lecture and the text. Even in math and science courses, your instructors want you not only to remember the correct theory, formula, or equation, but also to understand and apply what you have learned.

Knowing your preferred learning style will also help you decide the best ways for you to study, no matter what kind of text or exam you are facing. Remember your VARK score and review the material in chapter 3 that helps you link your learning style to strategies for exam preparation.

Getting Prepared for Tests and Exams

Believe it or not, you actually begin preparing for a test on the first day of the term. All of your lecture notes, assigned readings, and homework are part of that preparation. As the test day nears, you should know how much additional time you will need to review, what material the test will cover, and what format the test will take. It is very important to double-check your syllabi exam dates, as in Figure 8.1, and to incorporate these into your overall plans for time management, for example, in your daily and weekly to-do lists.

Here are some specific suggestions to help you prepare well for any exam:

1. Ask your instructor about the exam. Find out whether the test will be essay, multiple choice, true/false, fill-in-the-blank, short-answer, or another format. Ask how long the test will last and how it will be graded. Ask whether all questions will have the same point value. Talk with your instructor to clarify any misunderstandings

History 111, US History to 1865
Fall 2008

Examinations
Note: In this course, most of your exams will be on Fridays, except for the Wednesday before Thanksgiving and the final. This is to give you a full week to study for the exam and permit me to grade them over the weekend and return the exams to you on Monday. I believe in using a variety of types of measurements. In addition to those scheduled below, I reserve the right to give you unannounced quizzes on daily reading assignments. Also, current events are fair game on any exam! Midterm and final exams will be cumulative (on all material since beginning of the course). Other exams cover all classroom material and all readings covered since the prior exam. The schedule is as follows:

Friday, 9/1: Objective type

Friday, : Essay type

Friday, 1: Midterm: essay and objective

Friday, 1: Objective

Friday, 11/14: Open-book type

Wednesday, 11/26: Essay

Tuesday, 12/16: Essay and objective

◀ **Figure 8.1**
A Sample Course Syllabus

you might have about your reading or lecture notes. Some instructors might let you see copies of old exams so you can see the types of questions they use. Never miss the last class before an exam, because your instructor might summarize valuable information.

2. Manage your preparation time wisely. Create a schedule that will give you time to review effectively for the exam without waiting until the night before. Make sure your schedule has some flexibility to allow for unexpected distractions. If you are able to spread your study sessions over several days, your mind will continue to process the information between study sessions, which will help you during the test. Also, let your friends and family know when you have important exams coming up and how that will affect your time with them.

Write • DISCUSS • Compare • Ask • BLOG • Answer • *Journal*

How do you plan your study time for upcoming exams? Do you plan well in advance, or do you tend to wait until the last minute? What kinds of strategies could you use to do a better job in planning for exams? Create a study plan now for your next two upcoming exams.

3. Focus your study. Figure out what you can effectively review that is likely to be on the exam. Collaborate with other students to share information, and try to attend all test or exam review sessions offered by your professor.

4. Design an exam plan. Use the information about the test as you design a plan for preparing. Build that preparation into a schedule of review dates. Develop a to-do list of the major steps you need to take in order to be ready. Be sure you have read and learned all the material by one week prior to the exam. That way you will be able to use the final week to review and prepare for the exam. The week before the exam, set aside a schedule of one-hour blocks of time for review, and make notes on specifically what you plan to accomplish during each hour.

5. Join a study group. You've seen this suggestion in other chapters because joining a study group is one of the most effective strategies for doing well in college, especially preparing for exams. You can benefit from different views of your instructors' goals, objectives, and emphasis; have partners quiz you on facts and concepts; and gain the enthusiasm and friendship of others to help sustain your motivation.

Some instructors will provide time in class for the formation of study groups. Otherwise, ask your teacher, advisor, or campus tutoring or learning center to help you identify interested students and decide on guidelines for the group. Study groups can meet throughout the term, or they can just review for midterms or final exams. Group members should complete their assignments before the group meets and prepare study questions or points of discussion ahead of time. If your study group decides to meet just before exams, allow enough time to share notes and ideas.

6. Get a tutor. Most campus tutoring services are free. Ask your academic advisor or counselor or campus learning center. And many learning centers employ student tutors who have done well in the same courses you are taking. These students might have some good advice on how to prepare for tests given by particular

▲ **Your campus learning center might offer computer tutorials to help you prepare for exams.**

instructors. Learning centers often have computer tutorials that are available to help you refresh basic skills.

7. Prepare yourself emotionally; be confident. If you have given yourself adequate time to review, you will enter the classroom confident that you are in control. Study by testing yourself or quizzing others in a study group or learning community so that you will be sure you really know the material. Instead of telling yourself, "I never do well on math tests," or "I'll never be able to learn all the information for my history essay exam," make positive statements, such as "I have attended all the lectures, done my homework, and passed the quizzes. Now I'm ready to pass the test!"

Write • DISCUSS • Compare • Ask • BLOG • Answer • *Journal*

> Are there times when you engage in negative predictions about your academic performance? What do you think causes you to be so hard on yourself? Do you think that changing your predictions might change your performance? Why or why not? How can you reverse your thinking and give yourself a compliment on your work?

8. Practice relaxing. Some students experience upset stomachs, sweaty palms, racing hearts, or other unpleasant physical symptoms of test anxiety. See your counseling center about relaxation techniques. Some campus learning centers also provide workshops on reducing test anxiety. If this is a problem you experience, read the section on test anxiety later in this chapter.

▲ **Prepare for tests by studying with others.**

Confessions of a College Student

Name: Renee L. Barner

Age: 27

College: Salem Community College

Hometown: Pennsville, NJ

Major: Nursing

Favorite book: Anything

Favorite food: Chinese food

Favorite college course: All sciences

The person who inspires me the most or who I would most like to meet: My mother, who has been the best mother a person could ever want. We did not have a lot of money growing up, but my mother always made sure that we kids were taken care of. We always did fun things together as a family and she always made us feel that we could reach for the stars as long as we gave it our all. She is a wonderful mother, grandmother, and friend.

Heroes: Superman!!!

Favorite way to relax: Watch a movie with my family.

Are you the first to go to college in your family? Yes. Everyone is very proud of me and it has helped me push even harder to achieve.

Test-taking confession: Whenever I study for a test, I always read the material first. I then rewrite my notes and organize them. Then I make flash cards from the notes. If some notes are too long for flash cards, I carefully organize those on a separate sheet of paper. I always use mnemonic devices to help me remember. I make up fake tests and quiz myself on them. I have a friend review the flash cards with me and reread anything that still is not clear to me. Most of the time, it works very well!

Preparing for Math and Science Exams

Math and science exams might require additional preparation techniques. Here are some suggestions for doing well on these exams:

1. Do your homework regularly, even if it is not graded, and do all the assigned problems. Knowing how to solve the problem does not always guarantee being able to solve the problem.

2. As you do your homework, write out your work as carefully and clearly as you will be expected to on your tests. Doing this in your homework will give you one less thing to worry about.

3. Attend each class, and always be on time. Many instructors use the time at the beginning of class to review homework.

4. Create a review guide throughout the semester. As you begin your homework each day, write out a random problem from each homework section in a separate notebook. As you review later, you will be able to come back to these problems and be sure you have a good representation from each section you've studied.

5. Throughout the semester, keep a list of definitions or important formulas (great to put on flash cards). Review one or two as part of every study session. Another technique is to post the formulas and definition in prominent areas in your living space (e.g., on the bathroom wall, around your computer work area, or on the microwave door). Seeing this information so frequently will help embed the information in your mind.

Tips for Successful Test Taking

The following tips apply to any test situation:

1. Write your name on the test (unless directed not to) and answer sheet.

2. Analyze, ask, and stay calm. Take a long, deep breath and slowly exhale before you begin. Read all the directions so that you understand what to do. Ask the instructor or exam monitor for clarification if you don't understand something. Be confident. Don't panic. Answer one question at a time.

3. Make the best use of your time. Quickly survey the entire test and decide how much time you will spend on each section. Be aware of the point values of different sections of the test. Are some questions worth more points than others?

4. Answer the easy questions first. Expect that you'll be puzzled by some questions. Make a note to come back to them later. If different sections consist of different types of questions (such as multiple-choice, short answer, and essay), complete the types of question you are most comfortable with first. Be sure to leave enough time for any essays.

5. Before you even look at the test questions, turn the test paper over and take a moment to write down the formulas, definitions, and major ideas that you have been studying. This helps you go into the test with a feeling of confidence and knowledge—and it provides quick access to the information while you are taking the test. (Check with your instructor ahead of time to be sure that this is okay.)

6. If you feel yourself starting to panic or go blank, stop whatever you are doing. Take a long, deep breath and slowly exhale. Remind yourself you will be okay and that you do know your stuff and can do well on this test. Then take another deep breath. If necessary, go to another section of the test and come back later to the item that triggered your anxiety.

7. If you finish early, don't leave. Stay and check your work for errors. Reread the directions one last time. If you are using a Scantron answer sheet, make sure that all bubbles are filled in accurately and completely.

Essay Questions

Many college teachers have a strong preference for the essay exam for a simple reason: It promotes higher-order critical thinking, whereas other types of exams tend to be exercises in memorization. Generally, the closer you are to graduation, the more essay exams you'll take. To be successful on essay exams, follow these guidelines:

1. Budget your exam time. Quickly survey the entire exam, and note the questions that are the easiest for you, along with their point values. Take a moment to weigh their values, estimate the approximate time you should allot to each question, and write the time beside each item number. Be sure you know whether you must answer all the questions or choose among questions. Remember, it can be a costly error to write profusely on easy questions of low value, taking up precious time you might need on more important questions. Wear a watch so you can monitor your time, including time at the end for a quick review.

Write • DISCUSS • Compare • Ask • BLOG • Answer • Journal

Do you think that essay exams are more appropriate in upper-level courses and multiple choice exams in first-year courses? Why or why not?

2. Develop a very brief outline of your answer before you begin to write. Start working on the questions that are easiest for you, and jot down a few ideas before you begin to write. First, make sure that your outline responds to all parts of the question. Then use your first paragraph to introduce the main points, and subsequent paragraphs to describe each point in more depth. If you begin to lose your concentration, you will be glad to have the outline to help you regain your focus. If you find that you are running out of time and cannot complete an essay, provide an outline of key ideas at the very least. Instructors usually assign points based on your coverage of the main topics from the material. Thus, you will usually earn more points by responding briefly to all parts of the question than by addressing just one aspect of the question in detail.

3. Write concise, organized answers. Many well-prepared students write fine answers to questions that might not have been asked because they did not read a question carefully or did not respond to all parts of the question. Others hastily write down everything they know on a topic. Answers that are vague and tend to ramble will be downgraded by instructors.

4. Know the key task words in essay questions. Being familiar with the **key word** in an essay question will help you answer it more specifically. The following key task words appear frequently on essay tests. Take time to learn them, so that you can answer essay questions more accurately and precisely.

Analyze Divide something into its parts in order to understand it better; show how the parts work together to produce the overall pattern.

Compare Look at the characteristics or qualities of several things and identify their similarities or differences. Do not just describe the traits; define how the things are alike and how they are different.

Contrast Identify the differences between things.

Criticize/Critique Analyze and judge something. Criticism can be positive, negative, or both. A criticism should generally contain your own judgments (supported by evidence) and those of other authorities who can support your point.

Define Give the meaning of a word or expression. Giving an example sometimes helps to clarify a definition, but an example by itself is not a definition.

Describe Give a general verbal sketch of something, in narrative or other form.

Discuss Examine or analyze something in a broad and detailed way. Discussion often includes identifying the important questions related to an issue and attempting to answer these questions. A good discussion explores all relevant evidence and information.

Evaluate Discuss the strengths and weaknesses of something. Evaluation is similar to criticism, but the word "evaluate" stresses the idea of how well something meets a certain standard or fulfills some specific purpose.

Explain Clarify something. Explanations generally focus on why or how something has come about.

Interpret Explain the meaning of something. In science, you might explain what an experiment shows and what conclusions can be drawn from it. In a literature course, you might explain—or interpret—what a poem means beyond the literal meaning of the words.

Justify Argue in support of some decision or conclusion by showing sufficient evidence or reasons in its favor. Try to support your argument with both logical and concrete examples.

Narrate Relate a series of events in the order in which they occurred. Generally, you will also be asked to explain something about the events you are narrating.

Outline Present a series of main points in appropriate order. Some instructors want an outline with Roman numerals for main points followed by letters for supporting details. If in doubt, ask the instructor if he or she wants a formal outline.

Prove Give a convincing logical argument and evidence in support of some statement.

Review Summarize and comment on the main parts of a problem or a series of statements. A review question usually also asks you to evaluate or criticize.

Summarize Give information in brief form, omitting examples and details. A summary is short yet covers all important points.

Trace Narrate a course of events. Where possible, you should show connections from one event to the next.

Multiple-Choice Questions

Preparing for multiple-choice tests requires you to actively review all of the material covered in the course. Reciting from flash cards, summary sheets, mind maps, or the recall column in your lecture notes is a good way to review these large amounts of material.

Take advantage of the many cues that multiple-choice questions contain. Careful reading of each item might uncover the correct answer. Always question choices that use absolute words such as "always," "never," and "only." These choices are often (but not always) incorrect. Also, read carefully for terms such as "not," "except," and "but," which are introduced before the choices. Often the answer that is the most inclusive is correct. Generally, options that do not agree grammatically with the first part of the item are incorrect, but this is not always the case.

Some students are easily confused by multiple-choice answers that sound alike. The best way to respond to a multiple-choice question is to read the first part of the item and then predict your own answer before reading the options. Choose the letter that corresponds with the option that best matches your prediction.

If you are totally confused by a question, place a checkmark in the margin, leave it and come back later, but always double-check that you are filling in the answer for the right question. Sometimes another question will provide a clue for a question you are unsure about. If you have absolutely no idea, look for an answer that at least contains some shred of information. If there is no penalty for guessing, fill in an answer for every question, even if it is just a guess.

Fill-in-the-Blank Questions

In many ways preparing for fill-in-the-blank questions is similar to getting ready for multiple-choice items, but fill-in-the blank is harder because you do not have a choice of possible answers right in front of you. Not all fill-in-the-blank questions are constructed the same. Some teachers will provide a series of blanks to give you a clue regarding the number of words in the answer, but if just one long blank is provided you cannot assume that the answer is just one word. If possible, ask the teacher whether the answer is supposed to be a single word per blank or can be a longer phrase.

True/False Questions

Remember, for the statement to be true, every detail of the sentence must be true. Questions containing words such as "always," "never," and "only" are usually false, whereas less definite terms such as "often" and "frequently" suggest the statement might be true. Read through the entire exam to see if information in one question will help you answer another. Do not begin to second-guess what you know or doubt your answers because a sequence of questions appears to be all true or all false.

Matching Questions

The matching question is the hardest to answer by guessing. In one column you will find the term, and in the other, the description of it. Before answering any question, review all of the terms and descriptions. Match those terms you are sure of first. As you do so, cross out both the term and its description, and then use the process of elimination to assist you in answering the remaining items. Flash cards and lists that can be created from the recall column in your notes are excellent ways to prepare for matching questions.

Types of Tests

While you are in college, you will encounter many types of tests. Some tend to be used in particular disciplines; others can be used in any class you might take.

Problem-Solving Tests

In the physical and biological sciences, mathematics, engineering, statistics, and symbolic logic, some tests will require that you solve problems showing all steps. Even if you know a shortcut, it is important to document how you got from step A to step B. All that will matter on other tests is whether you have the correct solution to the problem, but doing all the steps will still help ensure that you get the right answer. For these tests you must also be very careful that you have made no errors in your scientific notation. A misplaced sign, parenthesis, bracket, or exponent can make all the difference.

If you are allowed to use a calculator, it is important to check that your input is accurate. The calculator does what you tell it to, and if you miss a zero or a negative sign, the calculator will not give you the correct answer to the problem.

Be sure that you read all directions carefully. Are you required to reduce the answer to simplest terms? Are you supposed to graph the solution? Be careful when "canceling terms," cross-multiplying, distributing terms, and combining fractions. Whenever possible, after you complete the problem, work it in reverse to check your solution, or plug your solution back into the equation and make sure it adds up. Also check to make sure that your solution makes sense. You cannot have negative bushels of apples, for example, or a fraction of a person, or a correlation less than negative 1 or greater than 1. Write out each step clearly, with everything lined up as the instructor has indicated in class (lining up the equal signs with each other, for example).

Machine-Scored Tests

It is important to carefully follow the directions for machine-scored tests. In addition to your name, be sure to provide all the information sought on the answer sheet, such as the instructor's name, the number for the class section, or your student ID number. Each time you fill in an answer, make sure that the number on the answer sheet corresponds with the number of the item on the test. If you have questions that you want to come back to (if you are allowed to do so), mark them on the test rather than on the answer sheet.

Although scoring machines have become more sophisticated over time, stray marks on your answer sheet can still be misread and throw off the scoring. When a machine-scored test is returned to you, check your answer sheet against the scoring key, if provided, to make sure that you receive credit for all the questions you answered correctly.

Computerized Tests

Your comfort with taking computerized tests might depend on how computer literate you are in general for objective tests, as well as your keyboarding skills for essay exams. If your instructor provides the opportunity for practice tests, be sure to take advantage of this chance to get a better sense of how the tests will be structured. There can be significant variations depending on the kind of test, the academic subject, and whether the test was constructed by the teacher or by a textbook company or other source.

For multiple-choice and other objective forms of computerized tests, you might be allowed to scroll down and back through the entire test, but this is not always the case. Sometimes you are only allowed to see one question at a time, and after you complete that question you might not be allowed to go back to it. In this situation you cannot skip questions that are hard and come back to them later, so be sure that you try to answer every question.

For computerized tests in math and other subjects that require you to solve each problem, record an answer, and then move to the next problem. Be sure to check each answer before you submit it. Also, know in advance what materials you are allowed to have on hand, including a calculator and scratch paper for working the problems.

Laboratory Tests

In many science courses and in some other academic disciplines, you will be required to take lab tests during which you rotate from one lab station to the next and solve problems, identify parts of models or specimens, explain chemical reactions, and complete other tasks similar to those that you have been performing in lab. At some colleges and universities, lab tests are now administered at computer terminals via simulations. To prepare for lab tests, always attend lab, take good notes, including diagrams and other visual representations as necessary, and be sure to study your lab notebook carefully prior to the test. If possible, create your own diagrams or models, and then see if you can label them without looking at your book.

You might also have to take lab tests in foreign language courses. These tests can have both oral and written components. Work with a partner or study group to prepare for oral exams. Ask each other questions that require using key vocabulary words. Try taping your answers to work on your pronunciation. You might also have computerized lab tests that require you to identify syllables or words and indicate the order and direction of the strokes required to create them, particularly in a foreign language that uses a different symbol system, such as Chinese. The best way to prepare for these tests is to learn the meaning and parts of the symbols and practice writing them regularly.

Open-Book and Open-Note Tests

If you never had open-book or open-note tests in high school, you might be tempted to study less thoroughly, thinking that you will have access to all the information you need during the test. This is a common misjudgment on the part of first-year students. Open-book and open-note tests are usually harder than other exams, not easier.

Most students do not really have time to spend looking things up during this type of exam. The best way to prepare is to begin the same way you would study for a test in which you cannot refer to your notes or text. But as you do so, develop a list of topics and the page numbers where they are covered in your text. You might want to use the same strategy in organizing your lecture notes. Number the pages in your notebook. Later type a three-column grid (or use an Excel spreadsheet) with your list of topics in alphabetical order in the first column and corresponding pages from your text and notebook in the second and third columns so that you can refer to them quickly if necessary. Or you might want to stick colored tabs onto your textbook or notebook pages for different topics. But whatever you do, study as completely as you

◀ **Open-book tests can be challenging. In order to use your time wisely, you'll need to review your reading in advance.**

would for any other test, and do not be fooled into thinking that you do not need to know the material thoroughly.

During the test, monitor your time carefully. Do not waste time unnecessarily looking up information in your text or notes to double-check yourself if you are confident of your answers. Instead, wait until you have finished the test, and then, if you have extra time, go back and look up answers and make any necessary changes. But if you have really studied, you probably will not find this necessary.

Sometimes the only reason a teacher allows open books or open notes is for students to properly reference their sources when responding to essay or short-answer tests. Make sure to clarify if you are expected to document your answers and provide a reference or Works Cited list.

Take-Home Tests

Like open-book and open-note tests, take-home tests are usually more difficult than in-class tests. Many take-home tests are essay tests, though some teachers will give take-home objective tests as well. Be sure to allow plenty of time to complete a take-home test. Read the directions and questions as soon as you receive the test in order to gauge how much time you will need. If the test is all essays, consider how much time you might allocate to writing several papers of the same length. Remember, your teacher will expect your essay answers to look more like assigned out-of-class papers than like the essays you would write during an in-class test.

Unfortunately, academic honesty issues can arise for take-home tests. If you are accustomed to working with a study group or in a learning community for the course, check with the teacher in advance to determine the extent to which collaboration is allowed on the test. One thing that can be very confusing for students is to be encouraged to work together throughout the academic term and then to be told that there should be no communication outside of class about a take-home test.

Overcoming Test Anxiety

Test anxiety takes many different forms. Part of combating test anxiety is understanding its sources and identifying its symptoms. Whatever the source, be assured that test anxiety is common.

Test anxiety has many sources. It can be the result of the pressure that students put on themselves to succeed. Without any pressure, students would not be motivated to study; some stress connected with taking exams is natural and can enhance performance. However, when students put too much pressure on themselves or set unrealistic goals for themselves, the result is stress that is no longer motivating, only debilitating.

The expectations of parents, a spouse, friends, and other people who are close to you can also induce test anxiety. Sometimes, for example, students who are the first in their families to attend college bear the weight of generations before them who have not had this opportunity. The pressure can be overwhelming!

Finally, some test anxiety is caused by lack of preparation, by not keeping up with assigned reading, homework, and other academic commitments leading

WIRED WINDOW

EVEN IF YOU ARE typically enrolled in traditional face-to-face courses, you will undoubtedly take an increasing number of your exams online through course management systems (like eCollege and Blackboard). Some of the same tips for successful test taking also apply to online exams. Ensure that you will be in a quiet area free of distractions while you take the exam. Learn about constraints (e.g., time limit, due date) before the exam by asking your professor or logging in early to see if the constraints are posted online. If you haven't already done so, take a practice test so that you are familiar with the testing interface. If there is no time limit, take a break after you complete the exam and then go back and recheck your answers. If there is a time limit and the course management system does not show a timer, use a stopwatch or countdown timer to track your progress (a good rule of thumb is to have the countdown timer sound once with enough time left for you to review the entire exam and then again with 5 minutes left). Since you won't have a paper exam, you'll be unable to take notes on the exam itself. Be prepared to have a notepad with you to jot down notes. You also won't be able to easily move back and forth between the pages of the exam to review your answers or skip questions for later. Therefore, when reviewing your answers or going back to previous questions, make sure that you have saved every page of the exam. If you save your exam and have not yet submitted it for grading, you can use your browser's back button to review questions and answers on previous pages.

up to the test. Procrastination can begin a downward spiral because after you do poorly on the first test in a course, there is even more pressure to do well on subsequent tests in order to pull up your course grade. This situation becomes even more dire if the units of the course build on one another, like in math and foreign languages, or if the final exam is cumulative. While you are trying to master the new material after the test, you are still trying to catch up on the old material as well.

Some test anxiety comes from a negative prior experience in taking any type of test, only certain types of test questions, or tests in a particular subject. Transcending the memory of negative past experiences can be a challenge for many students. But remember that the past is not the present. Perhaps there are good reasons that you performed poorly in the past. You might not have prepared for the test, you might not have read the questions carefully, or you might not have studied with others or sought prior assistance from your professor or a tutor. If you carefully follow the strategies in this chapter, you are very likely to do well on all your tests. Remember, a little anxiety is okay. But if you find it is getting in the way of your performance on tests and exams, be sure to seek help from your campus counseling center.

Write • DISCUSS • Compare • Ask • BLOG • Answer • *Journal*

> Do you experience any type of test anxiety? If so, what causes you to be anxious? If not, what strategies do you use to stay calm?

Types of Test Anxiety

Students who experience test anxiety under some circumstances do not necessarily feel it in all testing situations. For example, you might do fine on classroom tests, but feel anxious during standardized examinations like the SAT and ACT. One reason standardized tests are so anxiety provoking is the belief that they determine your future. Believing that the stakes are so high can create unbearable pressure. One way of dealing with this type of test anxiety is to ask yourself, "What is the worst that can happen?" Remember that it is not the end of the world. How you do on standardized tests might limit some of your options, but going into these tests with a negative attitude will certainly not improve your chances. Attending preparation workshops and taking practice exams not only can better prepare you for standardized tests, but also can assist you in overcoming your anxiety.

Some students are only anxious about some types of classroom tests. Practice always helps in overcoming test anxiety; if you fear essay exams, try predicting exam questions and writing sample essays as a means of reducing your anxiety.

Some students have difficulty taking tests at a computer terminal. Some of this anxiety might be related to lack of computer experience. On the other hand, not all computerized tests are user-friendly. You might only be allowed to see one item at a time. Often, you do not have the option of going back and checking over all your answers before submitting them. In preparation for computerized tests, ask the instructor questions about how the test will be structured. Also, make sure you take any opportunities to take practice tests at a learning center or lab.

Test anxiety is discipline-specific for some students. For example, some students have math test anxiety even if they do not suffer from test anxiety in other courses. It is important to distinguish the anxiety that arises from the subject matter itself from more generalized test anxiety. Perhaps subject-specific test anxiety relates to old beliefs about yourself, such as "I'm no good at math," or "I can't write well." Now is the time to try some positive self-talk and realize that by preparing well, you can be successful, even in your hardest courses. If the problem persists, talk to someone in your campus counseling center to develop some strategies to overcome irrational fears that can prevent you from doing your best.

Symptoms of Test Anxiety

Test anxiety can manifest itself in many ways. Some students feel it on the very first day of class. Other students begin showing symptoms of test anxiety when it is time to start studying for a test. Others do not get nervous until the night before the test or the morning of an exam day. And some students only experience symptoms while actually taking a test.

Symptoms of test anxiety can include butterflies in the stomach, queasiness or nausea, severe headaches, a faster heartbeat, hyperventilating, shaking, sweating, or muscle cramps. During the exam itself, students overcome with test anxiety can experience the sensation of "going blank," or being unable to remember what they know they know. At this point, students can undermine both their emotional and academic preparation for the test and convince themselves that they cannot succeed.

◀ **Sometimes test anxiety can cause you to forget what you have learned.**

© Mark Richards/PhotoEdit

Test anxiety can impede the success of any college student, no matter how intelligent, motivated, and prepared. That is why it is critical to seek help from your college or university's counseling service or another professional if you think that you have test anxiety. If you are not sure where to go for help, ask your advisor, but seek help promptly! If your symptoms are so severe that you become physically ill (with migraine headaches, hyperventilating, vomiting), you should also consult your physician or campus health service.

Strategies for Combating Test Anxiety

In addition to studying, eating right, and getting plenty of sleep, there are a number of simple strategies that you can employ to overcome the physical and emotional impact of test anxiety. First, any time that you begin to feel nervous or upset, take a long, deep breath and slowly exhale to restore your breathing to a normal level. This is the quickest and easiest relaxation device, and no one needs to know that you are doing it!

Before you go into the test room, especially prior to multi-hour final exams or sitting through several exams on the same day, it can help to stretch your muscles just as you would when preparing to exercise. Stretch your calf and hamstring muscles and roll your ankles. Stretch your arms; roll your shoulders. Tilt your head to the right, front, and left (but, to avoid injury, not to the back) to stretch your neck muscles.

Then when you sit down to take the test, pay attention to how you are sitting. Sit with your shoulders back and relaxed, rather than shrugged forward, and with your feet on the floor. Smooth out your facial muscles rather than wrinkling your forehead or frowning. Resist the temptation to clench your pencil or pen too tightly in your fist; take a break and stretch your fingers now and then.

Anxiety-reducing techniques that might be available through your campus counseling center include systematic desensitization, progressive muscle relaxation, and visualization. One of the most popular is creating your own peaceful scene and

▶ **Exercising before an exam will help you relax.**

© Big Cheese Photo/SuperStock

mentally taking yourself there when you need to relax. Try to use all five senses to recreate your peaceful scene in your mind: What would you see, hear, feel, taste, or smell?

These strategies can assist you in relaxing physically, but meanwhile, you must also pay attention to the mental messages that you are sending yourself. Focus on the positive! If you are telling yourself that you are not smart enough, that you did not study the right material, or that you are going to fail, you need to turn those messages around with a technique called **cognitive restructuring**. We all talk to ourselves, so make sure that your messages are encouraging rather than stress provoking. When you are studying, practice sending yourself positive messages: "I really know this stuff. I am going to ace this test!"

Similarly, do not allow others, including classmates, your spouse, parents, or friends, to undermine your confidence. If you belong to a study group, discuss the need to stay positive. Sometimes, getting to the test room early will expose you to other students asking questions or making comments that are only going to make you nervous. Get to the building early, but wait until just a few minutes before the exam begins to approach the classroom itself. If at any point during a test you begin to feel like you cannot think clearly, or you have trouble remembering, or you come to a question you cannot answer, stop for a brief moment and take another long, deep breath and slowly exhale. Then remind yourself of the positive self-messages you have been practicing.

Getting the Test Back

Students react differently when they receive their test grades and papers. For some students the thought of seeing the actual graded test produces high levels of anxiety.

But unless you look at the instructor's comments and your answers (the correct and incorrect ones), you will have no way to evaluate your own knowledge and test-taking strengths. You might also find that the professor made an error in the grade, an error that might have cost you a point or two.

It is important for you to review your graded test. You might find that your mistakes were caused by failing to follow directions, being careless with words or numbers, or by overanalyzing a multiple choice question. If you have any questions about your grade, be sure to talk to the professor. You might be able to negotiate a few points in your favor, but in any case, you will let your professor know that you are concerned and want to learn how to do better on graded tests and examinations.

Write • DISCUSS • Compare • Ask • BLOG • Answer • *Journal*

> What actions do you take when you look at graded tests? Take a look at the exam you got back from one of your classes. What can you learn from it? Would you ever challenge a professor if you thought he or she had made a mistake in your grade? Why or why not?

Academic Honesty & Misconduct

Imagine where society would be if researchers reported fraudulent results that were then used to develop new machines or medical treatments. Integrity is a cornerstone of higher education, and activities that compromise that integrity damage everyone: your country, your community, your college or university, your classmates, and yourself.

Cheating

Institutions vary widely in how they define broad terms such as lying or cheating. One university defines cheating as "intentionally using or attempting to use unauthorized materials, information, notes, study aids, or other devices. . . [including] unauthorized communication of information during an academic exercise." This would apply to looking over a classmate's shoulder for an answer, using a calculator when it is not authorized, procuring or discussing an exam (or individual questions from an exam) without permission, copying lab notes, purchasing term papers over the Internet, watching the video instead of reading the book, and duplicating computer files.

Plagiarism

Plagiarism, or taking another person's ideas or work and presenting them as your own, is especially intolerable in academic culture. Just as taking someone else's property constitutes physical theft, taking credit for someone else's ideas constitutes intellectual theft.

On most tests, you do not have to credit specific individuals. (But some instructors do require this; when in doubt, ask!) In written reports and papers, however, you must give credit any time you use a) another person's actual words; b) another person's ideas or theories—even if you don't quote them directly; or c) any other information not considered common knowledge.

Many schools also prohibit certain activities in addition to lying, cheating, unauthorized assistance, and plagiarism. Examples of prohibited behaviors include intentionally inventing information or results, earning credit more than once for the same piece of academic work without permission, giving your work or exam answers to another student to copy during the actual exam or before the exam is given to another section, and bribing in exchange for any kind of academic advantage. Most schools also outlaw helping or attempting to help another student commit a dishonest act.

Consequences of Cheating and Plagiarism

While you might see some students who seem to be getting away with cheating or plagiarizing, the consequences of such behaviors can be severe and life-changing. Recent cases of cheating on examinations and plagiarizing major papers have caused some college students to be suspended or expelled and even to have their college degrees revoked. Writers and journalists who have been found guilty of plagiarism have lost their jobs and their careers. Even college presidents are occasionally found guilty of "borrowing" the words of others and using them as their own in speeches and written documents. Such discoveries result not only in embarrassment and shame but also in lawsuits and criminal actions.

Because plagiarism can be a problem on college campuses, faculty are now using electronic systems such as **www.turnitin.com** to identify passages in student papers that have been plagiarized. Many faculty routinely check student papers to make sure that the writing is original. So even though the temptation to cheat or plagiarize might be strong, getting a potentially better grade isn't worth misrepresenting yourself or your knowledge and suffering the potential consequences.

Reducing the Likelihood of Academic Dishonesty

To avoid becoming intentionally or unintentionally involved in academic misconduct, consider the reasons it could happen.

▶ Ignorance. In a survey at the University of South Carolina, 20 percent of students incorrectly thought that buying a term paper wasn't cheating. Forty percent thought using a test file (a collection of actual tests from previous terms) was fair behavior. Sixty percent thought it was alright to get answers from someone who had taken an exam earlier in the same or in a prior term. What do you think?

▶ Cultural and campus differences. In other countries and on some U.S. campuses, students are encouraged to review past exams as practice exercises. Some student government associations maintain test files for use by students. Some campuses permit sharing answers and information for homework and other assignments with friends.

▶ Different policies among instructors. Because there is no universal code that dictates such behaviors, ask your instructors for clarification. When a student is caught violating the academic code of a particular school or instructor, pleading ignorance of the rules is a weak defense.

▶ A belief that grades—not learning—are everything, when actually the reverse is true. This might reflect our society's competitive atmosphere. It also might be the result of pressure from parents, peers, or teachers. In truth, grades are nothing if one has cheated to earn them. Even if your grades help you get a job, it is what you have actually learned that will help you keep the job and be promoted.

▶ Lack of preparation or inability to manage time and activities. Before you consider cheating, ask an instructor to extend a deadline so that a project can be done well.

Here are some steps you can take to reduce the likelihood of problems:

1. Know the rules. Learn the academic code for your college by going to its website. Also learn about any additional department guidelines on cheating or plagiarism. Study course syllabi. If a teacher does not clarify standards and expectations, ask exactly what they are.

2. Set clear boundaries. Refuse when others ask you to help them cheat. This might be hard to do, but you've got to say no. In test settings, keep your answers covered and your eyes down, and put all extraneous materials away, including cell phones. Now that many cell phones enable text messaging, instructors are rightfully suspicious when they see students playing with their cell phones during an exam.

3. Improve time management. Be well prepared for all quizzes, exams, projects, and papers. This might mean unlearning habits such as procrastination (see chapter 2, Time Management).

4. Seek help. Find out where you can obtain assistance with study skills, time management, and test taking. If your methods are in good shape but the content of the course is too difficult, see your instructor, join a study group, or visit your campus learning center or tutorial service.

5. Withdraw from the course. Your school has a policy about dropping courses and a deadline to drop without penalty. You might decide only to drop the course that's giving you trouble. Some students choose to withdraw from all classes and take time off before returning to school if they find themselves in over their heads or if a long illness, a family crisis, or some other unexpected occurrence has caused them to fall behind. Before you withdraw, you should ask about campus policies as well as ramifications in terms of federal financial aid and other scholarship programs. See your advisor or counselor.

6. Reexamine goals. Stick to your own realistic goals instead of giving in to pressure from family or friends to achieve impossibly high standards. You might also feel pressure to enter a particular career or profession of little or no interest to you. If so, sit down with counseling or career services professionals or your academic advisor and explore alternatives.

WHERE TO GO FOR HELP

On Campus

Learning Assistance Support Center Almost every campus has one of these, and studying for tests is one of their specialties. The best students, good students who want to be the best students, and students with academic difficulties use learning centers and tutoring services. These services are offered by both full-time professionals and highly skilled student tutors.

Counseling Services College and university counseling centers offer a wide array of services, often including workshops and individual or group counseling for test anxiety. Sometimes these services are also offered by the campus health center.

Fellow College Students Often the best help we can get is the closest to us. Keep an eye out in your classes, residence hall, extracurricular activities, and so forth for the best students, those who appear to be the most serious, purposeful, and directed. Hire a tutor. Join a study group. Students who do these things are much more likely to be successful.

Online

Read the following two websites. Take notes. Write a summary of what you believe to be the important facts.

The Academic Center for Excellence, University of Illinois at Chicago: **www.uic.edu/depts/counselctr/ace/examprep.htm**

Learning Centre of the University of New South Wales in Sydney, Australia: **www.lc.unsw.edu.au/onlib/exam.html**. Includes the popular SQ3R method.

My Institution's Resources

_____

_____

_____

_____

_____

_____

▶▶▶ BUILDING YOUR PORTFOLIO
A High Price to Pay

I desire so to conduct the affairs of this administration that if at the end, when I come to lay down the reins of power, I have lost every other friend on earth, I shall at least have one friend left, and that friend shall be down inside me.

–Abraham Lincoln (1809–1865), sixteenth President of the United States

To complete this portfolio activity electronically, please visit
academic.cengage.com/collsucc/Gardner/YCE8e.

Do you know the meaning of the words "academic integrity"? Academic integrity is a supreme value on college and university campuses. Faculty, staff, and students are held to a strict code of academic integrity, and the consequences of breaking that code can be severe and life-changing. Create a new entry in your portfolio with the title "A High Price to Pay." Record your work for this assignment there.

1. Imagine that you have been hired by your college or university to conduct a month-long academic integrity awareness campaign so that students will learn about and take your campus's guidelines for academic integrity seriously. To prepare for your new job,

   a. Visit your institution's website and use the search feature to find the Academic Integrity Code/Policy. Take time to read through the code, violations, and sanctions. *Note the website link here so it will be easy to find later:*

   _____

   b. Visit the judicial affairs office on your campus to learn more about the way your institution deals with violations of academic integrity policies.

   c. Research other online resources, such as the Center for Academic Integrity, hosted by Clemson University (**www.academicintegrity.org**), and read about its Fundamental Values Project.

   d. Check out other colleges' and universities' academic integrity codes and/or honor codes. How do they compare to your institution's code or policy?

2. Outline your month-long awareness campaign and include it in your portfolio. Here are a few ideas to get you started:

   - Plan a new theme every week; don't forget Internet-related violations.

   - Develop eye-catching posters to display around campus. For samples, check out the posters designed by students at Elizabethtown College in Pennsylvania (**www.rubberpaw.com/integrity**).

   - Think about guest speakers, debates, skits or other presentations.

   - Come up with catchy slogans or phrases.

   - Send students a postcard highlighting your institution's policies or honor code.

   - Consider the most effective ways to communicate your message to different groups on campus.

Academic Integrity Awareness Campaign	Events Plan
Week 1	
Week 2	
Week 3	
Week 4	

You might want to share your campaign ideas with other students in your class and even select the best ideas for presentation to your campus student affairs office or judicial board.

Effective Writing and Speaking

In this chapter YOU WILL LEARN

▶ That writing is a process leading to a product

▶ Why writing e-mail and other forms of electronic communication is not the same as writing a college paper

▶ How to review and revise your writing

▶ Six steps to success in preparing a speech

▶ How best to use your voice and body language

▶ How to sound organized when speaking on the spot

What is this speaker doing to communicate effectively?

© Vince Bucci/Getty Images

Constance Staley, University of Colorado at Colorado Springs, and R. Stephen Staley, Colorado Technical University, contributed their valuable and considerable expertise to the speaking portion of this chapter.

How Do Your WRITING AND SPEAKING Strategies Measure Up?

A?B?C?A?B?C?A?B?C?

Read the following questions and choose the answer that most fits you.

1 When you have a paper due, how long do you typically work on it?

A Usually, I start it the night before and work through the night until it's due.

B I try to get a head start by working on it a week ahead of time with some outlining, but other assignments take priority and I end up finishing most of the paper the night before.

C I start when the paper is assigned so that I can brainstorm on my topic, get a rough draft written, and have my roommate review it for me. This gives me plenty of time to improve the paper before it's due.

2 What types of revisions do you make to your papers?

A None—I'm lucky if I can finish writing it before it's due.

B I sometimes read it over for spelling and grammar mistakes, but my computer catches a lot of those.

C I like to think about my ideas and make sure that the paper flows logically, and then closer to my final draft, I look at the grammar and spelling.

3 How do you narrow a topic down for a paper?

A I just pick whatever first comes to mind; usually, I have a hard time writing about it, and I never seem to get a good grade.

B If it's something I'm interested in, I can narrow the topic down and do lots of research, but other times, I just can't seem to get myself interested enough to pick something interesting.

C I like to do lots of research on something I'm interested in and find a bunch of angles on the topic—that way I always find something I want to learn more about.

4 How do feel about speaking in front of a group?

A I never speak in class; I'm always "sick" on days that presentations are due.

B Depends on how large the class is and how prepared I am—I'm usually nervous, but I can get through it if I have to.

C I rehearse all my presentations and do a dry run with my friends so that I feel comfortable with what I'm going to say.

5 When you are asked an on-the-spot question, how do you respond?

A I usually answer with whatever comes into my mind first, but I find I usually want to change my mind afterwards.

B Sometimes I feel like I know the answer and other times I just stay silent rather than sounding dumb.

C I take a deep breath, say, "Let me think about that a moment," then either supply the answer or admit that I don't know.

Review your responses. **A** responses indicate that you need help with writing and speaking. **B** responses indicate that you have some ideas about how to write and speak effectively, but could use some assistance. **C** responses indicate that you have a good understanding about how to write and speak effectively. Whatever your responses, this chapter will help you learn more about these important skills that you will use while you're in college and in life beyond.

Writing and speaking are the two most common forms of communication. The ability to write well and speak well makes a tremendous difference in how the rest of the world perceives you and how well you will communicate throughout your life. But you will find that you often need to communicate differently depending on who is reading or listening to your words. Each time you speak or write, you are doing so to an audience. The audience might be one person—a friend, family member, professor, or a potential employer—or your audience might be a group, such as your classmates in college. Some audiences might be unknown to you. For instance, if you're writing a book or an article for publication, a blog or an entry in Facebook or MySpace, you never know who might read your words.

In order to communicate effectively, it's important to think about your audience, what they will understand and expect, and how they will react to what you are saying or writing. While it's generally okay to use informal language with your friends, family, and other college students, your professors and potential employers will expect more formal writing and speaking.

Experts suggest there's no single, universally accepted standard for how to speak or write American English. Even so, school systems, professional communicators, and businesses all have standards and, not surprisingly, the rules do not vary dramatically from place to place. If they did, we'd have a hard time understanding one another. Our purpose in this chapter is not to teach you grammar and punctuation (save that for your English classes), but to get you to think of writing and speaking as processes (how you get there) as well as products (the final paper or script) and to help you overcome those writer's and speaker's blocks we all encounter from time to time.

You might wonder, "Why can't more people express themselves effectively?" The answers vary, but all come back to the same theme: Most people do not think of writing and speaking as processes to be mastered step by step. Instead, they view writing and speaking as products; you knock them out and you're done. Nothing could be further from the truth

Whatever career you choose, you will be expected to think, create, communicate, manage, and lead. That means you will have to write and speak well. You will have to write reports about your work and the performance of others, e-mails to describe problems and to propose solutions, and position papers to explain and justify to your superiors why the organization must make certain changes. Often the decision makers in your organization will not know you personally. But they will know your writing, which is all the more reason to do it the right way.

As you lead and manage others, you also will need strong speaking skills in order to explain, report, motivate, direct, encourage, and inspire. You will likely give presentations in meetings to your superiors and their subordinates, and then frequently follow up with a written report or e-mail. So, as you prepare yourself for a career, you need to start thinking of yourself as a person who participates in the Information Age by being both a good thinker and a standout communicator.

Writing

William Zinsser,[1] author of several books on writing, claims, "The act of writing gives the teacher a window into the mind of the student." In other words, your writing provides tangible evidence of how well you think and how well you understand concepts related to the courses you are taking. Your writing might also reveal a good sense of humor, a compassion for the less fortunate, a respect for family, and many other things. Zinsser reminds us that writing is not merely

[1] William Zinsser, *On Writing Well* (New York: Harper Resource 25th Anniversary Edition, 2001).

something that writers do, but a basic skill for getting through life. He claims that far too many Americans cannot perform useful work because they never learned to express themselves. You might argue that television personalities are more renowned than writers—until you remember that writers come up with the words for most of them to speak.

Using Freewriting to Discover What You Want to Write About

Writing guru Peter Elbow[2] asserts that it's impossible to write effectively if you simultaneously try to organize, check grammar and spelling, and offer intelligent thoughts to your readers. He argues that it can't all be done at once, mainly because you use the right, or creative, side of your brain to create thoughts, while you use the left, or logical, side for grammar, spelling, organization, and so forth.

Elbow argues that we can free up our writing and bring more energy and voice into it by writing more like we speak and trying to avoid the heavy overlay of editing in our initial efforts to write. This preliminary step in the writing process is called "freewriting." By freewriting, he simply means writing that is temporarily unencumbered with mechanical processes, such as punctuation, grammar, spelling, context, and so forth. Freewriting is also a way to break the habit of trying to write and edit at the same time.

The freewriting process can be difficult because it goes against the grain of how we are accustomed to writing. We normally edit as we write, pausing to collect our thoughts, to recollect the correct spelling of a word, to cross out a sentence that does not belong, to reject a paragraph that doesn't fit with the argument that we are making, or to mentally outline a structure of the argument that we are trying to make.

Write • DISCUSS • Compare • Ask • BLOG • Answer • *Journal*

> Have you tried freewriting before? To see what freewriting feels like, write, "My writing speaks for me." Write for at least 10 minutes, nonstop, about that statement. Don't think about organization, grammar, punctuation, and spelling, but don't stop writing until the time's up. Discuss with your classmates your reactions to writing this way and what they wrote about.

[2] Peter Elbow, *Writing Without Teachers* (New York: Oxford University Press, 1973).

Narrowing Your Topic

In *Zen and the Art of Motorcycle Maintenance*,[3] Robert Pirsig tells a story about his first-year English class. Each week he assigned students a 500-word essay to write. One week, a student failed to submit her paper about the town where the college was located, explaining that she had "thought and thought, but couldn't think of anything to write about." Pirsig gave her an additional weekend to complete the assignment. As he said this, an idea flashed through his mind. "I want you to write a 500-word paper just about Main Street, not the whole town," he said. She gasped and stared at him angrily. How was she to narrow her thinking to just one street when she couldn't think of one thing to write about the entire town? On Monday she arrived in tears. "I'll never learn to write." Pirsig's answer: "Write a paper about one building on Main Street. The opera house. And start with the first brick on the lower left side. I want it next class."

The student's eyes opened wide. She walked into class the next time with a 5,000-word paper on the opera house. She had been freewriting but didn't realize it. "I don't know what happened," she exclaimed. "I sat across the street and wrote about the first brick, then the second, and all of a sudden I couldn't stop." What had Pirsig done for this person? He helped her find a focus and a place to begin. Getting started is what blocks most students from approaching writing properly. Faced with an ultimatum, she probably began to see the beauty of the opera house for the first time and had gone on to describe it, to find out more about it in the library, to ask others about it, and to comment on its setting among the other buildings on the block.

▲ **Find a comfortable and quiet spot to freewrite. It can help you narrow your topic.**

[3] Robert Pirsig, *Zen and the Art of Motorcycle Maintenance* (New York: Bantam Books, 1984).

Very few writers—even professionally published ones—say what they want to say on their first try. And the sad fact is that really good writers are in the minority. Yet through practice, an understanding of the writing process, and dedication, more people can improve their writing skills. And good writers can make good money.

Another way to think about writing is to distinguish between exploratory writing and explanatory writing. Those terms practically define themselves, but here is a clearer definition: **Exploratory writing**, like freewriting, helps you first discover what you want to say; **explanatory writing** then allows you to transmit those ideas to others. Explanatory writing is "published," meaning you have chosen to allow others to read it (your teacher, your friends, other students, or the public at large), but it is important that most or all of your exploratory writing be private, to be read only by you as a series of steps toward your published work. Keeping your early drafts under wraps frees you to say what you mean and mean what you say. Later, you will come back and make some adjustments, and each revision will strengthen your message.

Some writers say they gather their best thoughts through exploratory writing— by researching their topic, writing down ideas from their research, and adding their questions and reactions to what they have gathered. As they write, their minds begin to make connections between ideas. They don't attempt to organize, to find exactly the right words, or to think about structure. That might interrupt the thoughts that seem to magically flow onto the paper or computer screen. They frequently chide themselves—in writing—for not being able to find the right words. Of course, when they go from exploratory to explanatory writing, their preparation will help them form crystal clear sentences, spell properly, and have their thoughts organized so that their material flows naturally from one point to the next.

The Prewriting, Writing, and Rewriting Process

One of the more popular ways of thinking about the writing process includes the following steps:

1. Prewriting or rehearsing (freewriting). This step includes preparing to write by filling your mind with information from other sources. It is generally considered the first stage of exploratory writing.

2. Writing or drafting. This is when exploratory writing becomes a rough explanatory draft.

3. Rewriting or revision. This is when you polish your work until you consider it ready for your public because it clearly explains what you want to communicate

The reason many students turn in poorly written papers is that they skip the first and last steps and make do with the middle one. Perhaps it's a lack of time or putting off things until the night before the paper is due. Whatever the reason, the result is often a poorly written assignment since the best writing is usually done over an extended period of time, not as a last-minute task. Most professional writers and speakers would never begin to prepare an assignment only a day or hours before it's time to deliver. For one thing, the mere anxiety such a situation creates would be more than enough to close down any manner of intelligent thinking. Worrying about your grammar and spelling as you write what might be your only draft can lead to a low grade or a rejection from a career inquiry.

Describe your writing process. What steps do you go through when you write a major paper?

Prewriting: The Idea Stage

Many writing experts, such as Donald Murray[4], believe that, of all the steps, **prewriting** (or freewriting) should take the longest. You might question things that seem illogical. You might recall what you've heard others say. This should lead you to write more, to ask yourself whether your views are more reliable than those of others, whether the topic might be too broad or too narrow, and so forth.

What constitutes an appropriate topic, or thesis? When is it neither too broad nor too narrow? Test your topic by writing, "The purpose of this paper is to convince my readers that . . ." (but don't use that stilted line in your paper). Pay attention to the assignment. Know the limits of your knowledge, the limitations on your time, and your ability to do enough research.

Writing: The Beginning of Organization

Once you have completed your research and feel you have exhausted all information sources and ideas, it's time to move to the writing, or drafting, stage. It might be a good idea to begin with a **thesis statement** and an outline so that you can put things where they logically belong. A thesis statement is a short statement that clearly defines the purpose of the paper. For example:

Thesis: Napoleon's dual personality can be explained by examining incidents throughout his life.

1. Explain why I am using the term "dual personality" to describe Napoleon.

2. Briefly comment on his early life and his relationship with his mother.

3. Describe Napoleon's rise to fame from soldier to emperor. Stress the contradictions in his personality and attitudes

4. Describe the contradictions in his relationship with Josephine.

5. Summarize my thoughts about Napoleon's personality.

6. Possibly conclude by referring to opening question: "Did Napoleon actually have a dual personality?"

Once you have a workable outline, you can build your paper around a coherent topic, or thesis, and begin paying attention to the flow of ideas from one sentence to the next and from one paragraph to the next, including subheadings where needed. If you have carefully chosen the thesis at this stage, it will help you check to see that each sentence relates to your main idea. When you have completed this stage, you will have the first draft of your paper in hand.

---

[4] Donald Murray, *Learning by Teaching: Selected Articles on Writing and Teaching* (Portsmouth, NH: Boynton/Cook, 1982).

WIRED WINDOW

WIKIPEDIA is an online encyclopedia that obtains content from its users. You might have used Wikipedia to do research for term papers in high school. Unlike traditional encyclopedias, the content found on Wikipedia is never systematically reviewed by topic experts. So, who can add or edit content on Wikipedia? The answer is *anyone*. Sometimes, this can create chaos on Wikipedia pages when users spend a lot of time quarreling over facts. Theoretically, these discussions can lead to better content on the more popular Wikipedia pages; however, on less popular pages, information can be grossly inaccurate. Knowing this, it should be no surprise that many of your professors will not allow the use of Wikipedia as a source for your research papers. The discussion of using Wikipedia as a legitimate source continues in the academic world with many faculty members at one extreme of the debate arguing that Wikipedia is nothing more than an opinion-based website, while those on the other end arguing that Wikipedia is the ultimate form of peer review. The main point of the argument is that Wikipedia arrives at knowledge by bypassing the established process of scientific inquiry, which includes conducting research that meets certain criteria and publishing that research in periodicals that are reviewed by experts in the field (also referred to as "peer review"). So, before you begin your research papers, check with your professors to see if they will allow you to use Wikipedia as a reference and if they do, use Wikipedia sparingly.

Rewriting: The Polishing Stage

Are you finished? Not by a long shot. Here comes the stage where you take a good piece of writing and potentially make it great. The essence of good writing is rewriting. You read. You correct. You add smoother transitions. You slash through wordy sentences or paragraphs that add nothing to your paper. You substitute stronger words for weaker ones. You double-check spelling and grammar. It also might help to share your paper with one or more of your classmates to get their feedback. This is typically called "peer review." Once you have talked with your reviewers about their suggested changes, you can either accept or reject them. At this point, you are ready to finalize your writing and "publish," or rather, turn in your paper.

The "Write, Read, Observe, Experience, Research, Vocabulary, Grammar, Play, Read Aloud, and Edit" Process

Despite its cumbersome name, the process described by fiction writer and editor Niko Silvester of **www.about.com**[5] is very logical and easy to follow.

▶ Write. That's it. Write every day. Write as much as you can. The more you write, the better you'll write.

[5] Niko Sylvester, *Top 10 Ways to Become a Better Writer.* (teenwriting.about.com/od/thewritingprocess/tp/BetterWriting.htm).

▶ Read. After you read to understand or enjoy the material, do a second read-through, taking enough time to discover how the writer structured the chapter, book, or article. You won't want to copy the author's style, of course, but you can learn a lot by studying good writing.

▶ Observe. Observe yourself and others. Notice how things look and how their appearance can change.

▶ Experience. Try new things. Do the usual things in unusual ways. Each experience you have gives you more material to write about.

▶ Research. If you can't experience it, look it up. Research what you need, research anything else that appeals to you. You never know when you can use it.

▶ Vocabulary. Learn at least one new word every day. A good resource for accomplishing this is **www.wordsmith.org**. You can subscribe at no cost and each day you'll receive an e-mail with a new word and definition.

▶ Grammar. Bad grammar is a clue that the writer is less than sharp. Bad grammar can obscure the meaning of a word, a sentence, or a paragraph. Take a grammar course or purchase a grammar book if you're somewhat shaky with grammar.

▶ Play. Write just for fun, not for an assignment. Your nonrequired writing—no pressures attached—will help you make discoveries that will improve your writing assignments.

▶ Read aloud. Read your own writing aloud to hear how it sounds. If you stumble over some words, your readers probably will stumble, too.

▶ Edit. The editing process takes much longer than the writing itself. Editing is the time to slow down and see if what you've written makes sense and is easy to read. It is your last chance to get it right. If you've followed all the right steps, you ought to be in good shape.

◀ **You might choose to use your laptop during class to take notes, or you might write them out and transfer them to your laptop after class. This is another way of embedding the material in your mind.**

© David Pollack/CORBIS

Allocating Time for Each Writing Stage

When writer Donald Murray was asked how long a writer should spend on each of the three stages, he suggested:

Prewriting: 85 percent (including research and rumination)

Writing: 1 percent (the first draft)

Rewriting: 14 percent (revising till it's right)

If the figures surprise you, here's a true story about a writer who was assigned to create a brochure. He had other jobs to do and kept avoiding that one. But the other work he was doing had a direct bearing on the brochure he was asked to write. So as he was putting this assignment off, he was also "researching" material for it.

After nearly three months, he finally decided it was time to move forward. He sat at his computer and dashed the words off in just under 30 minutes. The more he wrote, the faster the ideas popped into his head. He actually was afraid to stop until he had finished. He read his words, made revisions, sent it around the office for a peer review, accepted some suggestions, and the brochure was published.

He had spent a long time prewriting (working with related information without trying to write the brochure). He went through the writing stage quickly because his mind was primed for the task. As a result, he had time to polish his work before the first draft.

With a few changes, you can do the same. Begin writing the day you get the assignment, even if it's only for 10 or 15 minutes. That way, you won't be confronting a blank paper later. Write something every day; the more you write, the better you'll write. Dig for ideas. *Reject nothing* at first, then revise later. Read good writing; it will help you find your own writing style. Above all, know that becoming a better thinker and writer takes hard work, but practice—in this case—can make near perfect.

Choosing the Best Way to Communicate to Your Audience

Before you got to college, you spent much more time writing informally than writing formally. Perform a quick calculation. Think about all of the time you have spent writing e-mails, MySpace and blog comments, text messages, and instant messages (IM). Now think about all of the time you spent writing papers for school. Typically, writing for wired communications is informal. This can be a real detriment to your writing skills. The grammar and structure of e-mails, MySpace and Facebook messages, IM, and text messages resemble a conversation instead of a formal piece of writing. Additionally, communications via IM and text messaging use spelling and grammar all their own. As a shortcut, people often condense text messages and IM by using abbreviations like "brb," "lol," "y?," and "ttyl." They are abbreviated for good reason—imagine how long it would take to thumb this sentence into a text message. The downside of text message and IM shortcuts is that they have gradually caused many of us to become careless in our formal writing.

Confessions of a College Student

Name: Sarah Bivens

Age: 28

College: Nassau Community College

Hometown: Rosedale, NY

Major: Liberal Arts/Nursing

Favorite book: *Confession of an Economic Hitman* by John Perkins

Favorite college courses: Math and Psychology

Favorite way to relax: Foot soaks/massages

Are you the first to got to college in your family? If so, what impact has that had on your experience? Yes, and it has made a tremendous impact because all eyes are on me.

Favorite food: Baked chicken

Writing and speaking confession: The amount of writing I did when I attended Freeport High School was nothing compared to the writing expected of me in college. In high school I could remember writing only two book reports, one for *A Streetcar Named Desire* and the other for *Of Mice and Men.* So it was a shock to find that in Sociology alone, I've got five book reports due by the end of the term. To write a critically effective book review or report, I must possess strong writing skills—the ability to use correct grammar and punctuation and to be able to organize my thoughts in a logical manner. My English class meets twice a week and most of our work is devoted to writing practice.

I never used to like to write, but after my first year in college, I found that my writing and vocabulary skills had improved tremendously. Good skills to have when you want to communicate clearly!

When you write to your friends via e-mail, MySpace and Facebook messaging, IM, and text messaging, you use informal language. Indeed, the nature of these types of messages dictates that they be quick, to the point, and not convey much in terms of tone. Have you ever been offended by a message a friend sent to you, later to find out that the intended meaning was completely different from the way you read it? For example, take the statement "whatever" when used by itself. When "whatever" is used in an IM, it can take on a wide variety of meanings. It could be dismissive, as in "Whatever. I'm angry and I don't really care," or it could be a relaxed affirmation, as in "I'm in agreement with whatever you'd like to do." Researchers have found that people can't guess e-mail tone correctly even when they are certain that they can.

Being aware of the differences in formal and informal writing will help you build the formal writing skills that you need for college. How would you write an e-mail to friends telling them about the volunteer work you did this past weekend? Now, how would you write that same e-mail to a potential employer who might hire you for your first job out of college? Another way to improve your formal writing is to consider the reader's point of view. For the next week, before sending any MySpace or Facebook messages, e-mails, or text messages, reread them and consider how the person receiving them will perceive your tone. What kind of mood will they think you are in? Will they feel like you are happy to have them as a friend? How many different ways might your message be interpreted?

BLOG, et cetera • *Write* • DISCUSS • *Journal* • Ask • Answer

> Have you ever sent or received an e-mail or text message that could be interpreted in more than one way? What did you learn from that experience?

Writing formally for class projects might be a challenge at first. Visit your institution's writing center when you are starting to work on your paper. Ask your professor for examples of papers that have received good grades. Don't be afraid to ask your professor to help you review your writing after you have worked with the writing center. Most importantly, you can practice by using a more formal tone when IMing and messaging. You'll find that your friends won't fault you for it. (Have you ever seen an IM complaining, "Can you please stop using proper grammar"?) Since you spend more time with online forms of communication, it's a great way to get real-world practice in the art of academic writing.

Speaking

The advice given here about writing also applies to speaking in public. The major difference, of course, is that you not only have to write the speech; you also have to present it vocally to an audience.

Successful speaking involves six fundamental steps:

Step 1: Clarify your objective.
Step 2: Analyze your audience.
Step 3: Collect and organize your information.
Step 4: Choose your visual aids.
Step 5: Prepare your notes.
Step 6: Practice your delivery.

Step 1: Clarify Your Objective

Begin by identifying what you want to accomplish. Do you want to persuade your listeners that your campus needs additional student parking? Inform your listeners about the student government's accomplishments? What do you want your listeners to know, believe, or do when you are finished?

Step 2: Analyze Your Audience

You need to understand the people you'll be talking to. Ask yourself:

▶ **What do they already know about my topic?** If you're going to give a presentation on the health risks of fast food, you'll want to know how much your listeners already know about fast food so you don't risk boring them or wasting their time.

▶ What do they want or need to know? How much interest do your classmates have in nutrition? Would they be more interested in some other aspect of college life?

▶ Who are they? What do they have in common with me?

▶ What are their attitudes toward me, my ideas, and my topic? How are they likely to feel about the ideas I am presenting? What attitudes have they cultivated about fast food?

Step 3: Collect and Organize Your Information

Now comes the critical part of the process: building your presentation by selecting and arranging blocks of information. One useful analogy is to think of yourself as guiding your listeners through the maze of ideas they already have to the new knowledge, attitudes, and beliefs you would like them to have. You can apply the same suggestions from earlier in this chapter about creating an outline for writing to composing an outline for a speech.

Step 4: Choose Your Visual Aids

When visual aids are added to presentations, listeners can absorb 35 percent more information, and over time, they can recall 55 percent more. You might choose

▲ **Imagine your audience. What do they already know about my topic? What do I need to tell them?**

to prepare a chart, show a video clip, write on the board, or distribute handouts. You might also use your computer to prepare overhead transparencies or dynamic PowerPoint presentations. As you select and use your visual aids, consider these rules of thumb:

▶ Make visuals easy to follow. Use readable lettering, and don't crowd information.

▶ Explain each visual clearly.

▶ Allow your listeners enough time to process visuals.

▶ Proofread carefully. Misspelled words hurt your credibility as a speaker.

▶ Maintain eye contact with your listeners while you discuss visuals. Don't turn around and address the screen.

Although a fancy PowerPoint slideshow can't make up for inadequate preparation or poor delivery skills, using clear, attractive visual aids can help you organize your material and help your listeners understand what they're hearing. The quality of your visual aids and your skill in using them can contribute to making your presentation as effective as possible.

Step 5: Prepare Your Notes

If you are like most speakers, having an entire written copy of your speech in front of you might tempt you to read much of your presentation. And even if it doesn't, your presentation could sound canned. On the other hand, your memory might fail you. A better strategy is to memorize only the introduction and conclusion so that you can maintain eye contact and therefore build rapport with your listeners.

© image100/SuperStock

▲ **Visual aids help draw your audience into your presentation.**

The best speaking aid is a minimal outline, carefully prepared, from which you can speak extemporaneously. Rehearse thoroughly in advance and you'll be better prepared for how and when you want to present your points. Because you are speaking from brief notes, your words will be slightly different each time you give your presentation. That's okay; you'll sound prepared, but natural. You might wish to use some unobtrusive note cards. It's not a bad idea to number them, just in case you accidentally drop the stack; it has happened to the best of speakers! After you become more comfortable with speaking, you might want to let your visuals serve as notes. A handout or PowerPoint slide listing key points might also serve as your basic outline. Eventually, you could find you no longer need notes.

Step 6: Practice Your Delivery

As you rehearse, form a mental image of success rather than failure. Practice your presentation aloud several times beforehand to harness that energy-producing anxiety.

Begin a few days before your target date, and continue until you're about to "go on." Rehearse aloud. Talking through your speech can help you much more than thinking through your speech. Practice before an audience—your roommate, a friend, your dog, even the mirror. Talking to something or someone helps simulate the distraction listeners cause. Consider audiotaping or videotaping yourself to pinpoint your own mistakes and to reinforce your strengths. If you ask your practice audience to critique you, you'll have some idea of what changes you might wish to make.

Write • DISCUSS • Compare • Ask • BLOG • Answer • *Journal*

> Think about public speakers you hear either in person or on TV. Which ones are the most effective and why? What are some of the specific ways that the best public speakers communicate with an audience?

Using Your Voice and Body Language

Let your hands hang comfortably at your sides, reserving them for natural, spontaneous gestures. Unless you must stay close to a fixed microphone, plan to move comfortably and casually about the room. Some experts suggest changing positions between major points in order to punctuate your presentation, signaling to your audience, "I've finished with that point; let's shift topics."

Also:

▶ Make eye contact with as many listeners as you can. This helps you read their reactions, demonstrate confidence, and establish command.

▶ A smile helps to warm up your listeners, although you should avoid smiling excessively or inappropriately. Smiling through a presentation on world hunger would send your listeners a mixed message.

▶ **What suggestions for improvement would you offer this presenter?**

© Christina Micek

▶ As you practice, pay attention to the pitch of your voice, your rate of speech, and your volume. Project confidence and enthusiasm by varying your pitch. Speak at a rate that mirrors normal conversation—not too fast and not too slow. Consider varying your volume for the same reasons you vary pitch and rate—to engage your listeners and to emphasize important points.

▶ Pronunciation and word choice are important. A poorly articulated word (such as "gonna" for "going to"), a mispronounced word ("nuculer" for "nuclear"), or a mis-used word ("anecdote" for "antidote") can quickly erode credibility. Check meanings and pronunciations in the dictionary if you're not sure, and use a thesaurus for word variety. Fillers such as "um," "uh," "like," and "you know" are distracting, too.

▶ Consider your appearance. Convey a look of competence, preparedness, and success by dressing professionally.

The GUIDE Checklist For Acing Your Presentation

Imagine you've been selected as a campus tour guide for next year's prospective first-year students and their families visiting campus. Picture yourself in front of the administration building with a group of people assembled around you. You want to get and keep their attention in order to achieve your objective: raising their interest in your school. Using the GUIDE method shown in Figure 9.1, you would:

G: Get Your Audience's Attention You can relate the topic to your listeners: "Let me tell you what to expect during your college years here—at the best school in the state."

Or you can state the significance of the topic: "Deciding on which college to attend is one of the most important decisions you'll ever make."

◄ **Figure 9.1** The GUIDE Checklist

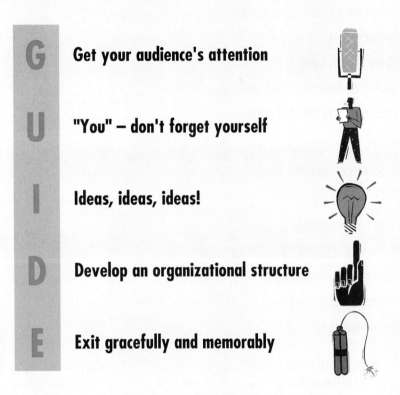

Or you can arouse their curiosity: "Do you know the three most important factors that students and their families consider when choosing a college?"

You can also tell a joke (but only if it relates and isn't offensive), startle the audience, tell a story, or ask a rhetorical question (a question asked to produce an effect, especially to make an assertion, rather than to elicit a reply). Regardless of which method you select, remember that a well-designed introduction must not only gain the attention of the audience but also develop rapport with them, motivate them to continue listening, and preview what you are going to say during the rest of your speech.

U: You (U)—Don't Forget Yourself In preparing any speech, don't exclude the most important source of your presentation—you. Even in a formal presentation, you will be most successful if you develop a comfortable style that's easy to listen to. Don't play a role. Instead, be yourself at your best, letting your wit and personality shine through.

I: Ideas, Ideas, Ideas! Create a list of all the possible points you might want to make. Then write them out as conclusions you want your listeners to accept. For example, imagine that on your campus tour for prospective new students and their parents, you want to make the following points:

1. Tuition is reasonable.

2. The faculty is composed of good teachers.

3. The school is committed to student success.

4. College can prepare you to get a good job.

5. Student life is awesome.

6. The library has adequate resources.

7. The campus is attractive.

8. The campus is safe.

9. Faculty members conduct prestigious research.

10. This college is the best choice.

For a typical presentation, most listeners can process no more than five main points. After considering your list for some time, you decide that the following five points are critical:

1. Tuition is reasonable.

2. The faculty is composed of good teachers.

3. The school is committed to student success.

4. The campus is attractive.

5. The campus is safe.

Try to generate more ideas than you think you'll need so that you can select the best ones. As with writing, don't judge them at first; rather, think up as many possibilities as you can. Then use critical thinking to decide which are most relevant to your objectives.

As you formulate your main ideas, keep these guidelines in mind:

▶ Main points should be parallel, if possible. Each main point should be a full sentence with a construction similar to the others. A poor, nonparallel structure might look like this:

1. Student life is awesome. (a full-sentence main point)

2. Tuition (a one-word main point that doesn't parallel the first point)

For a parallel second point, try instead:

2. Tuition is low. (a full-sentence main point)

▶ Each main point should include a single idea. Don't crowd main points with multiple messages, as in the following:

1. Tuition is reasonable, and the campus is safe.

2. Faculty are good teachers and researchers.

Ideas rarely stand on their own merit. To ensure that your main ideas work, use a variety of supporting materials. The three most widely used forms of supporting materials are **examples**, **statistics**, and **testimony**.

▶ Examples include stories and illustrations, hypothetical events, and specific cases. They can be powerful, compelling ways to dramatize and clarify main ideas, but make sure they're relevant, representative, and reasonable.

▶ Statistics are widely used as evidence in speeches. Of course, numbers can be manipulated, and unscrupulous speakers sometimes mislead with statistics.

▶ If you use statistics, make sure they are clear, concise, accurate, and easy to understand.

▶ Testimony includes quoting outside experts, paraphrasing reliable sources, and emphasizing the quality of individuals who agree with your main points. When you use testimony, make sure that it is accurate, expert, and credible.

Finally, because each person in your audience is unique, you are most likely to add interest, clarity, and credibility to your presentation by varying and combining the types of support you provide.

D: Develop an Organizational Structure For example, you might decide to use a chronological narrative approach, discussing the history of the college from its early years to the present. Or, you might wish to use a problem-solution format in which you describe a problem (such as choosing a school), present the pros and cons of several solutions (the strengths and weaknesses of several schools), and finally identify the best solution (your school!).

Begin with your most important ideas. Writing an outline might be the most useful way to begin organizing. List each main point and sub-point separately on a note card. Spread the cards out on a large surface (such as the floor), and arrange, rearrange, add, and delete cards until you find the most effective arrangement. Then simply number the cards, pick them up, and use them to prepare your final outline.

As you organize your presentation, remember that your overall purpose is to guide your listeners. This means you must not neglect transitions between your main points. For example:

"Now that we've looked at the library, let's move on to the gymnasium."

"The first half of my presentation has identified our recreational facilities. Now let's look at the academic hubs on campus."

"So much for the academic buildings on campus. What about the campus social scene?"

In speaking, as in writing, transitions make the difference between keeping your audience with you and losing them at an important juncture.

E: Exit Gracefully and Memorably Plan your ending carefully, realizing that most of the suggestions for introductions also apply to conclusions.

Whatever else you do, go out with style, impact, and dignity. Don't leave your listeners asking, "So that's it?" Subtly signal that the end is in sight (without the overused "So in conclusion . . ."), briefly summarize your major points, and then conclude confidently.

Speaking on the Spot

Most of the speaking you will do in college and after will be on the spot. When your instructor asks your opinion on last night's reading, when a classmate stops you in the hall to find out your position on an issue, or when your best friend asks you to defend your views, you have to give impromptu speeches.

When you must speak on the spot, it helps to use a framework that allows you to sound organized and competent. Suppose your instructor asks, "Do you think the world's governments are working together effectively to ensure a healthy environment?" One of the most popular ways to arrange your thoughts is through the PREP formula[6]. Short for "preparation," this plan requires the following:

P: Point of View Provide an overview—a clear direct statement or generalization: "After listening to yesterday's lecture, yes, I do."

R: Reasons Broadly state why you hold this point of view: "I was surprised by the efforts of the United Nations General Assembly to focus on the environment."

E: Evidence or Examples Present specific facts or data supporting your point of view: "For example, the industrialized nations have set stringent goals on air pollution and greenhouse gases for the year 2010."

P: Point of View, Restated To make sure you are understood clearly, end with a restatement of your position: "So, yes, the world's governments seem to be concerned and working to improve the situation."

Write • DISCUSS • Compare • Ask • BLOG • Answer • *Journal*

Write about your experience of speaking in front of a group. Is public speaking something you enjoy or dread? Are you an anxious or a comfortable speaker? What strategies could you suggest to anyone who wants to become more comfortable in speaking in front of a group?

What If All Else Fails?

What if you plan, organize, prepare, and rehearse, but calamity strikes anyway? What if your mind goes completely blank, you drop your note cards, or you say something totally embarrassing? Don't forget that people in your audience have been in your position and empathize with you. Accentuate the positive, rely on your wit, and keep speaking. Your recovery is what they are most likely to recognize; your success is what they are most likely to remember.

---

[6] Kenneth Wydro, *Think on Your Feet* (Englewood Cliffs, NJ: Prentice-Hall, 1981).

▷ WHERE TO GO FOR HELP

On Campus

Writing Center Most campuses have one of these. Frequently it is found within the English Department.

Learning Assistance Center In addition to help on many other topics, these centers offer help on writing.

Departments of Speech, Theater, and Communications These offer both resources and specific courses to help you develop your speaking skills.

Student Activities One of the best ways to learn and practice speaking skills is to become active in student organizations, especially those like the Student Government Association and the Debate Club.

Online

Writing tips: www.sfsu.edu/~lac/uselinks_writitng.htm
Check out these writing resources from San Francisco State University.

Plain language Ever been confused by government gobbledygook? Here's a guide to writing user-friendly documents for federal employees: www.plainlanguage.gov/ Go to the bottom of the page, and under "How to/ Tools," click on "Writing Reader-Friendly Documents." Toastmasters International offers public speaking tips at http://www.toastmasters.org/pdfs/top10.pdf

My Institution's Resources

_____

_____

_____

_____

_____

_____

_____

_____

▸▸▸ BUILDING YOUR PORTFOLIO
In The Public Eye

According to most studies, people's number one fear is public speaking. Number two is death. Death is number two. Does that sound right? This means to the average person, if you go to a funeral, you're better off in the casket than doing the eulogy.

-Jerry Seinfeld (b. 1954), American actor and comedian

To complete this portfolio activity electronically, please visit academic.cengage.com/collsucc/Gardner/YCE8e.

The media provide ample opportunities for celebrities and public figures to show off their public speaking skills. As you've probably noticed, some celebrities are much better speakers than others! However, being a good public speaker is not just important for those in the public eye. Whether you want to be a movie star or a marine biologist, potential employers tend to put excellent communication skills at the top of their "must have" list for job applicants.

1. Create a new entry in your portfolio with the title "In the Public Eye." Record your work for this activity there.

2. Identify a public figure (e.g., David Letterman, Host, the Late Show with David Letterman; Katie Couric, host of the CBS Evening News) who, in your opinion, is a good public speaker and explain why it is important for that person to speak well.

3. List the specific qualities (e.g., humor, eye contact) that you think make that person a good public speaker.

4. Remember the last time you gave a presentation in front of a group, and, using a scale of 1-5 (five being excellent), rate yourself as a public speaker using the guidelines below:

Public Speaking Skills	1 Poor	2 Fair	3 Average	4 Good	5 Excellent
Level of Preparedness (well prepared and confident, last minute technology check)					
Professional Appearance (appropriate business attire, including shoes)					
Effective Vocal Presentation Style (clear and persuasive; good pitch of your voice, rate of speech, and volume; correct grammar)					
Appropriate Behavior and Speech (no chewing gum; avoided fillers such as "um," "uh," "like," and "you know")					
Natural Body Language (good eye contact with audience, appropriate facial expressions, relaxed posture)					
Note your lowest scores: those are areas you probably need to work on as you prepare for your next presentation.					

Research and College Libraries

In this chapter YOU WILL LEARN

▶ The difference between research and simply finding information

▶ What membership and participation in the Information Society require of us

▶ Why information literacy is the survival skill for the twenty-first century

▶ How to employ information literacy in the library, in the classroom, and in life

▶ How to focus on a topic, narrow it, and shape it

▶ Specific search strategies

▶ How to ask librarians for help

▶ How plagiarism can doom a paper, a course, or a career

What key words could you use to search for more information about this image of Mt. St. Helens, taken from space?

Courtesy of the National Aeronautics and Space Administration.

Charles Curran and Rose Parkman Marshall, both of the University of South Carolina, and Margit Watts of University of Hawaii, Manoa contributed their valuable and considerable expertise to the writing of this chapter.

What Do You Know about RESEARCH AND COLLEGE LIBRARIES?

Read the following questions and choose the answer that most fits you.

1 *How do you usually navigate your library when beginning a research paper?*

A I never use the library. Google is my preferred method of research.

B I sometimes check out the library's online catalog to search for my topic, but there's so much to choose from that I usually get overwhelmed and pick the first two books that appear in the catalog.

C I talk with a librarian who helps me decide what types of sources I should be looking at–the librarian is my best resource for navigating my institution's large library.

2 *How do you check your sources for accuracy?*

A Anything I find on the Internet is accurate as long as it's not from someone's personal web page.

B As long as the writing is clear, the source seems accurate to me.

C I take a look at the author's credentials, the publisher, and the date. If a source is really dated, I try to find current material.

3 *What's the difference between popular magazines and scholarly publications?*

A Magazines are more fun to read.

B Magazines are something I would buy in a bookstore, but I wouldn't buy a scholarly publication.

C Popular magazines are not always written by experts in the field, whereas scholarly publications are.

4 *How do you narrow your topic for a research paper?*

A Are you supposed to narrow a topic beyond what the instructor gives you? I never thought to do that.

B I take a look online to see what's popular about my topic.

C I talk to my instructor or the librarian to get ideas and then explore some books and online sources to discover what aspect of the topic interests me most and can be the focus of my paper.

5 *Do you do research in any other aspects of your life?*

A No way–research is just for papers I do in college.

B Is checking movie times on a Friday night research?

C When I bought a car, I compared the Toyota to the Subaru to find out more about the differences that I might not recognize immediately.

Review your responses. **A** responses indicate that you need a lot of help in understanding the importance of research and using the library. **B** responses indicate that you have some ideas about research, but you will benefit from learning more. **C** responses indicate that you know a great deal about how to use information resources and conduct research on a particular topic. However you responded, you will find this chapter helpful as you learn to take maximum advantage of the information resources available today.

Most colleges and universities describe their three major missions as teaching, research, and service. While each of those missions is vital, we know that without the ability to find and evaluate information quickly the world would come to a standstill. Information feeds research, and research produces discoveries that improve our quality of life.

Those who ignore the importance of information or lack the skills to find and use information will also lack the ability to keep up, to participate, and to succeed in college, career, and community. Finding and using information means more than learning how to operate a computer or visiting the library. It means learning the basic research and critical thinking skills needed to make sense of the vast amount of information at your fingertips. It means developing information literacy skills. That holds true for whatever career path you choose.

What's Research–and What's Not?

Some of the steps you will go through in the name of research might turn out not to be research after all. See if you can tell the difference:

1. You complete an assignment that requires you to demonstrate how to use a library's electronic book catalog, electronic periodical index, e-mail delivery system, government documents collection, map depository, and electronic interlibrary loan service.
   _____ Research _____ Not Research

2. You are assigned to do a report on ethics; so you go to an encyclopedia, copy selected portions of an article without giving citations, and submit that as your report.
   _____ Research _____ Not Research

3. You are assigned to find a definition of ethics, a book on ethics, a journal article on ethics, and one Internet item on ethics.
   _____ Research _____ Not Research

4. Your assignment in ethics requires you to use at least five sources; you find five items on the Internet, treat them as equally reliable sources, patch them together without commentary, compose and attach an introduction, and submit your paper.
   _____ Research _____ Not Research

5. Assigned to select and report on an ethical issue, you pick ethics in politics, accumulate a dozen sources, interpret them, evaluate them, select a few and discard a few, organize the keepers into a coherent arrangement, extract portions that hang together, write a paper that cites your sources, compose an introduction that explains what you have done, draw some conclusions of your own, and submit the results.
   _____ Research _____ Not Research

◀ **Not being able to find the information you need can be frustrating.**

If you were good at #1, you might be well prepared to conduct a research project in a library, but just performing those steps with no specific purpose in mind is not conducting research.

If you were good at #2, chances are you might flunk the paper. Your instructor might teach you a new word: **plagiarism**. Copying information, or using just some of it, even changing the words around, requires that you give credit to the originator. If you were good at #3, that means you are a good retriever. While retrieving and research are not the same, retrieving is an essential research skill.

If you were good at #4, you might be in more trouble than the person in #2. First, you are plagiarizing by not crediting your sources. Second—and a much more important flaw insofar as research is concerned—is the indiscriminate use of sources that might be new or old, useful or dangerously in error, reliable or shaky, research based or anecdotal, or biased beyond credibility.

If you are good at #5, especially in the analysis and drawing of conclusions, then you have experienced the rush that comes with discovery and the pleasure that accompanies making a statement or taking a stand. The conclusion that you composed is your triumph; it is new information!

The Information Age, the Information Explosion, and the Information Society

During the Agricultural Age, most people farmed. Now only a tiny fraction of us work the land, but our abundance fills our silos and granaries. During the Industrial Age, we made things. We still do, of course, but we have automated industry so that fewer people can produce more goods. In addition, we have shipped much of our manufacturing overseas to cheaper labor markets. Other nations have joined the game and compete strenuously these days. Now we live in the Information Age, a name we concocted because it signifies the primacy of information in our everyday lives. Here are some key Information Age observations:

▶ Information, having overtaken things, is the new commodity. Consider TV, the Internet, and your computer. Information companies such as Microsoft and Apple, Google and Alta Vista have earned billions by simply offering or selling information to you.

▶ America's gross national product (GNP) is substantially information based.

▶ There is more information than ever before. It doubles at ever shortening intervals. This abundance has not made information easier to get, although the abundance creates that illusion.

▶ Because abundance and electronic access combine to produce prodigious amounts of retrievable information, people need highly developed **sorting** skills to cope.

▶ Most of the American workforce is employed at originating, managing, or transferring information.

▶ Information has value; you can determine its benefits in dollars, and you can compute the cost of not having it.

▶ Information literacy is the survival skill for your generation.

▶ The information professionals at your library are leading authorities on how to find information. And most important, they not only know where to find it, they also have the wonderful ability to help you use information to meet your needs, solve problems, provide explanations, open up new possibilities, and ultimately create new knowledge. Some campuses even have a first-year librarian, someone who is especially able to help new students with the kinds of questions they are most likely to ask.

Write • DISCUSS • Compare • Ask • BLOG • Answer • *Journal*

> Why do you think the chapter authors state, "Information literacy is the survival skill for [this] generation"? Do you agree? Why or why not?

Making Sense of It All

What is the role of information in our everyday lives? How do we cope with the daily challenge of finding the right information to solve a given problem before it defeats us? Which airline or travel service really offers the cheapest airfare? Is it true that certain professors always ask true/false questions? On third down when the football team lines up with a slot receiver, do they always pass, and is the slot receiver always the first (and maybe only) target? Which variety of poisonous serpent bit the patient, and which antivenin is required to treat the victim? Which is likely to give me better service, a Subaru or a Toyota? What are the relationships between social class and mental illness? At what stress levels will bridge cables snap? What is iambic

◀ **Research can take many forms, as these students demonstrate.**

© PureStock/Alamy

▶ **Information plays a key role in vastly different projects.**

© Mark Richards/PhotoEdit

pentameter? Who steals most from a chain store, the customers who lift displayed products or the employees who help themselves to inventory? What is the best way to shave time from the manufacture and delivery of tractors?

These questions all share some common factors. Although some of these questions are academic and others are down-to-earth questions that people ask as part of their jobs, they share a particular common characteristic. The answers to each are available in information agencies and/or in electronic formats. An inquirer needs instant answers for the question about snake bites because a life hangs in the balance. Other situations might not be so critical.

Galloping New Ignorance (GNI)

You have probably heard the phrase "Knowledge is power." While knowledge can contribute to power, it is only true if knowledge is put to use. And in order to have power, knowledge must be timely and relevant. When you retrieve, sort, interpret, analyze and synthesize sources from an information center, whether it is the library or a computer database, you will produce a product that has power.

Galloping New Ignorance (GNI) drains power. What is Galloping New Ignorance? It is the assumption that the huge amounts of manageable information available electronically provide valuable knowledge. While some students might rejoice at the discovery of 12,456 hits from a search on fossil fuels, shock takes hold if and when they realize their discovery is totally unsorted, and they frequently respond by settling—using the first five hits, irrespective of quality or authenticity. GNI can affect anyone, including smart decision makers who should know better and whose decisions suffer as a consequence. People who believe that they are informed because they are wired contribute to GNI.

© Anton Vengo/SuperStock

◀ **Librarians can help you narrow your search for information to the best resources.**

Write • DISCUSS • Compare • Ask • BLOG • Answer • *Journal*

How do you find sources for an important paper? Do you go to the first five hits on Google, or do you take a more deliberate process? What strategies could you use to make sure your Internet or library research results in valid information?

Confusing mounds of information for valuable information is a common GNI symptom. People marvel at the information explosion, the paper inflation, and the Internet. They conclude that they are or can easily become informed. Many are unprepared for the blurring of lines between subjects, the huge number of available publications, and the unsorted, unevaluated mass of information that pours down upon them at the press of a button. What is the antidote for GNI? How can one become an informed and successful user of information?

Learning to Be Information Literate

Here are four things to remember about information:

1. Know that information matters. It helps empower people to make good choices. The choices people make often determine their success in business, their happiness as partners, and their well-being as citizens on this planet.

2. Know how and where to find it. If you are sick, you must know whose help to seek. If you are poor, you need to know where to get assistance. If you want to study

chemistry, you need to know which schools offer degrees, how much they charge, if there are scholarships, and who will hire you when you graduate.

3. Know how to ask the right questions. Once you find where to go and whom to ask, you'll need to possess the skills to ask good questions and to make educated searches of information systems, such as the Internet, libraries, and databases. You'll also want to cultivate relationships with information professionals, such as librarians so they can help you frame good questions, broaden and narrow searches, and retrieve the information you need. You must be able to identify and define your need and to use the kinds of inquiry terminology that will give you hits instead of misses.

Write • DISCUSS • Compare • Ask • BLOG • Answer • *Journal*

> Do you think the library is a necessary resource for learning in college? Why or why not?

4. Learn how to interpret the information you find. While it is very important to retrieve information, it is even more important to know what to do with it. What does the information mean? Have you selected a source you can understand? Is the information accurate? Is the author/provider a reliable source? How can you determine this?

How Does the Information Fit Your Need?

▶ Is it introductory? Introductory information is very basic and elementary. It does what its name implies: it introduces and provides a first impression. It often neither assumes nor requires prior knowledge about the topic. Example: A snake is a long-bodied, legless animal.

▶ Is it definitional? Definitional information provides some descriptive details about a topic. Example: Snakes are either venomous or nonvenomous. The venom may be of three types: neurotoxic, hemotoxic, or a combination of both.

▶ Is it analytical? Analytical information supplies data about origins, behaviors, differences, and uses. Example: While some snakes are shy and prefer to retreat when disturbed, some are aggressive. People often mistake venomous varieties for harmless ones, and they suffer the deadly consequence.

▶ Is it current or dated? Is it someone's opinion, or is it a rigorously researched document? Can you lay it out in a logical sequence? Can you conclude anything? Use the "so what?" test: How important is this discovery?

▶ Who are you going to tell about your discovery, and how? Will you write a report? What guidelines for construction will you follow? Will you respect the intellectual property of others by giving appropriate credit to sources? Will you give your report orally? If you transfer this information orally, what principles for making presentations will you identify, practice, and master? Or will you just wing your presentation without much forethought?

Information literacy has many facets, among them:

▶ Computer literacy, the abilities associated with using electronic methods (search language), both for inquiry and for constructing presentations for others of what you have found and analyzed.

▶ Media literacy, which is facility with various formats: film, tape, CDs, and the machines that operate them.

▶ Cultural literacy, knowing what has gone on and is going on around you. If someone remarks about the Great Bambino or a feat of Ruthian proportion, you have to know about George Herman (Babe) Ruth, or you will not get the point.

You have to know the difference between the Civil War and the Revolution, U2 and Y2K, Eminem and M&Ms, or you will not understand everyday conversation.

The Association of College and Research Libraries (ACRL) has developed the following five best practices for the information-literate student:

1. The information-literate student determines the nature and extent of the information needed by:

   ▶ defining and articulating the need for information

   ▶ identifying a variety of types and formats of potential sources for information

2. The information-literate student accesses needed information effectively and efficiently by:

   ▶ selecting the most appropriate research methods

   ▶ creating and using effectively designed search strategies

   ▶ finding information online or in person using a variety of methods

   ▶ refining the search strategy along the way if necessary

   ▶ extracting, recording, and managing the information and its sources.

3. The information-literate student evaluates information and its sources critically and incorporates selected information into his or her knowledge base and value system by:

   ▶ summarizing the main ideas from the information gathered

   ▶ applying criteria for evaluating both the information and its sources

   ▶ synthesizing main ideas to construct new concepts

   ▶ comparing new knowledge with prior knowledge

   ▶ determining the value added, contradictions, or other unique characteristics of the information

   ▶ determining whether the new knowledge has an impact on the individual's value system and taking steps to reconcile differences

   ▶ validating, understanding, and interpreting the information through discourse with other individuals, subject-area experts, and/or practitioners

   ▶ determining whether the initial query should be revised

4. The information-literate student, individually or as a member of a group, uses information effectively to accomplish a specific purpose by:

   ▶ applying new and prior information to planning and creating a particular product or performance

   ▶ revising the development process for the product or performance

   ▶ communicating the product or performance effectively to others

5. The information-literate student understands many of the economic, legal, and social issues surrounding the use of information and accesses and uses information ethically and legally by:

▶ following laws, regulations, institutional policies, and etiquette related to the access and use of information resources.

▶ acknowledging the use of information sources in communicating the product or performance.

Information Literacy Competency Standards for Higher Education (2000). **www.ala.org/ala/acrl/ acrlstandards/standards.pdf**

Narrowing and Researching an Assigned Topic

If you are fortunate to have an instructor who understands that information literacy skills are best practiced and learned when you have a reason for gathering information, that instructor will give you a research assignment to discover, interpret, organize, and present some findings to your classmates. Let's assume that your assignment is to research the topic of political ethics. What steps should you take to conduct your research? If you wanted to forgo the opportunity to improve your information literacy skills, you could manage this from your own computer and pick the first hits you get on the Internet or from *Readers' Guide Abstracts.* But that's not a good idea. Doing research requires that you follow these steps:

Step 1: Define the Topic in General Terms

Since your job is to define and introduce, you will be well served by general and specific dictionaries and encyclopedias. Any respected general dictionary can define ethics for you, but it would be a good idea to get your topic defined in context. Since your topic is political ethics, consult a political dictionary and an encyclopedia that would consider the political aspects of your ethics topic. For example, you would most likely find a great article on lobbies in the *Encyclopedia of American Political History.* Find out what the best source would be for your topic, and ask your librarian or course instructor for help in identifying the best resources.

Step 2: Specify and Narrow Your Topic

After you have retrieved a definition that you determine to be complete and understandable, you are ready to search for a good introduction—some basic information that guides you toward a further understanding of the nature of your topic. You have a decision to make. What aspects of political ethics will you pursue? Even if you launch the most general of inquiries, you will discover very quickly that your topic is vast and that there are many related subtopics. Talk to your librarian about the particular components of the topic that interest you most, and what kinds of sources you might expect to find.

Whether you are searching the library or the Internet, narrowing your search is a critical step so you can focus and retrieve highly relevant items. Remember those 12,456 hits on fossil fuels? What you want is 12 or so specific, highly relevant hits on an aspect of political ethics that you can fashion into a coherent five-minute presentation, or a lucid, well-organized essay or opinion piece.

When you look up "political ethics" in the Library of Congress Subject Headings (LCSH) or when you check "political ethics" in the library's electronic catalog, you will discover some choices:

Civil service, ethics	Judicial ethics
Conflict of interests	Justice
Corporations—corrupt practices	Legislative ethics
Ethics, modern	Political corruption
Environmental ethics	Political ethics
Fairness	Social ethics
Gifts to politicians	

Note two things. First of all, because your topic is broad, every one of these headings leads to books and articles on political ethics. The good news is there's lots of information; the bad news is there's lots of information. Remember what you read in chapter 9 on writing about the importance of narrowing your topic. To complete this research project, you'll need to narrow the topic of political ethics and get much more specific. Ask the librarians for help in identifying related topics, and do a subject or keyword search using your institution's online library catalog. Learning more about all the areas related to a general topic will actually help you narrow your search.

Some databases permit searching by using keywords. A keyword is a single word that would appear in the topic you are investigating. Your library's catalog probably has the keyword option. Other databases permit searching of phrases. A few databases allow a natural language search that uses regular spoken language—you can ask the search engine a question or type in a sentence that describes what you are looking for. Some indexes such as the *New York Times* Index and ERIC (Education Resources Information Center) have their own legal subject terms and their own approved lists of search terms that you should consult before searching.

Because you might know about the efforts of lobbyists and political action committees to influence legislation, and because this subtopic interests you, you might decide that gifts to politicians and political corruption will be your target topics. Of course, "lobbyists" opens up a new subject area that you might explore if you are interested in the ethical aspects of a legitimate practice that is common in the American political process.

Encyclopedic sources will help you craft an introduction to your three-pronged topic: gifts to politicians, political corruption, and lobbyists. For instance, two editions of the previously cited and very useful specific subject encyclopedia, *The Encyclopedia of American Political History*, can supply some interesting information. It has a good "lobbies and lobbyists" piece, and also a major article on "political corruption." If an encyclopedia has an index, use it. Your chances of finding something useful are increased significantly if you check the index first.

If you consult your notes and your topic breakdown, you will see that you have narrowed your broad topic to a manageable size. From dictionaries and encyclopedias, you have found definitions, introductory materials, some current and historical examples of political ethics in action, and related information on your topic. You are now ready to launch a broader search.

Step 3: Launch Your Search

It is decision time. Are you going to search print or electronic sources? For best results, decide to do both. Where you begin is up to you. Let's say you decide upon periodicals, journals, and magazines first.

Your library will probably subscribe to electronic and print versions of *Readers' Guide*, Social Science Index, and PAIS (Public Affairs Information Service). Also consider reviewing the serial *Editorials on File*, a publication printed twice monthly that contains about 200 editorials per issue. *Editorials on File* will give you some different points of view on a variety of topics. You will have to search more cleverly in this publication, for the topics you seek will be embedded in more general subject headings. Check the indexes bound at the end of a yearly volume. You might not find gifts to politicians, political corruption, or lobbying, but under politics you can find current news stories, each of which produces numerous columns of editorial reporting. It's important to always be flexible in your search terms or think creatively about how to reword your topic to find what you are looking for.

In searching for articles, you should realize that there can be a heavy dose of bias or point of view in some of them. Although nothing is inherently wrong with someone's point of view, it is dangerous for a reader not to know that the bias is there. A great source for keeping you informed about potential bias is *Magazines for Libraries*,[1] which will tell you about a periodical's editorial leanings. Here are some examples:

Periodical Title	**Perspective**
America	Jesuit/Catholic
Church and State	Historically Protestant
Commentary	American Jewish Committee
Commonweal	Catholic
Time	Major newsweekly; not opinion-free
New Republic	"Even-handed"
National Review	Conservative

By recognizing bias among your sources, you will begin to find where you stand on your topic. Although it's reassuring to find others who agree with your views, is it just as essential that you consider different opinions so that you can speak intelligently to those points.

> *Write • DISCUSS • Compare • Ask • BLOG • Answer • Journal*
>
> In your opinion, what newspapers, magazines, or TV networks are biased? Does a biased point of view make you more or less likely to read or watch? Why do you think many people only expose themselves to opinions or viewpoints like their own?

[1] Cheryl LaGuardia, Bill Katz, and Linda S. Katz, *Magazines for Libraries, 13th ed.* (New Providence, NJ: RR Bowker LC, 2004).

Using Electronic Sources

Online periodical databases, online catalogs, and the World Wide Web allow you to quickly locate materials in the vast universe of electronic information. Let's begin with some general information to help you search more effectively.

First, know the difference between searching online catalogs or periodical databases, and the web. Online catalogs and online periodical databases such as LexisNexis are accessed via the Internet; however, the web only acts as a host to disseminate the information. Information on a database is usually stored in a single location or server that is owned by a company such as Gale Research. Remember, much of the information found in online periodical databases might also be found in print. Human beings, not computers, do the indexing, so you can be fairly sure the information meets certain criteria for inclusion. The indexer might have made a determination as to the accuracy, timeliness, and authoritativeness of the article under consideration. Be careful to choose key words relevant to your investigation as this will help you retrieve material you can use. You don't want to have to sort through a lot of sources as you did when you were narrowing your topic. Searching online catalogs and online periodical databases is a lot like searching the print version of *Readers' Guide*—only much quicker.

You should know that an index and a catalog have completely different uses. The former card catalogs that were common in libraries until recent years have been replaced by OPAC (online public access catalogs). These catalogs tell you what books, magazines, newspapers, videos, and other materials are available in a particular library. An index such as InfoTrac College Edition, Readers' Guide, or America: History and Life allows you to search for articles within many periodicals such as newspapers, magazines, journals, or even book chapters. While some of these sources will be in your library, you can retrieve others through an online database system or interlibrary loan. Ask your librarian for help with locating articles or books not available in your campus library.

Searching the web, on the other hand, is a totally different story. You get different results from what you retrieve from a database. The information searched by googling is not found in a single location; it is an aggregation of information from the vast universe of servers around the globe. Anybody can have a website and more are added every day, which means you cannot be sure of the website owner's credibility and reliability. So the information you retrieve from the web might be written by anyone—a fifth grader, a distinguished professor, a professional society, or a biased advocate! In a search using the keywords "smoking consequences," uninformed comments on smoking and health could appear in a Google list just above or below results from a rigorous scientific study.

A recent Google search on the subject "political corruption" generated over 25 million hits. The first page yielded these interesting results:

A great collection of links on politics and political corruption

A Libertarian Party legislative program on political corruption

Two **www.amazon.com** ads

Two sources on political corruption in Illinois

A site that offers "research" on gambling and political corruption

An article by a political activist on corporate greed and political corruption

A university site offering information about political corruption in South Africa

An offer to sell you books on political corruption

While this is not quite a hodgepodge of suspect and reliable information, it surely demonstrates that one must be alert when examining Internet sources. Mixed in with credible reporting are sales promotions, a piece aimed at making you feel guilty for riding around in a fancy car, some antigambling exhortations, and useful links to other sources. It isn't always easy to evaluate the quality of Internet sources. You will want to check pages 208-209 in this chapter to read some helpful strategies you can use to determine whether sources are credible and authentic.

To become a successful and savvy user of electronic resources, you need to establish and follow certain guidelines such as these:

1. Write out your topic or problem as a statement or question. "Is it right for politicians to take gifts from lobbyists?" Or, "The influence of lobbyists or PACs has dramatically changed American political ethics."

2. Understand Boolean operators. Boolean operators are the words "and," "or," and "not." The Bowling Green State University Library website describes these terms this way:

A search for rock AND roll will locate all records containing both the word "rock" and the word "roll." It will locate items about rock and roll music. It might also locate records that contain both words in a different context, such as "It recommends you roll the rock quickly."

A search for rock OR roll will locate all records containing either the word "rock" or the word "roll"–not necessarily both. It will retrieve items about bakery rolls, tumbling, rocks, music, gemstones, etc.

A search for rock NOT roll will locate records containing the word "rock" but NOT the word "roll." It will retrieve items about rocks, gemstones, diamonds, etc." (**www.bgsu.edu/colleges/library/infosrv/lue/boolean.html**)

3. Write down several terms or synonyms for your topic so that if one search does not yield any hits, you have some backup terms on hand. Search in a variety of ways. Will you get more hits by using a natural language search–"ethics in politics"–or using Boolean operators, such as "politics AND ethics AND gifts"?

4. The first time you use any electronic resource, be sure to consult the Help link provided by the catalog, database, or search engine to learn specific searching techniques. You will get better results if you use the tips and strategies suggested by the database provider.

5. Understand whether you need scholarly publications, popular magazines, or both. Do you know the difference?

<u>Scholarly Journals</u>	<u>Popular Magazines</u>
Long articles	Shorter articles
In-depth information on topic	Broad overview of topic

Written by experts in subject/field	Written by journalists or staff reporters
Graphs, tables, or photographs to support text	Lots of color photos of people and events
Articles "refereed" or reviewed	Articles evaluated by peers in field
Documented by Works Cited or References page	No bibliography, but sources credited

6. Select the correct database for your particular subject or topic. Most libraries subdivide their databases by broad general categories such as Humanities, Social Sciences, Science and Technology, Business, Health and Medicine, and Government Information, or by major. Each library loads its subscription list onto its electronic resources page. Under "Social Sciences," for example, one might find International Political Science Abstracts (PAIS); America: History and Life; and over 20 other databases. There are also multidisciplinary databases that provide excellent material on most topics you encounter during your first years of college. Ask your librarian about the databases that are most relevant to your needs.

7. After you scan several entries, decide if (and how) you need to limit your search. You can often limit by date, language, journal name, full-text, refereed, or word(s) in title. If you get too many hits, you might want to add additional search terms. The search "lobbyists OR political action committees AND gifts" yielded more than 400 hits. Adding "politicians" in a new search reduced the results to a manageable number. (Hint: If you get too few hits, omit a search term. It is really better to use a building-blocks approach to searching. Begin with the general, and add terms to refine and limit search.) For certain current topics, your instructors often prefer information that is no more than five years old, and limiting by date helps you comply with this instruction.

8. Does the database have a thesaurus of terms you can search? Many databases—such as ERIC and PsychINFO—have online and print thesauri to help you select the best search terminology and learn related terms.

9. Learn the quirks of databases or search engines you use often. In Google, for example, should you use Boolean operators (e.g., "politicians AND lobbyists")? Can you use natural language to search "ethics in politics" or "gifts to politicians"? You can truncate a word by using an asterisk to retrieve broader results. For instance, "Lobby*" will search for "lobby," "lobbying," "lobbyist," and "lobbyists." (Hint: Be careful not to truncate too drastically; otherwise, you will get results you do not need; for example, "Lobb*" will also retrieve "lobbed" and "lobbing.")

10. Check your library's electronic resources page to see what else is available to you online. Most libraries have links to other commonly used electronic reference tools. These include online encyclopedias, dictionaries, almanacs, style guides, biographical and statistical resources, and news sources.

Write • DISCUSS • Compare • Ask • BLOG • Answer • *Journal*

> Talk to a faculty member, a parent, or an older friend who went to college. Ask them how they conducted research before the Internet, before Google. Write a short review of the strategies used by former generations to access and use information.

Nine C's for Evaluating Internet Sources

The library at the University of Wisconsin at Eau Claire offers these suggestions for checking Internet sources:

Content. What is the intent of the content? Are the title and author identified? Is the content juried? Is the content popular or scholarly, satiric or serious? What is the date of the document or article? Is the edition current? Do you have the latest version? Is this important? How do you know?

Credibility. Is the author identifiable and reliable? Is the content credible? Authoritative? Should it be? What is the purpose of the information? Is it serious, satiric, humorous? Is the URL extension .edu, .com, .gov, or .org? What does this tell you about the publisher?

Critical Thinking. How can you apply critical thinking skills, including previous knowledge and experience, to evaluate Internet resources? Can you identify the author, publisher, edition, and so on, as you would with a traditionally published resource? What criteria do you use to evaluate Internet resources?

Copyright. Even if the copyright notice does not appear prominently, someone wrote, or is responsible for, the creation of a document, graphic, sound, or image, and the material falls under the copyright conventions. "Fair use" applies to short, cited excerpts, usually as an example for commentary or research. Materials are in the public domain if this is explicitly stated. Internet users, as users of print media, must respect copyright.

Citation. Internet resources should be cited to identify sources used, both to give credit to the author and to provide the reader with avenues for further research. Standard style manuals (print and online) provide some examples of how to cite Internet documents, although these standards are not uniform.

Continuity. Will the Internet site be maintained and updated? Is it now and will it continue to be free? Can you rely on this source over time to provide up-to-date information? Some good .edu sites are now .com, with possible cost implications. Other sites offer partial use for free and charge fees for continued or in-depth use.

Censorship. Has your discussion list been evaluated? Messages posted to a moderated list are reviewed by a "moderator" before they are distributed to the entire list. Does your search engine or index look for all words or are some words excluded? Is this censorship? Does your institution, based on its mission, parent organization, or space limitations, apply some restrictions to Internet use? Consider censorship and privacy issues when using the Internet.

Comparability. Does the Internet resource have an identified comparable print or CD-ROM data set or source? Does the Internet site contain comparable and complete information? (For example, some newspapers have partial but not full text information on the Internet.) Do you need to compare data or statistics over time? Can you identify sources for comparable earlier or later data? Comparability of data might or might not be important, depending on your project.

Context. What is the context (frame of reference) for your research? Can you find commentary, opinion, narrative, statistics, and so forth? Are you looking for current or historical information? Definitions? Research studies or articles? How does Internet information fit in the overall context of your subject? Before you start searching, define the research context and research needs, and decide what sources might best fill information needs without data overload.

▷ WHERE TO GO FOR HELP

On Campus

Your Instructor Be sure to ask your instructor for help with your information search, especially if you need to narrow your topic.

Library Libraries offer a variety of forms of help, including library orientation sessions, workshops, and, on some campuses, credit-bearing courses to develop your library search and retrieval skills.

Specialized Libraries/Collections If you are at a large university it will be very common to find multiple libraries that are part of separate schools or colleges. For example, if you are a business administration major, your university will probably have a separate business library that you will need to learn to use in addition to the central library. This is true of many majors.

Technology Support Centers Many campuses have such units staffed by personnel responsible for the institution's entire technology infrastructure. These units frequently offer noncredit workshops, help sessions, and so on. In addition, many of the departments in larger universities will have their own separate technology labs and centers where you can work and get assistance. It won't surprise you to find that much of the help provided to students comes from fellow students who are often ahead of their faculty in these skills! Some campuses also provide such assistance in residence halls, where there might even be a "computing assistant" on a parallel with the resident assistant.

Discipline-Based Courses Many majors will offer specialized courses in discipline-based research methods. You will find these listed in your campus catalog/bulletin. Usually you don't take these in your first year, but check them out. And, of course, for those interested in for-credit courses dealing with technology, check out the courses in computer science.

Online

Research and documenting sources: **http://owl.english. purdue.edu/owl/resource/584/02/**
Purdue University has an excellent resource on documenting sources, both print and electronic.

My Institution's Resources

_____

_____

_____

_____

_____

_____

Other Sources for Information and Assistance

What if the library does not have the journal or book you really need for your research or project? The interlibrary loan department will be happy to borrow the materials for you. Most libraries allow you to submit your interlibrary loan requests online. Ask about this free service at your reference desk.

Are you a distance education student who cannot come into your college library in person? Libraries provide proxy access to their electronic materials to distance education students. To learn how, e-mail or call the reference desk.

Be sure to use the handouts and guides available in print at the reference desk or online. You will also find online tutorials and virtual tours of the library that enable you to become familiar with the collections, service points, and policies of your library.

▶ **If your city has a good library, use it as well as your campus library. You can find a world of additional information sources.**

© Will & Deni McIntyre/CORBIS

Ask a Librarian—Librarians Thrive on Helping You

In your quest for information, you need to begin by assessing what you already know and explore for a while on your own. After 10 or 20 minutes, however, you might decide to get some help. Ask a librarian. Librarians are information experts who are trained to assist and guide you to the resources you need. The librarians assigned to reference work or the ones who patrol the computer stations might look busy. That's because they are! But they are busy helping students with projects just like yours. You will not interrupt them when you ask for assistance, and 99 percent of them will help you promptly and ably.

Today, you can contact a reference librarian in several ways. You can e-mail a reference librarian and receive a quick reply. Or you can call the reference desk to ask a question, such as, "Do you have a copy of the report *Problems with the Presidential Gifts System*"? Third, you can have a "live chat" online with a library staffer in real time. Fourth, you can come to the reference desk in person. (Hint: You will be most successful if you know your assignment and have negotiated it with your instructor. To be on the safe side, bring any written instructions you have to your meeting with the librarian. Tell the librarian what you have already tried—if anything.) If you are not successful in your first attempts at retrieving relevant information, ask for additional help. Finally, you might make an appointment to see a reference librarian. Remember, there are no silly questions. The information staff has heard them all, probably several times today, and a good librarian will treat your inquiry with respect. Most libraries have websites with lots of help available. Some also have tutorials on writing research papers, and conducting online searches.

About Plagiarism

In recent history, a serious candidate for the American presidency was forced to withdraw from the race when opponents discovered he had failed to give proper credit to a source he used in one of his speeches. Everyone from songwriters to book

Confessions of a College Student

Name: Katie Anderson

Age: 20

University: Missouri State University at Springfield

Hometown: Fulton, MO

Major: Psychology with minors in Criminology and Biomedical Science

Favorite book(s): *Tuesdays With Morrie* by Mitch Albom, *Blue Like Jazz* by Donald Miller, and any Dr. Seuss book

Favorite college course: So far? Probably my CRM 210 (Intro to the Criminal Justice System). It's what made me decide to be a CRM minor.

Favorite food: Nothing could beat my grandma's cooking, but I'm really just a sucker for anything homemade. Other than that, nothing beats good Italian, Chinese, or sushi.

The person who inspires me the most: After the horrible shooting at Virginia Tech in 2007, many inspiring stories have emerged. One that pulled at my heart the strongest was that of Liviu Librescu, a 76-year-old professor of engineering at Virginia Tech and Holocaust victim, who barricaded the door to his classroom long enough for his students to jump to safety from the upper-story windows of Norris Hall, and who subsequently was killed by the assassin.

Favorite way to relax: If I'm stressed, I enjoy running until I can't run anymore. Then I shower and change into comfortable clothes and hang out with my friends.

Library confession: My first visit to our campus library was for my Freshman Honors Seminar. We had the chance to receive 10 bonus points if we toured the library within the first few weeks of classes. Since this was my first time in the library, I left without learning my way around. But when I was required to actually use the library in the spring, I still found it tough to find what I was looking for. I hate asking questions and feeling stupid (big mistake!), so I just picked up a map and wandered until I found what I needed.

The library also is a place where I can study with very few distractions. I have a hard time concentrating in my room, but if I study at the library, I leave the rest of my life in my room and take only what I'll need for studying. It really works.

---

authors to website developers is on guard against idea thievery. When ideas are put on paper, film, screens, or tape, they become intellectual property. Using those ideas without permission or without saying where you got them, and sometimes without paying for them, can cost you a grade, a course, a degree, maybe even a career. Plagiarism can mess you up big time and get you in trouble with your school. But, it is so easy to avoid. Just remember:

▶ If you use somebody else's exact published words, you have to give that person credit.

▶ If you use somebody else's published ideas, even if you use your words to express the ideas, you must give that person credit.

Your instructor will indicate the preferred method for citation: footnotes, parenthetical references embedded in the text of your paper, and/or endnotes of

WIRED WINDOW

YOU MIGHT BE FAMILIAR with downloading music using peer-to-peer file sharing programs (popular programs use networks such as Gnutella, Ares, and BitTorrent). The Recording Industry Association of America recently started to sue individual students for downloading and sharing music. Your college professors have been enforcing ownership rights in a similar way for much longer—they have been catching students plagiarizing since there were papers to plagiarize. Interestingly, professors have seen a rise in plagiarism. In some high schools, the concept of plagiarism is rarely explained and students might arrive at college with an incomplete understanding of how to cite others' work. The web also makes it easier for students to "cut and paste" text and pass that work off as their own—a practice that is considered unethical and, at some institutions, grounds for dismissal. With the advent of new technologies, it is becoming easier to catch offenders. Some colleges and universities use a website called www.TurnItIn.com, where a student will upload a paper to a website. The instructor will then have the paper checked against a large database of student papers and against the web (it's like doing a Google search on every paper ever written and on the Internet at the same time). The website then provides instructors with an originality report for each student. To avoid plagiarism when doing online research, review this section and make sure that you know the correct way to cite someone else's work when you paraphrase or use direct quotes.

some kind. Even a novice student can meet the challenge of putting together information about complex topics composed by experts.

Most instructors and most college officials consider plagiarism cheating. They seldom accept "I didn't know" as a defense. They might not acknowledge that plagiarism can be inadvertent or an "oops!" thing. The Internet, which can be a tempting repository of ideas to pilfer, now offers programs that help instructors identify plagiarized assignments. The websites **www.Turnitin.com** and **www.Plagiarism.org** are examples of Internet help available to professors.

Submitting a term paper purchased from an Internet source or from an individual will cause you to:

1. Miss out on the discovery and analysis that information literacy activities provide. You are in college to learn and you are cheating yourself of that opportunity.

2. Give a false impression that you know something you do not, a fakery that will catch up with you in school and certainly on the job.

3. Flunk.

4. Get by, if the ruse is successful, but learn little or nothing. Remember why you are in college and your goals for the future.

As a student of English composition, comparative literature, or public relations, your task will be to manage information for projects and presentations, oral and written. In a few years, as a technical writer for IBM, a teacher of English at a school or university, or a campaign manager for a gubernatorial candidate, your task will be the same—to manage and present information for oral and written projects. The information literacy skills you learn and employ as a student are the same ones that will serve you well as a successful professional.

▶▶▶ BUILDING YOUR PORTFOLIO
In the Know

I find that a great part of the information I have was acquired by looking something up and finding something else on the way.

–Franklin P. Adams (1881–1960), American journalist and radio personality

To complete this portfolio activity electronically, please visit
academic.cengage.com/collsucc/Gardner/YCE8e.

Reviewing multiple sources of information can help you to get the whole story. This is especially important when using the Internet as a research tool. While the Internet is becoming a primary source of worldwide news, there is no overarching quality control system for information posted on the Internet. Regardless of where you are gathering your information, you need to read with a discerning eye to make sure the source is credible.

1. Create a new entry in your portfolio with the title "In the Know." Record your work for this assignment there.

2. Choose a national current event.

a. Carefully read about it on your favorite news website (e.g., **www.cnn.com**).

b. Also read about the event in a traditional national newspaper (e.g., *The New York Times, Wall Street Journal, Christian Science Monitor,* or *USA Today*). Your campus library or local community library will have these newspapers.

Website used: _____

Newspaper used: _____

3. Compare and contrast the differences in the ways these two sources portrayed the event.

▶ Is the author's name or another source provided?

▶ Are there clues that the authors are biased in their reporting? If so, describe these clues.

▶ Who do you think the authors were writing for (intended audience)? (For example, were they writing for a general audience or for people of a certain age or educational level?)

_____	_____
_____	_____
_____	_____
_____	_____
_____	_____
_____	_____

▶ Were the facts presented the same way by both the Internet and the print source?

_____
_____
_____

Explain your answer.

▶ Did one source cover more details than the other? If so, explain your answer.

_____
_____
_____

▶ Were the writers' information sources listed? If so, what were those sources?

_____	_____
_____	_____
_____	_____
_____	_____
_____	_____
_____	_____

Majors and Careers: Making the Right Choice

In this chapter YOU WILL LEARN

▶ Tips for thriving in the current economy

▶ How majors, interests, and careers are linked—but not always

▶ How to plan a career itinerary for each year of college

▶ The skills employers seek in college graduates

▶ How to search for a job

How many careers can you find in this photo?

© Lester Lefkowitz/CORBIS

Philip Gardner of Michigan State University contributed his valuable and considerable expertise to the writing of this chapter.

What Do You Know ABOUT YOUR MAJOR and INTENDED CAREER?

Check the items below that apply to you:

1 *Do you plan to visit your campus's career center or your career advisor?*

A I will so that they can help me prepare for what I'll need to do to meet my goals after graduation.

B I've thought about it, but I'm a little nervous because I'm not really sure I know what I want to do.

C No–I already know what job I want. I don't see how they can help me.

2 *Do you think it would be a good idea to work while you're in college?*

A If I could find a job on campus or a part-time job that relates to my major, it would be a good idea.

B I'm not sure. I could use some extra money, but I don't know what kind of job to look for.

C I'd rather not work; that will cut into my social life. But if I have to work, I want a job that will pay me a lot of money.

3 *Why is networking important in deciding on and advancing in a career?*

A If you make connections with people who are doing what you think you want to do, you can learn more about the job and maybe have an "in" on a future job.

B I know networking is important, but I always feel funny about introducing myself to someone I don't know.

C Networking is important because success is all about who you know, not what you know. My motto is "fake it and make it."

4 *What kinds of questions are good to ask during an interview for a job?*

A I like to ask what the work environment is like to determine if I would like to work there.

B I usually just let them ask me all the questions–I can never think of anything to ask.

C Mostly I want to know how much vacation and sick leave I get.

5 *How did you decide on, or how do you plan to choose, your major?*

A I have thought about both my personal interests and what the job market is offering in the way of my interests.

B I am getting a handle on what my interests are by taking a wide range of courses, but beyond that I haven't thought about it much.

C I guess I'll just major in whatever kinds of courses I get the best grades in.

Review your responses. **A** responses indicate that you are already making plans while you're in college for what you'll do when you graduate. **B** responses indicate that you're beginning to think about the links between college and career, but you're not doing everything you could. **C** responses indicate that you're not taking the link between college and career very seriously. However you responded, this chapter will offer you important information about how your college education can prepare you for the future.

Students come to college for many reasons, but for many a central purpose of college is gaining the knowledge and skills necessary for future employment. Your success in your work life will often depend on whether the profession or career you think you want to pursue is really right for you. But sometimes success in the workplace also depends on your ability to do simple things well, such as being on time, being honest, and doing your best. Let's look at the work experiences of two college students, Sara and John.

Sara entered college with thoughts of majoring in the sciences because she enjoyed working in the laboratory at her hometown hospital. Her concern for helping others led her to choose nursing as a major; it was a good career path that combined her two primary interests. Sara sailed through the first two years, excelling in her science classes. During her junior year, she began her nursing courses and spent more time observing nursing practice in her university's teaching hospital. After a summer working in various departments of her hometown hospital, Sara made an appointment with a career counselor. She confessed that she did not like being around sick people every day and wanted to change her major but had no idea what she wanted to do. Sara was wise to change her major before she began what would have been a frustrating career as a nurse.

John explored several majors during his first two years in college by choosing his elective courses with careers in mind and talking to his friends. He settled on business as a major, focusing on finance. John had high aspirations of working for a Fortune 500 company and earning a six-figure salary within five years of graduation. He performed above average in his academic work, although he was occasionally slack with assignments and frequently missed class. He interned with two prominent companies and eventually accepted a position at a Fortune 500 company. To his surprise, he was laid off nine months later because he was frequently late for work and missed important deadlines on two occasions. Although John had high aspirations while he was in college, he somehow never learned, or took seriously, the basic habits of career success.

Like Sara and John, students planning for careers frequently encounter bumps along the way. Choosing a career is a process of discovery, involving a willingness to remain open to new ideas and experiences. Why begin thinking about your career now? Because many of the decisions you make during your first year in college will have an impact on where you end up after you graduate.

Careers and the New Economy

In your lifetime, companies have restructured and taken on new shapes to remain competitive. As a result, major changes have taken place in how we work, where we work, and the ways we prepare for work while in college. In many ways, the following characteristics define today's economy:

▶ Global. Increasingly, national economies have gone multinational, not only moving into overseas markets but seeking cheaper labor, capital, and resources abroad. Factories around the world built to similar standards can turn out essentially the same products. Your career is bound to be affected by the global economy, even if you never leave the United States. For example, when you call an 800 number for customer service, the person who talks to you might be answering your call in Iowa, Ireland, or India. In his recent best-selling book, *The World is Flat*, Thomas Friedman reminds his readers that talent has become more important than geography in determining a person's opportunity in life. College graduates in the U. S. are now competing for jobs with others around the world who are often willing to work longer hours for less money than American workers. And this is true not only for manufacturing jobs, which are routinely being outsourced to other countries, but also for professional occupations such as medicine and accounting.

▶ Innovative. The economy depends on creativity in new products and services to generate consumer interest around the world. We are witnessing an unprecedented expansion of entrepreneurial businesses that have become the foundation for new job growth.

▶ Boundaryless. Teams of workers within an organization need to understand the missions of other teams because they most likely will have to work together. U.S. companies also have partners throughout the world. In 2006, the French telecommunications company, Alcatel, acquired the American company, Lucent, to create one of the world's major suppliers of telecommunications equipment. Domestically, Time Warner's merger with American Online created the largest communications group in the country. Crossing boundaries has other implications. You might be an accountant and find yourself working with the public relations division of your company, or you might be a human resources manager who does training for a number of different divisions and in a number of different countries. You might even find yourself moved laterally—to a unit with a different function—as opposed to climbing the proverbial career ladder.

▶ Customized. More and more, consumers are demanding products and services tailored to their specific needs. For example, you surely have noticed the seemingly endless varieties of a single brand of shampoo or cereal crowding your grocer's shelves. Such market segmentation requires constant adaptation of ideas to identify new products and services as new customer demands emerge.

▶ Fast. When computers became popular, people rejoiced because they believed the computer would reduce their workloads. Actually, the reverse happened. Whereas secretaries and other support workers once performed many tasks for executives, now executives are designing their own PowerPoint presentations because, as one article put it, "It's more fun to work with a slide show than to write reports." For better or worse, "We want it now" is the cry in the workplace, with product and service delivery time cut to a minimum (the "just-in-time" policy). Being fast requires constant thinking outside the lines to identify new approaches to designing and delivering products.

▶ Unstable. Scandals within the highest ranks of major companies and constant mergers and acquisitions of companies have destabilized the work force. Increases in oil prices have had a ripple effect through many sectors of the economy. The global marketplace is constantly changing, so it's important to keep up to date on economic trends as they relate to your prospective major and career.

According to *Fast Company* magazine, the new economy has changed many of the rules about work. Leaders are now expected to teach and encourage others as well as head up their divisions. Careers frequently zigzag into other areas. People who can second-guess the marketplace are in demand. Change has become the norm. Workers are being urged to continue their learning, and companies are volunteering to play a critical role in the welfare of all people through sponsorship of worthy causes. With the lines between work and life blurring, workers need to find healthy balance in their lives. Bringing work home might be inevitable at times, but it shouldn't be the rule.

As you work, you'll be continually enhancing and expanding your skills and competencies. You can accomplish this on your own by taking evening courses or by attending conferences and workshops your employer sends you to. As you prepare over the next few years to begin your career, remember that:

▶ You are, more or less, solely responsible for your career. At one time, organizations provided structured ladders that employees could climb in their moves to higher professional levels. In most cases, such ladders have disappeared. Companies might assist you with assessments and information on available positions in the industry, but the ultimate task of creating a career path is yours.

▶ To advance your career, you must accept the risks that accompany employment and plan for the future. Organizations will continually restructure, merge, and either grow or downsize in response to economic conditions. As a result, positions might be cut. Because you can be unemployed unexpectedly, it will be wise to keep other options in mind.

▶ A college degree does not guarantee employment. Of course, you'll be able to hunt for more opportunities that are rewarding, financially and otherwise, than if you did not have a degree. But just because you want to work for a certain organization doesn't mean there will always be a job for you there.

▶ A commitment to lifelong learning will help keep you employable. In college you have been learning a vital skill: how to learn. Gradus, the Latin root of graduation, means moving to a higher level of responsibility. Your learning has just begun when you receive your diploma.

Now the good news. Thousands of graduates find jobs every year. Some might have to work longer to get where they want to be, but persistence pays off. If you start now, you'll have time to build a portfolio of academic and **cocurricular experiences** that will begin to add substance to your career profile. Rudyard Kipling's verse from *Just So Stories* (1902) is an easy device for remembering how to navigate the fast economy for career success:

> *I keep six honest serving-men;*
> *(They taught me all I knew);*
> *Their names are What and Why and When*
> *And How and Where and Who.*

The knowledge to manage your career comes from you (why, who, how) and from an understanding of the career you wish to enter (what, where, when).

◀ Networking is an important skill for opening the door to a future job.

© PhotoAlto/SuperStock

Confessions of a College Student

Name: Mary Ann Williams

Age: 45

College: Midlands Technical College

Hometown: Columbia, SC

Major: Nursing

Favorite books(s): *Of Mice and Men, Lonesome Dove*

Favorite college course: Intro to Psychology

Heroes: Celia Bowman, a coworker who returned to school to get her nursing degree.

Favorite way to relax: Reading at the beach

Your proudest moment or biggest accomplishment: Returning to college at the age of 45.

Favorite food: Dark chocolate

Career center confession: One of the assignments in my freshman seminar was to take a career

assessment inventory at the career center. I'd never taken a career placement test before and didn't know what to expect. I was surprised to learn that I scored high in several career areas other than my chosen field. While I plan to remain in my chosen field of nursing, it was helpful to know that I have other options, should I decide to change my major. The career center and the programs it offers gave me the opportunity to learn something new and helpful about myself.

Aligning Your Sense of Purpose and Your Career

Why Why do you want to be a _____ ? Knowing your goals and values will help you pursue your career with passion and an understanding of what motivates you. When you speak with an interviewer, avoid clichés like "I'm a people person" or "I like to work with people." Sooner or later, most people have to work with people. And your interviewer has heard this much too often. Instead, be sure that you have crystallized your actual reasons for following your chosen career path. An interviewer will want to know why you are interested in the job, why it feels right for you at this time in your life, and if you are committed to this career for the future.

Who Network with people who can help you find out what you want to be. Right now, those people might be instructors in your major, an academic advisor, or someone at your campus career center. Later, network with others who can help you attain your goal. Someone will always know someone else for you to talk to.

How Have the technical and communications skills required to work effectively. Become a computer whiz. Learn how to do PowerPoint presentations, build web pages, and create Excel spreadsheets. Take a speech course. Work on improving your writing. Even if you think your future job doesn't require these skills, you'll be more marketable with them.

What Be aware of the opportunities an employer presents, as well as such threats as **outsourcing** jobs. Clearly understand the employment requirements for the career field you have chosen. Know what training you will need to remain in your chosen profession.

Where Know the points of entry into the field. For example, you can obtain on-the-job experiences through internships, co-ops, or part-time jobs.

When Know how early you need to start looking. Find out if certain professions hire at certain times of the year.

Connecting Your Major and Your Interests with Your Career

Some students are sure about their major when they enter college, but many others are at a loss. Either way, it's okay. At some point you might ask yourself, "Why am I in college?" Although it sounds like an easy question to answer, it's not. Many students would immediately respond, "So I can get a good job or education for a specific career." The problem is that most majors do not lead to a specific career path or job. You actually can enter most career paths from any number of academic majors. Marketing, a common undergraduate business major, is a field that recruits from a wide variety of majors including advertising, communications, and psychology. Sociology majors find jobs in law enforcement, teaching, and public service.

Today English majors are designing web pages, philosophy majors are developing logic codes for operating systems, and history majors are sales representatives and business managers. You do not have to major in science to gain admittance to medical school. Of course, you do have to take the required science and math courses, but medical schools seek applicants with diverse backgrounds. Only a few technical or professional fields, such as accounting, nursing, and engineering, are tied to specific majors.

Exploring your interests is the best way to choose an academic major. If you're still not sure, take the advice of Patrick Combs, author of *Major in Success*, who recommends that you major in a subject that you are really passionate about. Most advisors would agree.

Write • DISCUSS • Compare • Ask • BLOG • Answer • *Journal*

> Would you describe your major as something you're really passionate about? Why or why not? If your answer is no, why are you pursuing this particular major?

Chapter 1 in this book suggested that you think very seriously about your purpose for being in college. Here are some additional questions to ask yourself as you continue thinking about why you're at this particular college or university.

▶ Am I here to find out who I am and to study a subject that I am truly passionate about, regardless of whether it leads to a career?

▶ Am I here to engage in an academic program that provides an array of possibilities when I graduate?

▶ Am I here to prepare myself for a graduate program?

▶ Am I here to obtain specific training in a field that I am committed to?

▶ Am I here to gain specific skills for a job I already have?

Some students will find they're not ready to select an academic major in the first year. You can use your first year, and even your second year, to explore your interests and see how they might connect to various academic programs. In the process of your exploration, you might later answer the question differently than you would during your first term.

You can major in almost anything. As this chapter will emphasize, it is how you integrate your classes with extracurricular engagement and work experience that prepares you for a successful transition into your career. Try a major you think you'll like, and see what develops. But keep an open mind, and don't pin all your hopes on finding a career in that major alone.

Selecting a major and a career ultimately has to fit with your overall life goals, purposes, values, and beliefs.

Exploring Your Interests

Dr. John Holland, a psychologist at Johns Hopkins University, developed a number of tools and concepts that can help you organize the various dimensions of yourself so that you can identify potential career choices.

Holland separates people into six general categories based on differences in their interests, skills, values, and personality characteristics—in short, their preferred approaches to life:[1]

▶ **With so many majors to choose from, it might be wise to do some exploring before you actually declare one.**

© Sheri Blaney/Cengage

[1] Adapted from John L. Holland, *Self-Directed Search Manual* (Odessa, FL: Psychological Assessment Resources, 1985).

Realistic (R) These people describe themselves as concrete, down-to-earth, and practical doers. They exhibit competitive/assertive behavior and show interest in activities that require motor coordination, skill, and physical strength. They prefer situations involving action solutions rather than tasks involving verbal or interpersonal skills, and they like to take a concrete approach to problem solving rather than rely on abstract theory. They tend to be interested in scientific or mechanical areas rather than cultural and **aesthetic** fields.

Investigative (I) These people describe themselves as analytical, rational, and logical problem solvers. They value intellectual stimulation and intellectual achievement and prefer to think rather than to act, to organize and understand rather than to persuade. They usually have a strong interest in physical, biological, or social sciences. They are less apt to be people oriented.

Artistic (A) These people describe themselves as creative, innovative, and independent. They value self-expression and relations with others through artistic expression and are also emotionally expressive. They dislike structure, preferring tasks involving personal or physical skills. They resemble investigative people but are more interested in the cultural or the aesthetic than the scientific.

Social (S) These people describe themselves as kind, caring, helpful, and understanding of others. They value helping and making a contribution. They satisfy their needs in one-to-one or small-group interaction using strong speaking skills to teach, counsel, or advise. They are drawn to close interpersonal relationships and are less apt to engage in intellectual or extensive physical activity.

Enterprising (E) These people describe themselves as assertive, risk taking, and persuasive. They value prestige, power, and status and are more inclined than other types to pursue it. They use verbal skills to supervise, lead, direct, and persuade rather than to support or guide. They are interested in people and in achieving organizational goals.

Conventional (C) These people describe themselves as neat, orderly, detail oriented, and persistent. They value order, structure, prestige, and status and possess a high degree of self-control. They are not opposed to rules and regulations. They are skilled in organizing, planning, and scheduling and are interested in data and people.

Holland's system organizes career fields into the same six categories. Career fields are grouped according to what a particular career field requires of a person (skills and personality characteristics most commonly associated with success in those fields) and what rewards those fields provide (interests and values most commonly associated with satisfaction). Here are a few examples:

Realistic (R) Agricultural engineer, electrical contractor, industrial arts teacher, navy officer, fitness director, package engineer, electronics technician, computer graphics technician

Investigative (I) Urban planner, chemical engineer, bacteriologist, flight engineer, genealogist, laboratory technician, marine scientist, nuclear medical technologist, obstetrician, quality-control technician, computer programmer, environmentalist, physician, college professor

Artistic (A) Architect, film editor/director, actor, cartoonist, interior decorator, fashion model, graphic communications specialist, journalist, editor, orchestra leader, public relations specialist, sculptor, media specialist, librarian, reporter

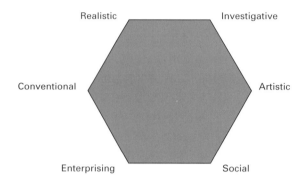

▶ **Figure 11.1**
Holland's Hexagonal Model of
Career Fields

Social (S) Nurse, teacher, social worker, genetic counselor, marriage counselor, rehabilitation counselor, school superintendent, geriatric specialist, insurance claims specialist, minister, travel agent, guidance counselor, convention planner

Enterprising (E) Banker, city manager, FBI agent, health administrator, judge, labor arbitrator, salary and wage administrator, insurance salesperson, sales engineer, lawyer, sales representative, marketing specialist

Conventional (C) Accountant, statistician, census enumerator, data processor, hospital administrator, insurance administrator, office manager, underwriter, auditor, personnel specialist, database manager, abstractor/indexer

Your career choices ultimately will involve a complex assessment of the factors that are most important to you. To display the relationship between career fields and the potential conflicts people face as they consider them, Holland's model is commonly presented in a hexagonal shape (Figure 11.1). The closer the types, the closer the relationships among the career fields; the farther apart the types, the more conflict between the career fields.

Holland's model can help you address the problem of career choice in two ways. First, you can begin to identify many career fields that are consistent with what you know about yourself. Once you've identified potential fields, you can use the career library at your college to get more information about those fields, such as daily activities for specific jobs, interests and abilities required, preparation required for entry, working conditions, salary and benefits, and employment outlook. Second, you can begin to identify the harmony or conflicts in your career choices. This will help you analyze the reasons for your career decisions and be more confident as you make choices.

Never feel you have to make a decision on the results of only one assessment. Career choices are complex and involve many factors; furthermore, these decisions are reversible. Take time to talk your interests over with a career counselor. Another helpful approach is to shadow an individual in the occupation that interests you to obtain a better understanding of what the occupation entails in terms of skills, commitment, and opportunity.

Factors Affecting Career Choices

Some people have a definite self-image when they enter college, but most of us are still in the process of defining (or redefining) ourselves throughout life. We can look at ourselves in several useful ways with respect to possible careers:

▶ Values. Today, more than ever, knowing your core values (your most important beliefs) will be important in shaping your career path. In a fast economy, having a strong rudder will help you steer through the turbulent times.

▶ Interests. Your interests will develop from experiences and beliefs and can continue to develop and change throughout your life. You might be interested in writing for the college newspaper because you wrote for your high school paper. It's not unusual to enter Psych 101 with a great interest in psychology and realize halfway through the course that psychology is not what you imagined.

▶ Skills. The ability to do something well can usually be improved with practice.

▶ Aptitudes. Your inherent strengths, or aptitudes, are often part of your biological heritage or the result of early training. We each have aptitudes we can build on.

▶ Personality. Your personality makes you you and can't be ignored when you make career decisions. The quiet, orderly, calm, detail-oriented person probably will make a different work choice than the aggressive, outgoing, argumentative person.

▶ Life goals and work values. Each of us defines success and satisfaction in our own way. The process is complex and very personal. Two factors influence our conclusions about success and happiness: a) knowing that we are achieving the life goals we've set for ourselves, and b) finding that we gain satisfaction from what we're receiving from our work. If your values conflict with the organizational values where you work, you might be in for trouble.

Your Career Planning Timetable

The process of making a career choice begins with

▶ Understanding your values and motivations

▶ Identifying your interests

▶ Linking your personality and learning styles to those interests

▶ Using this information to decide on an appropriate academic major

This is a process you will begin in your first college year, and you will gradually complete it as you move closer to graduation. So don't worry about finishing this now. Not every student will fall into this pattern. While this is one way to begin investigating career possibilities, circumstances might force you to digress from this plan. Such circumstances might be a change of major or an unforeseen opportunity to intern. You will need to periodically reevaluate your plan to better suit your needs and any special characteristics of your major.

Creating a Plan

A good career plan should eventually include:

▶ Researching possible occupations that match your skills, interests, and academic major

▶ Building on your strengths and developing your weaker skills

▶ Preparing a marketing strategy that sells you as a valued member of a professional team

▶ Writing a convincing résumé and cover letter

Table 11.1 on page 225 provides a guide to what you should be doing during each year of college; if you are in a two-year associate degree program, you will have to do more during your second year than this table suggests.

Write • DISCUSS • Compare • Ask • BLOG • Answer • *Journal*

What kind of "marketing strategy" could you develop to sell yourself to a potential employer? Which of your characteristics or aptitudes would you emphasize?

You might proceed through these steps at a different pace than your friends, and that's okay. What you want is to develop your qualifications, make good choices, and take advantage of any opportunities on campus to learn more about the career search. Keep your goals in mind as you select courses and seek employment, but also keep an eye out for unique opportunities; the route you think you want to take ultimately might not be the best one for you.

Planning for Two-Year College Students

If you are a student attending a two-year college and you plan to transfer to a four-year college or university, your career planning timeline will be compressed. You might find that once you get to the four-year institution, you have less time to make adjustments in your course work and career opportunities. The major stumbling block is the fact that transfers often arrive on their new campus with enough credits to declare a major; at this point changing your major again can be costly, because it will mean adding time, and therefore expense, before graduation.

Consider these early steps during your first three terms at your two-year college:

▶ Take a career interest inventory, and begin focusing on the career paths that most interest you.

Students attending community colleges face additional academic and career choices.

▶ Visit with a career counselor to develop a short-term strategy to test your career interests.

▶ Enroll in a career decision-making class.

▶ Job shadow a professional in the occupation(s) that you wish to enter.

▶ Attend a local job fair (if possible) to learn about potential job opportunities.

Table 11.1   Your Career Itinerary

A. NO MATTER WHAT YEAR

▶ Get a job. Even a part-time job will develop your skills and might help you to make decisions about what you like—and what you don't—in a work environment. In any job, you can learn vital skills such as teamwork, communication, and interpersonal, computer, and time management skills.

Write • DISCUSS • Compare • Ask • BLOG • Answer • *Journal*

> What kinds of part-time jobs have you had, either for pay or as a volunteer? Which of your jobs was your favorite; which did you dislike? What do your experiences tell you about your preferences for work in the future?

▶ Register with your college's online job listing system to find listings for part- and full-time, internship, co-op, and seasonal employment.

▶ Find on-campus interviewing opportunities for internships in your early years and for full-time employment after graduation.

▶ Network with family, friends, instructors, friends of family, and acquaintances to find contacts in your field(s) of interest so that you can learn more about those areas.

▶ Volunteer! This can help you explore careers and get some experience in an area that interests you as you help others.

▶ Conduct occupational and industry research for your field or area of geographic interest. Look for other options within and beyond those fields.

▶ Explore career options through informational interviews (interviewing to find out about a career) and job shadowing (observing someone at work—with their permission, of course).

▶ Prepare a draft of your résumé and have it critiqued by a career counselor and perhaps by a professional in your chosen field.

▶ Get involved in clubs and organizations; work toward leadership positions.

▶ Explore study possibilities in other countries to gain a global perspective and learn a foreign language.

▶ Attend career fairs to connect with employers for internships and other career-related opportunities as well as to develop a professional network.

B. FIRST YEAR OF COLLEGE

▶ Take the Holland Self-Directed Search or a similar interest inventory at your career center.

▶ Take a variety of classes to get exposure to various skill and knowledge areas.

▶ Attend your campus's annual career fair to see what is being offered.

▶ Talk to a career counselor about your skills, aptitudes, and interests. Find out what the career center offers.

Write • DISCUSS • Compare • Ask • BLOG • Answer • *Journal*

> Have you explored your institution's career center? If so, what did you learn? If not, when in your college experience do you think going to the career center will be most important? Why?

Continued

C. SECOND YEAR OF COLLEGE

▶ Attend career fairs to learn more about employers who hire graduates in your major.

▶ Spend some time talking with your college advisor or career counselor to discuss your career plans.

D. THIRD YEAR OF COLLEGE

▶ Take an advanced computerized career assessment to discover further career options and to refine your career plans. Visit your career center.

▶ Take on a leadership role in a club or organization.

▶ Participate in mock interview activities to improve your interviewing skills.

▶ Attend workshops to learn more about résumé writing, looking for an internship, interviewing, and other job search skills.

▶ Explore the option of graduate school.

▶ Develop a top-10 list of employers of interest.

E. LAST YEAR OF COLLEGE

▶ Check on-campus interviewing opportunities on a daily basis, beginning in the fall term. Interview with organizations recruiting for your major.

▶ Research organizations of interest to you, interview with those coming to campus, and contact human resources professionals who represent organizations that won't be on campus. Find out if you can interview.

▶ Attend career fairs to network with employers and set up interviewing opportunities.

▶ If you're thinking about graduate school, request applications early in the fall, and send them out throughout the fall term.

▶ Target your geographic areas of interest by contacting local chambers of commerce and using local newspapers, phone books, and Internet resources.

Used by permission of Career Passport, Michigan State University.

During your last term at your two-year college, consider these options:

▶ Determine what academic majors best match your occupational interests.

▶ Investigate whether the college or university you will attend next has the majors you need and any prerequisite requirements you will have to meet before you can enroll in your chosen major.

▶ If you still find you do not have a clear career focus by the time you transfer, meet again with the college's career advisor.

▶ Visit the campus you are transferring to prior to registration. Meet with both a career advisor and an academic advisor as soon as possible.

Starting Your Search for a Major and a Career

Some first-year students come to college with a strong sense of self-knowledge and a focus on a specific interest. Others have no idea what their interests might be and are in the process of sorting through their values, interests, and skills in an attempt to define themselves. Such self-definition is an ongoing experience that, for many of us, continues well beyond college. It helps to keep a journal of such thoughts because

◀ **A campus career fair is the ideal place to explore a variety of careers with professionals.**

reviewing these early interests later in life might lead to long-forgotten career paths just when you need them.

As you start examining your aspirations and interests, keep in mind these simple do's and don'ts:

<u>**Do's**</u>

1. Do explore a number of career possibilities and academic majors.

2. Do get involved through volunteer work, study abroad, and student organizations—especially those linked to your major.

3. Do follow your passion. Learn what you love to do, and go for it.

<u>**Don'ts**</u>

1. Don't just focus on a major and blindly hope to get a career out of it. That's backward.

2. Don't be motivated primarily by external stimuli, such as salary, prestige, and perks. All the money in the world won't make you happy if you hate what you're doing every day.

3. Don't select a major just because it seems cool.

4. Don't choose courses simply because your roommate or friend said they were easy. That's wasting your valuable time, not to mention tuition.

Getting Experience

Now that you have a handle on your interests, it's time to test the waters and do some exploring. Your campus has a variety of activities and programs in which you can participate to confirm those interests and your values, and gain valuable skills. Here are some examples:

▶ Volunteer/service learning. Some instructors build service learning into their courses. **Service learning** allows you to apply academic theories and ideas to actual practice. Volunteering outside of class is also a valuable way to encounter different life situations and to gain work knowledge in areas such as teaching, health services, counseling, and tax preparation. A little time spent each week can provide immense personal and professional rewards.

▶ Study abroad. Spend a term taking courses in another country, and learn about a different culture at the same time. Learn to adapt to new traditions and a different pace of life. Some study abroad programs also include options for both work and service learning experiences.

▶ Internships and co-ops. Many employers now expect these work experiences. They want to see that you have experience in the professional workplace and have gained an understanding of the skills and competencies necessary to succeed. Check with your academic department and your career center on the internships that are available in your major. Many majors offer academic credit for internships. And remember: with an internship on your résumé, you'll be a step ahead of students who ignore this valuable experience.

▶ On-campus employment. On-campus jobs might not provide as much income as off-campus jobs, but on-campus jobs give you a chance to practice good work habits. On-campus employment also brings you into contact with faculty and other academic professionals who you can later consult as mentors or ask for references.

▶ Student projects/competitions. In many fields, students engage in competitions based on what they have learned in the classroom. Civil engineers build concrete

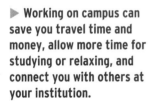

▶ **Working on campus can save you travel time and money, allow more time for studying or relaxing, and connect you with others at your institution.**

© SW Productions/Getty Images

canoes, and marketing majors develop campaign strategies, for example. They might compete against teams from other colleges or universities. In the process, they learn teamwork, communication, and applied problem-solving skills.

▶ Research. An excellent way to extend your academic learning is to work with a faculty member on a research project. Research extends your critical thinking skills and provides insight on a subject above and beyond your books and class notes.

Skills Employers Look For

One of the many important purposes and outcomes of your college experience is the acquisition of a combination of knowledge and skills. Two types of skills are essential to employment and to life: content (mastery) skills and transferable skills.

Content Skills

Content skills, often referred to as cognitive, intellectual, or "hard" skills, are acquired as you gain mastery in your academic field and include writing proficiency, computer literacy, and foreign language skills. Computing knowledge and ability are now perceived as core skills of equal importance to reading, writing, and mathematics. In fact, employer expectations for computer knowledge and application continue to rise.

Content skills include specific types of information, facts, principles, and rules. For instance, perhaps you have knowledge of civil engineering related to dam construction, or you have extensive experience working with telescopes. Maybe your work in the library and study of library science has trained you in several library databases. Or you might know the most common clinical diagnoses in psychology. We often forget some of the preparation we have gained that augments our mastery of specific academic material, especially statistics, research methods, foreign language aptitude, and computer literacy. You can apply all of this specific knowledge to jobs in a particular field or occupation.

Certain types of employers will expect extensive knowledge in your academic major before they will consider hiring you; for example, to get a job in accounting you must demonstrate knowledge of that field. However, for most college students, it's sufficient to have some fundamental knowledge; you will learn more on the job as you move from entry-level to more advanced positions.

Transferable Skills

Transferable skills are those that are general and apply to or transfer to a variety of settings. Examples of transferable skills include excellent public speaking, interpersonal understanding, seeing the big picture, grasping the application of a software program to a task, using available software to maintain home pages and transfer information, and providing leadership while working in a team environment. By category, these transferable skills are:

▶ Communication skills that demonstrate solid oral and listening abilities in addition to a good foundation in the basic content skill of writing

▶ Presentation skills, including the ability to justify and persuade as well as to respond to questions and serious critiques of your presentation material

▶ Leadership skills, or the ability to take charge or relinquish control according to the needs of the organization

▶ Team skills, or the ability to work collaboratively with different people while maintaining autonomous control over some assignments

▶ Interpersonal abilities that allow you to relate to others, inspire others to participate, or ease conflict between coworkers

▶ Personal traits, including showing initiative and motivation, being adaptable to change, having a work ethic, being reliable and honest, possessing integrity, knowing how to plan and organize multiple tasks, and being able to respond positively to customer concerns

▶ Critical thinking and problem solving, or the ability to identify problems and their solutions by integrating information from a variety of sources and effectively weighing alternatives

▶ A willingness to learn quickly and continuously

Transferable skills are valuable to many kinds of employers and professions. They give you flexibility in your career planning. You can gain transferable skills through a variety of activities. For example, volunteer work, study abroad, involvement in a student professional organization or club, and the pursuit of hobbies or interests can all build teamwork, leadership, interpersonal awareness, and effective communication abilities. Internships or career-related work are also valuable opportunities to practice these skills in the real world.

Key Competencies

While employers expect skills and related work experience from today's college graduates, they also have begun to focus on additional key competencies that are critical for success in the new knowledge economy.

▶ Integrity. Your employment will depend on being able to act in an ethical manner at work and in the community.

▶ Innovation. You should also be able to evaluate, synthesize, and create knowledge that will lead to new products and services. Employers seek individuals who are willing to take some risks and explore innovative and better ways to deliver products and services.

▶ Initiative. A great employee is able to recognize the need to take action, such as helping a team member, approaching a new client, or taking on assignments without being asked. Employers do not want employees who will wait passively for a supervisor to provide work assignments; they want people who will see what they have to do and do it.

▶ Commitment. Both employers and graduate schools look for a candidate's commitment to learning. They want you to express what you really love to study and are willing to learn on your own initiative. The best foundation for this competency is to be engaged in an academic program where you wake up every morning and are eager to go to class.

Finding a Job While in College

Do you hope to get a job while you are in college? Before you do, be really honest with yourself: is this something you must do in order to pay for college or is this something you want to do to maintain your lifestyle and acquire things you want? Or is it a combination of both? Most students work. Here are some things you should know about working in college.

Work can support the attainment of your college goals, provide you with the financial means to complete college, and help structure your time so that you are a much better time manager. It can help you meet people who will later serve as important references for graduate school and/or employment. Yet working too much can interfere with your college success, your ability to attend class, do homework, and participate in many other valuable college activities, such as group study, foreign study and travel, and group activities. Take some time to determine how much you need to work, and stay within reasonable limits.

Stated very simply, students who work more than 15 hours a week have a lower chance of success in college. And, students who work on campus are also more likely to graduate from college than students working off campus.

On-Campus Jobs

If you want or need to work, explore on-campus opportunities as soon as (or even before) you arrive. If you have a **work-study award,** check with your student employment office for a listing of possible campus jobs for work-study students. Your career center can tell you how to access your college's online employment system. It probably handles all types of jobs. You might have to register, but that is easy, especially if you have a draft résumé to upload to the web-based form. College employment systems generally channel all jobs collected from faculty, advisors, and career counselors into one database, so it is convenient for you to identify the sorts of jobs you are looking for.

Many campuses offer an on-campus job fair early in the fall term. Even if you might not be interested at the time, a visit to the job fair will give you a great idea of the range and type of jobs available on campus. You will be pleasantly surprised to learn that there are more opportunities than washing dishes in the cafeteria. Job fairs usually include off-campus community employers as well, in part because your institution must spend some of the work-study funds it receives supporting off-campus work by students.

Off-Campus Jobs

The best places to start looking for off-campus jobs are your campus career center and/ or your financial aid office. They might well have listings or websites with off-campus employment opportunities. Feel free to speak to a career counselor for suggestions.

▶ Learn the names of the major employers in your college's geographic area: manufacturers, service industries, resorts, etc. For example, some campuses are near UPS distribution centers, which are well known for favoring college students for lucrative part-time union-scale wage jobs. Once you know who the major employers are, check them out, visit their websites, and learn the details.

▶ Every state in the country has a state agency to collect and disseminate information about available employment opportunities. Check out the relevant website and see if your state agency has an office in the community where you are attending college.

▶ Visit employment agencies, particularly those that seek part-time, temporary workers. This is a convenient, low-risk (for both you and the employer) way to "shop" for a job, and to obtain flexible, short-term, low-commitment employment.

▶ Visit online job boards, and look at the classified ads in the local newspaper, in print or online. Also, don't forget the classifieds in the national press. Some national firms will have jobs that can be done part-time in your area or even from your own living space!

▶ Check your campus student newspaper. Employers who favor hiring college students often advertise there.

▶ Most jobs are never posted. Employers find it easier to hire people recommended to them by current employees, friends, or the person vacating the position. Faculty often hire students for their research labs based on performance in the classroom.

▶ Who you know is important. Your friends who already work on campus or who have had an internship can be the best people to help you when you are ready to search for your job. In fact, nearly 50 percent of all student jobs are found through family and friends.

College students often view the choice of a career as a monumental and irreversible decision. But, in its broadest sense, a career is the sum of the decisions you make over a lifetime. There is no right occupation just waiting to be discovered. Rather, there are many career choices you might find fulfilling and satisfying. The question to consider is: "What is the best choice for me now?"

Steps to Obtaining a Job and Beginning a Career

Building a Résumé

Before you finish college, you'll need a résumé —whether it's for a part-time job, for an internship or co-op position, or for a professor who agrees to write a letter of recommendation for you. Typically, there are two types of résumés: one is written in chronological format, and the other is organized by skills. Generally, choose the chronological résumé if you have related job experience, and choose the skills résumé if you can group skills from a number of jobs or projects under several meaningful categories. Try for one page, but if you have a number of outstanding things to say that won't fit on a single page, add a second page.

Writing a Cover Letter

When sending a cover letter, heed the following suggestions:

▶ Find out whom to write. It's not the same in all fields. If you were seeking a marketing position at an advertising agency, you would write to the director of account services. If you were approaching General Motors regarding a position in the engineering department, you might write to either the director of human resources for the entire company or to a special human resources director in charge of engineering. Your academic advisor or career counselor can help you here. So can the Internet.

▶ Get the most recent name and address. Advisors or career counselors can guide you to references in your campus or career library. Never write, "To whom it may concern."

▶ Use proper format for date, address, and salutation.

Interviewing

The first year of college does not seem like a time to be concerned about interviews, certainly not for a job. However, students often find themselves in interview situations shortly after arriving on campus: vying for positions on the student residence governing board, finding an on-campus job, competing for a second-year scholarship, applying for a residence hall assistant position, choosing a summer job opportunity, and being selected for an internship or as a research assistant. Preparing for an interview begins the moment you arrive on campus because the interview is about you and how college has changed you. Students who haven't clarified their sense of purpose or who have only taken a little time to actually reflect on who they are and how they have changed can feel lost in an interview.

The purpose of the interview is to exchange information. The interviewer's goal is to evaluate you on your abilities and competencies in terms of what the company is looking for. For you, the interview is an opportunity to learn more about the employer and whether the job would be a good fit with your aptitudes and preferences. Ideally, you will want to find a match between your interests and abilities and the position or experience you are seeking.

Here are some important tips as you prepare for an interview:

▶ Check with a career counselor to see if you can attend a mock interview. Usually designed only for seniors as they prep for their on-campus interviews, mock interviews help students strategize and feel comfortable with an interview. Even if a mock interview session is not available to you, the career center can offer tips for you on handling an interview situation. Check your career center website for sample interview questions so that you can practice before an interview.

▶ Understand the nature of the **behavioral interview**. In a behavioral interview, the interviewer assumes that your past experiences are good predictors of your future abilities and performance. Interviewers want to hear stories about things that you have done that can help them assess your skills and behaviors. Often there is not a right or wrong answer. Answering a behavioral question can be hard. A method used at Michigan State University and other campuses to help students think through possible answers is the PARK method, which helps to focus on the most relevant aspects of your experience.

P: The problem or situation (What happened?)
A: The actions you took (What did you do?)
R: The results or outcomes (What was the result of the actions you took?)

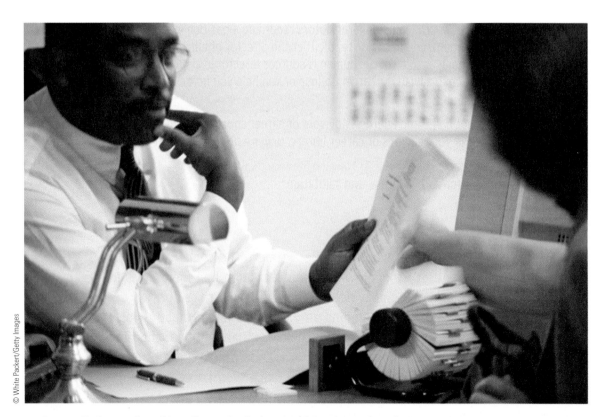

▲ **Be sure that your résumé is well-organized, clear, and free of any misspelled words or incorrect use of language.**

K: The knowledge you gained and applied through the experience (What did you learn? How did you apply it?)

▶ Dress appropriately. Dress codes vary depending on the location of the interview, and the type of interview (e.g., professional, student focused). First impressions matter, so as a rule of thumb always dress neatly and conservatively. You can be somewhat casual for some types of employers, but it is better to dress too professionally (in a dress suit and polished shoes) than too informally.

Getting Off to a Good Start in the Workplace

This textbook has been designed to assist you in achieving success in college. This chapter extends the lessons you've learned about college to making a successful transition into the workplace. You learned that the workplace is dynamic, changing constantly, and it is very different from the college classroom. Employers want their new college hires to start fast and adapt quickly to their work environments. The skills mentioned in this section support this rapid transition. The behaviors and competencies highlighted in this chapter are those on which employers focus to identify new employees ready for promotion or more challenging assignments. And some behaviors can quickly lead to disciplinary actions, even dismissal.

Your career can get off to a rocky start if you display inappropriate behavior or make poor ethical choices. Perhaps little or nothing happened when you missed a

⌐⌐IRED ⌐⌐INDO⌐⌐

IN ADDITION TO CHECKING your résumé and references, potential employers will also use online resources to learn more about you. In a recent national survey of college employers, slightly more than 11% said that they review candidate profiles on social networking sites like MySpace and Facebook and more than 60% said that the information they find has at least some influence on their hiring decisions. Since a user outside of your Facebook network cannot see your profile, companies have asked their employees who are recent graduates or their college interns to research potential candidates. On profile pages, employers can find discrepancies between a candidate's résumé and their actual academic and work experience. Potential employers might even spot other kinds of information or see pictures that would make them think twice about hiring you. Keep in mind that most of the people making hiring decisions at companies don't understand social networking websites the way you do—they are wary of sharing any personal information online. When they find that a potential candidate is comfortable sharing his or her party pictures, describing personal escapades that some might consider inappropriate, or allowing friends to post crude comments, they will seriously question the judgment of that applicant. Knowing this, what would you change about your Facebook and/or MySpace profile to make it more appropriate for viewing by potential employers?

Now that you know what employers are looking for when they search social networking websites to research potential employees, pretend you are an employer. Pick either Facebook or MySpace and search for your friends—what did you find? How many of your friends would you hire based solely on their profile page? How many would you not hire based on the information or pictures on their profile page? Why? What about your own profile? What would a potential employer find there, and how might he or she react?

class or two. Your professor might have been willing to give you an extension on a paper or project deadline. Maybe you were pushed to get an assignment completed and so you copied material from several websites and dropped the material in your paper without proper citations or original thought. The consequences might have been minimal—maybe you received a B- rather than a B. You might have been involved in a team project although you were not very enthusiastic about the topic or the other members of the group. Your contribution was minimal, but you got a great grade because everyone else covered for you. While these behaviors occasionally are overlooked in college, they will quickly get you in trouble at work. In the workplace, you might not get a second chance.

Employers, in response to a series of questions on how they have to discipline new hires, listed the following most frequent behaviors leading to disciplinary actions:

Reason for disciplinary action	Occurrence: Fairly to Very Often (%)
Lack of commitment to work	52
Unethical behavior	46
Failure to follow instructions	41
Ineffective in teams	41
Missing assignments/deadlines	33

Source: CERI Research Brief 1-2007, *Moving Up or Moving Out of the Company?* Michigan State University.

Not all inappropriate behavior will result in a dismissal or firing. Most employers want new hires to succeed and might give young adults the opportunity to make corrections in their behaviors. When asked which behaviors could result in firing, employers indicated repeatedly being late to work or missing assignment deadlines probably would result in termination. However, unethical behaviors, poor work attitude, and inappropriate use of technology would result in immediate dismissal. Technology use is a ticklish problem for many employers. The rapid increase in e-mail, text messaging, social networking websites like MySpace and Facebook, and blogs have challenged acceptable business communication. New hires need to be aware that the material they place in these environments is part of the public record and can be found by anyone. Companies are sensitive to their brand image and have little tolerance for comments that are derogatory to the company. A more serious problem for employers is the hacking done by new employees, not of external sites, but within the company's own systems. Hacking might be the top ethical breach that companies face today. Avoid these behaviors if you do not want to be fired.

TOP SIX REASONS NEW COLLEGE HIRES ARE FIRED
Unethical behavior
Lack of motivation at work
Inappropriate use of technology
Failure to follow instructions
Being late for work
Missing assignment deadlines

Write • DISCUSS • Compare • Ask • BLOG • Answer • *Journal*

If you were an employer, what behaviors would cause you to fire an employee? Are any of those behaviors like some of those you see in college? What advice would you give to a new hire who was working for you?

Employers quickly identify the individuals they want to promote or move to more challenging assignments. When asked what behaviors or competencies grab their attention, two skill sets stood out. The most important attribute you can bring into the workplace is a willingness to take the initiative. Employers are looking for individuals who will accept responsibilities above and beyond the stated job, who will volunteer for additional activities, who will promote new ideas, and who will be self-starters (needing little stimuli from a supervisor).

Another important attribute is "self-management." Self-management embodies skills that establish your accountability to the company. Skills include the ability to:

▶ Monitor and regulate work commitments (set priorities)

▶ Manage time

▶ Establish high performance levels (including completing work on time, understanding the quality indicators of work performance)

▶ Handle stress

▶ Provide and develop rapport with customers and coworkers

▶ Cope effectively with change

Four additional skill sets round out the characteristics cited by employers as key to promotion or job assignments:

▶ Personal attributes (dependable, friendly, patient, reliable, and respectful of diversity)

▶ Commitment and passion for work

▶ Leadership

▶ Ability to present ideas persuasively in written and oral forms (being good at show-and-tell)

These are all transferable skills from your college experience. Look back to the section on transferable skills and the key competencies and you will see that every one of them is an important ingredient to your future success in whatever path you choose after graduation.

Top Characteristics and Competencies that Employers Seek in Promotion/Job Assignments
Taking initiative
Self-management
Personal attributes
Commitment and passion for work
Leadership
Show-and-tell

▶ WHERE TO GO FOR HELP

On Campus

Your College Website Search your campus career resources. Larger campuses might have specialized career service centers for specific professional schools and clusters of majors. Often student professional organizations, academic advisors, and departments will provide relevant career information on their websites.

Career Center Almost every college campus has a career center where you can obtain free counseling and information on careers. A career professional will work with you to help you define your interests, interpret results of any assessment you complete, coach you on interview techniques, and critique your résumé. It's important to schedule an appointment. By the end of your first year you should be familiar with the career center—where it is located and the counselor responsible for your academic major or interests. You might also find opportunities for internships and practica here.

Academic Advising More and more advisors have been trained in what is known as "developmental" advising, or helping you see beyond individual classes and working to help you initiate a career search. Talking to your advisor is often the best place to start. If you have not declared a major—which is true of many first-year students—your advisor might be able to help you with that decision as well.

Faculty On many campuses, faculty take an active role in helping students connect academic interests to careers. A faculty member can recommend specific courses that relate to a particular career. Faculty in professional curricula, such as business and other applied fields, often have direct contact with companies and serve as contacts for internships. If you have an interest in attending graduate school, faculty sponsorship is critical to admission. Developing a faculty mentor can open a number of important doors.

Library Some campuses have a separate library in the career center staffed by librarians whose job is to help you locate career-related information resources. Of course, all campuses have a main library containing a wealth of information on careers. The person who will be glad to help you is your reference librarian at the main desk. If you are a student on a large university campus, you might find additional libraries that are specific to certain professional schools and colleges within the university, such as business, education, law, medicine, music, and engineering; these are also excellent sources for career information.

Upper-class Students: Ask if they can help you navigate courses and find important resources. Upper-class students might also have practical experience gained from internships and volunteering. Since they have tested the waters, they can alert you to potential pitfalls or inform you of opportunities.

Student Organizations Professional student organizations that focus on specific career interests meet regularly throughout the year. Join them now. Not only will they put you in contact with upper-class students, but their programs often include employer representatives, helpful discussions on searching for internships or jobs, and exposure to current conditions in the workplace.

Online

Career Center Go to your career center's home page and check its resources, such as hot links to useful pages. For example: Occupational Information Network: **http://online.onecenter.org**. This federal government site has information on occupations, skill sets, and links to professional sites for selected occupations. This is a great place to get started thinking about your interests.

Mapping Your Future: **www.mapping-yourfuture.org**. This comprehensive site provides support for those who are just starting to explore careers.

The Riley Guide: **www.rileyguide.com**. One of the best sites for interviewing, job search strategies, and other critical career tips.

My Institution's Resources

_____

_____

_____

_____

_____

▶▶▶ BUILDING YOUR PORTFOLIO
Investigating Occupations

The best career advice to give to the young is
'Find out what you like doing best and get someone to pay you for doing it.'
-Katherine Whitehorn (b. 1926), British writer and journalist

To complete this portfolio activity electronically, please visit
academic.cengage.com/collsucc/Gardner/YCE8e.

How do you know how to select a major if you are not sure what you want to do when you graduate? College classes, out-of-class activities, and part-time jobs will help you narrow your choices and make decisions about a major and a potential career.

1. Create a new entry in your portfolio with the title "Investigating Occupations." Record your work for this assignment there.

2. List at least two majors that you are considering right now or that you would like to know more about. Why do you find these majors interesting?

3. What are two careers that you think you might be interested in after you graduate? Explain your answer.

4. The U.S. Bureau of Labor Statistics publishes the online Occupational Outlook Handbook, which provides details for hundreds of jobs. You can search for a specific job and learn about the training and education needed, median earnings, job prospects, roles and responsibilities on the job, and working conditions.

   a. Visit the Occupational Outlook Handbook online at www.bls.gov/oco and type the first career name that you listed above in the search field.

   b. Look through the search results to find the specific career that you are interested in learning more about.

   c. In the chart below, note the training/degree required, describe the job outlook, and list the median earnings for each career. Look through the other descriptions to learn more about the career.

Occupational Outlook Handbook	Example Career: Computer Software Engineers	Career 1:	Career 2:
Training Required	Bachelor's degree, computer science/software engineering		
Job Outlook	One of the fastest-growing occupations from 2004 to 2014		
Earnings	Median annual earnings: about $74,980		

Even in your first year of college it is important that you begin to think about what you are going to do after graduation. The more you investigate different types of careers, the easier it will be for you to identify a major or help you decide what kind of internship, part-time job, or service learning opportunity you want to experience while you are still in college. Exploring your strengths, interests, and goals will help you to find a career that you enjoy and that meets your lifestyle expectations.

CHAPTER 12

Relationships

In this chapter YOU WILL LEARN

▶ How relationships are important to your success in college

▶ How to determine whether a serious relationship is right for you

▶ What kinds of relationships should be off-limits for college students

▶ What guidelines to use in establishing electronic relationships

▶ How relationships with parents or family members change

▶ How to live safely on campus and online

What clues can you find to the relationship between these two people?

© Bill Aron/PhotoEdit

Tom Carskadon of Mississippi State University and Reynol Junco of Lock Haven University contributed their valuable and considerable expertise to the writing of this chapter.

How Well Do You HANDLE RELATIONSHIPS?

A?B?C?A?B?C?A?B?C?

Read the following questions and choose the answer that most fits you.

1 How important to you is making new friends in college?

(A) I have a good circle of friends from home, so if I meet a few new people here, that's great, but I don't really need any more friends.

(B) It's really important to me because having good friends in college is a good support system, emotionally and academically, since we are all going through the same thing at this school.

(C) I don't make friends easily, so I'd rather just tough it out by myself.

2 Do you know why having a romantic relationship with your professor is off limits?

(A) I think there is probably a rule about this, but I really don't know why it matters.

(B) Romantic relationships with professors, or supervisors for that matter, are dangerous because those people have power over you, your grades, or your job. If you broke up, you wouldn't want your ex to have that kind of power.

(C) I really don't see a problem if both of you are consenting adults.

3 Do you think it's important to maintain good communication with your family members while you are in college?

(A) I guess sometimes it is when they give me money, but sometimes they pry too much into my life.

(B) Yes—they just want to be sure I am making the right decisions and are there to support me.

(C) They just get in the way of my independence—I'll see them over the holidays.

4 What might be dangerous about online relationships?

(A) I think they are the best way to meet new people, although sometimes it's creepy when strangers reveal that they know something about me I didn't know they knew.

(B) If I reveal too much about what I'm doing, someone could easily stalk me without my even knowing.

(C) Nothing—I've met tons of people in person whom I first met online and nothing bad has happened to me yet.

5 What strategies can you use to be safe on campus?

(A) I'll try to remember to lock my car and the door of my residence hall room, but basically I think college is a safe place.

(B) Even though there are no guarantees, I'm going to do everything I can to protect myself and my property.

(C) I just leave my doors unlocked. If somebody wants to steal something of yours, they'll find a way. I'd rather they just take something than break into my car.

Review your responses. (A) responses indicate that you have some idea about how to form good relationships and be safe on campus. (B) responses indicate that you understand how to make the most of your college experience through your relationships and behaviors. (C) responses indicate that you need additional help in negotiating both relationships and safety concerns. Whatever your responses, you'll find this chapter provides good information that will improve your college experience.

What does success in college have to do with relationships? As college instructors, we have learned from our own experiences and the experiences of others that the quality of the relationships students develop in college can have positive or negative effects on their concentration, self-confidence, and academic success.

Relationships take many forms. If you live on campus, one of your primary relationships, for better or worse, will be with your roommate or suitemates. Another important set of relationships will be with your instructors. You might choose to get to know your instructors or to ignore them, but the quality of the interaction you have with them might affect how well you do academically.

Whether you live on or off campus, you will continue a relationship with your parents, spouse, children, or other family members. Sometimes the assumptions and expectations that define family interactions will change, and negotiating that change is not always easy. Parents sometimes have trouble letting go of a son or daughter, and you might feel that they still want to control your life. If you are an adult with a spouse or partner, going to college will give you a new identity that might be uncomfortable or threatening to your partner. If you have children, they might not understand what's going on as your needs for study time become as important as their need for your undivided attention.

If your friends also go to college, you will have a great deal to share and compare. But if your friends are not college students, they, too, might be threatened as you take on a new identity. And of course, romantic relationships can support you or can create major conflict and heartbreak, depending on whether your partner shares your feelings and whether the relationship is healthy and affirming or dysfunctional.

This chapter will help you to think about all the different kinds of relationships that affect college students, including those that are established, maintained at a distance, or operate online.

Write • DISCUSS • Compare • Ask • BLOG • Answer • *Journal*

At this point in your life, what are your three most important relationships? Write about each of those three people and what makes them special to you.

▲ **You'll begin to make friends on the very first day of your college experience.**

Friendships in and Beyond College

One of the best things about going to college is meeting new people. In fact, scholars who study college students have found that you'll learn as much—or more—from other students you meet as you'll learn from professors. Although not everyone you hang out with will be a close friend, you will likely find a few relationships that are really special and might even last a lifetime. Although in the beginning it's tempting to associate with other students who dress like you dress, talk like you talk, and listen to the same music you enjoy, you will be missing out on one of the best aspects of college life if you associate only with people just like you. It's a good idea to diversify—to make friends with students who are from another state, another country, or a different racial or ethnic group.

Roommates

Adjusting to a roommate is another significant transition experience. You might make a lifetime friend or an exasperating acquaintance you wish you'd never known. A roommate doesn't have to be a best friend—just someone with whom you can share your living space comfortably. Your best friend might not make the best roommate. In fact, many students have lost friends by rooming together.

With any roommate, it's important to establish your mutual rights and responsibilities in writing. Many colleges provide contract forms that you and your roommate can use. If things go wrong later, you will have something to point to.

If you have problems, talk them out promptly. Talk directly—politely but plainly. If problems persist, or if you don't know how to talk them out, ask your residence hall counselor for help; he or she is trained to help resolve roommate conflicts.

Normally, you can tolerate (and learn from) a less than ideal situation; but if things get really bad and do not improve, insist on a change. If you are on campus, talk to your resident assistant (RA) or to a professional counselor in your campus's counseling center.

Online Connections

MySpace, Facebook, Second Life, Skype, instant messaging, dating sites, and e-mail all allow you to form new relationships with people you have never met and to maintain relationships with old friends. Meeting new people online can be both fun and educational. You can interact with a variety of people you might never have had the opportunity to meet otherwise.

For instance, imagine having regular online chats with the following people as one student does, who all met online: an aspiring screenwriter in New Jersey, an undercover narcotics agent in Michigan, a professional animator in Georgia, a college teacher in Connecticut, a high school student in Arizona, a librarian in California, a strip-club bartender in Tennessee, a mother in Pennsylvania, a police officer in Australia, a flight attendant in Illinois, an entrepreneur in Louisiana, a psychologist in Colorado, a physician in training in Texas, a schoolteacher in Canada, and college students in five states and three countries.

▲ **Your first-year roommate can become your lifelong friend.**

The downside? Meeting people online might lead to more transient and unpredictable relationships than those you would have in the "real world." People might not be what they seem. Meeting them in real life could be delightful—or disastrous. Some people assume false identities online (this is the norm on Second Life). You could be corresponding with someone who wants to harm you. Be very cautious about letting strangers know your name, address, telephone number, or other personal information, and be wary of face-to-face meetings.

Maintaining your former relationships online can be a way to help ease the transition to college. More than likely, you already have friends from high school on your buddy and friends lists. Using the Internet to maintain your relationships and build new ones is helpful; however, be wary of socializing online to the exclusion of socializing with those around you. If you find that you haven't made many, if any, new friends in person at your college or university, you might be socializing online too much. Try to strike a balance between your online and real social worlds. College counselors have experience helping students who need help socializing in the "real world."

Write • DISCUSS • Compare • Ask • BLOG • Answer • Journal

Have you met someone online whom you consider interesting? If so, describe that person. If not, describe the kind of person you would like to meet online.

WIRED WINDOW

IN A RECENT SURVEY, between 3 and 10 percent of college students lied on their social networking website profiles about their age, gender, what they do for a living, or their interests. The popular media frequently report on people who use social networking websites to prey on others. A recent investigation by a popular news magazine found that almost 750 registered sex offenders had MySpace profiles. Imagine how many offenders are on MySpace who don't list their real names. Even though the percentage of people who use MySpace to prey on others is small relative to the number of total users, it is important to consider ways of protecting yourself. Use common-sense precautions (like not giving out your location or contact information) and adjust your privacy settings accordingly. As the aforementioned survey found, the level of deceit on social networking sites varies based on the significance of the lie the person is telling. The chances that people will lie about a criminal background are greater than the chances they will lie about their age or gender. Even if you are careful to avoid offenders online, you can be hurt emotionally by someone who is deceitful. You might already know people who found that some of their MySpace friends weren't who they thought they were. Try your own MySpace investigation. Find a MySpace profile of someone you think is not who they portray themselves to be. What are your reasons for selecting this profile? Why do you think this person is representing himself or herself in this way?

Getting Serious with Relationships

Not only does college present an opportunity to make lots of new friends, it is also a place where romantic relationships flourish. Although some beginning college students are married or are already in long-term committed relationships, others might have their first serious romance with someone they meet on campus. If you are gay, lesbian, bisexual, or transgendered, you might find it much easier to meet romantic partners in college than you ever have before. Whatever your sexual orientation, the opportunities are like a banquet table; some people will sample lots of different choices, and others settle in with just one person. Either way, you'll grow and learn a great deal about yourself and those with whom you become involved. You'll also get insight on what it would be like to live with or marry your partner before you take that life-changing step.

You might have a relationship you feel is really special. Should you make it exclusive? Don't do so just because being with each other exclusively has become a habit. Ask yourself why you want this relationship to be exclusive. For security? To prevent jealousy? To build depth and trust? As a prelude to a permanent commitment? Before you make the decision to see only each other, make sure it is the best thing for each of you. You might find that you treat each other better and appreciate each other more when you feel free to explore other relationships.

If you are seriously thinking about marriage or a long-term commitment, consider this: Studies show that the younger you are, the lower your odds of a successful marriage. Also, a "trial marriage" or living together does not decrease your risk of later divorce.

Above all, beware of what might be called the "fundamental marriage error": marrying before both you and your partner are certain about who you are and what you want to do in life. Many 18- to 20-year-olds change their outlook and life goals drastically as they get older. If you want to marry, the person to marry is someone you could call your best friend—the one who knows you inside and out, the one you don't have to play games with, the one who prizes your company, the one who, over a period of years, has come to know, love, and respect who you are and what you want to be.

Long-Distance Relationships

Relationships change significantly when they turn into long-distance romances. Many students arrive at college while still romantically involved with someone back home or at another college or university.

College is an exciting scene with many social opportunities, and it might be hard to maintain a long-distance relationship when you are constantly meeting new people. You and your long-distance partner will need to be candid with each other about whether continuing your relationship is a good idea. If you decide to maintain your romantic relationship with an absent partner, look for other ways to get involved in campus life and meet people. An important part of your college education will come from people—faculty, staff and other students. Those relationships don't have to be romantic in order to be meaningful and long lasting.

Breaking Up

In a national study of 5,000 college students conducted in 2001 by researchers at the University of California, Los Angeles, 29 percent reported they ended a romantic relationship during their first year in college.

▲ **Ending a relationship is never easy.**

© Myrleen Ferguson Cate/PhotoEdit

Breaking up is hard, but if it is time to end a relationship, do it cleanly and calmly. Don't be impulsive or angry. Explain your feelings and talk them out. If you don't get a mature reaction, take the high road; don't join someone else in the mud. If you decide to reunite after a trial separation, be sure enough time has passed for you to evaluate the situation effectively. If things fail a second time, you really need to move on.

If your partner breaks up with you, you might find yourself sad, angry, or even depressed. If your partner breaks up with you online, or you learn about an imminent breakup through IM away messages or profile pages, social networking websites, or blog postings, it is best to ask to discuss the matter over the phone or in person. It is very difficult, if not impossible, to tell someone's tone via online communication, which might lead to more hurt for both partners. Remember that you're not alone. Almost everyone has been rejected or "dumped" at one time or another. Let some time pass, be open to moral support from your friends and your family, and if necessary, pay a visit to your college counselor or a chaplain. These skilled professionals have assisted many students through similar experiences, and they can be there for you as well. Bookstores and your library will also have good books on the topic of surviving a breakup.

You might want to remain friends with your partner, especially if you have shared and invested a lot in your relationship. It will be difficult to be friends, however, until both of you have healed from the hurt and neither of you wants the old relationship back. That usually takes a year or two.

Write • DISCUSS • Compare • Ask • BLOG • Answer • *Journal*

> Based on your experience or the experience of someone close to you, what advice would you give other students dealing with a breakup?

Off-Limits!

Some romantic relationships are strictly off-limits. Never become romantically involved with your professor or someone who works above or for you. If your partner is a person who has power and influence over you, the romance might really represent that person's need for power. Many of these relationships end in a breakup. And imagine how you would feel if your ex, who might be hurt or bitter or even want you back, still had control over your grades or your job! If you date a subordinate and the relationship ends, you might find yourself accused of sexual harassment, fired, or sued. Even dating coworkers is risky; it will be much harder to heal from a breakup if you must continue to work together.

Marriage and Parenting during College

Can marriage and parenting coexist with being a college student? The answer, of course, is yes, although linking all of these identities—student, spouse, parent—will not be easy. If you are married or in a long-term relationship, with or without children,

▲ **Being a parent while going to college is a major challenge.**

you will need to be an expert at time management. The expectations of your roles might come into conflict, and you'll need to know what comes first and when. Most college instructors will be flexible with requirements if you have genuine problems with meeting a deadline because of family obligations. But it's important that you explain your situation; don't expect your instructors to be able to guess what you need if you don't tell them. As the demands on your time increase, it is important that you and your partner share the burdens equally. You can't expect to be spoiled or pampered just because you're a student.

Occasionally, deciding to go to college can create conflict within a family. Partners and children can be threatened and intimidated if you take on a new identity and set of responsibilities. Financial pressures are likely to put an extra strain on your relationship, so both you and your partner will have to work hard at attending to each other's needs. Be sure to involve your family members in your decision to go to college; bring them to campus at every opportunity, let them read your papers and other assignments, and see if your partner can take a course too. Finally it's very important to carve out time for your partner and your family just as carefully as you schedule your work and your classes.

Relationships with Your Parents

Whether you live on campus or at home, becoming a college student will change your relationship with your parents. Home will never be quite the same, and you will not be who you were before. You might find that your parents hover over you and try to make your decisions on your behalf, such as your major, where and how much you work, and

Confessions of a College Student

Name: Matt D'Anna

Age: 19

College: Siena College

Hometown: Nanuet, NY

Major: Finance

Favorite book: *Juiced* by Jose Canseco

Favorite college course: History

The person I would most like to meet: Michael Jordan

Heroes: My dad

Favorite way to relax: Playing video games or watching any type of sporting event

Your proudest moment or biggest accomplishment: Graduating high school

Favorite food: Anything not from the school cafeteria

Relationships confession: My parents are probably the most influential people at this point in my life. I call home every day and talk to at least one of my parents. I believe a college student's bond with parents will only strengthen as each college year goes by. I also believe it is important for students to have at least one close friend to lean on. A good relationship with your roommate is also very important. You don't have to be best friends with your roommate, but it is important that you be able to get along. While my roommate and I are not close friends, we don't seem to bother one another, which I note is the case with other roommates, too.

what you do on weekends. In fact, some instructors and administrators have coined the term "helicopter parents" to describe these hovering behaviors. You also might find that it's really hard for you to make any decisions without talking to your parents first. While communication with your parents is important, don't let them make all your decisions. Your college or university will help you draw the line between what decisions should be yours alone, and what decisions your parents should help you make.

Many college students are living in blended families so that more than one set of parents is involved in their college experience. If your father or mother has remarried, you will have to negotiate with both family units.

So how can you have a good relationship with your parents during this period of transition? A first step in establishing a good relationship with them is to be aware of their concerns. The most common are:

▶ Parents fear you'll harm yourself. You might take risks that make older people shudder. You might shudder, too, when you look back on some of your stunts. Sometimes your parents have reason to worry.

▶ Parents think their sons or daughters are still young and innocent. And yes, the old double standard (differing expectations for men than women, particularly regarding sex) is alive and well.

▶ Parents know you're older but might continue to picture you as a child. Somehow, the parental clock always lags behind reality. Maybe it's because they loved you so much as a child, they can't erase that image.

▶ Parents mean well. Most love their children, even if it doesn't always come out right; very few are really indifferent or abusive.

▶ Parents fear that you might change in some negative way and lose the values that characterize your family unit and your culture.

▶ Finally, parents fear that you might never come home again, and for some college students, this is exactly what happens.

Remember that parents have genuine concerns that you will understand even better when you become a parent yourself. To help your parents feel more comfortable with your life in college, try setting aside regular times to update your parents on how college and your life in general are going. Ask for and consider their advice. You don't have to take it.

Not every family is ideal. If your family is close and supportive, you are blessed. If it is even halfway normal, you will succeed. But some families are truly dysfunctional. If love, respect, enthusiasm, and encouragement are just not in the cards, look around you. Other people will give you these things, and you can create the family you need. With your emotional needs satisfied, your reactions to your real family will be much less painful.

What should you do if the family falls apart? Divorce happens, and sometimes it happens when a son or daughter goes to college. It's hard to proceed with life as usual when the family foundation seems to be cracking under you. But remember that your parents are adults. If your father and mother decide to go their separate ways, it's not your fault, and you should not feel responsible for their happiness.

◀ **College students often talk to family and friends several times a day.**

© age/fotostock/SuperStock

Even if you're successful in determining appropriate boundaries between your life and theirs, it's hard not to worry about what's happening at home. So seek help from your campus's counseling center or from a chaplain if you find yourself in the midst of a difficult family situation.

Write • DISCUSS • *Compare* • Ask • BLOG • Answer • *Journal*

How is your family reacting to your college experience? Are they supportive, fearful, meddling, remote?

Developing Relationships through On-Campus Involvement

Colleges and universities can seem huge and unfriendly places, especially if you went to a small high school or grew up in a small town. To feel comfortable in this new environment, it is important for you to find your comfort zone or niche. It's not hard to find the place where you belong, but it will take some initiative on your part. Consider your interests, the high school activities that you enjoyed most, and choose some activities to explore. You might be interested in joining an intramural team, performing community service, running for a student government office, or getting involved in the residence hall. Or you might prefer joining a more structured campuswide club or organization.

Almost every college has numerous organizations you can join; usually you can check them out through activity fairs, printed guides, open houses, web pages, and so on. Or even better, consider attending a meeting before you make the decision to join. See what the organization is like, what the expectations of time and money are, and whether you feel comfortable with the members. And remember, new students who become involved with at least one organization are more likely to survive their first year and remain in college.

Be careful not to overextend yourself when it comes to campus activities. While it is important to get involved, joining too many clubs or organizations will make it difficult to focus on any given activity and will make it difficult to get your school-work done. Future employers will see a balance in campus involvement and academics as a desirable quality in prospective employees. Don't fall into the trap of thinking that more is better. In the case of campus involvement, as in many things, quality is much more rewarding than quantity.

Write • DISCUSS • *Compare* • Ask • BLOG • Answer • *Journal*

Have you already become involved in campus organizations? What kinds of involvement have you already experienced? If you haven't become involved, what club or organization most interests you? Explain why.

To Greek or Not to Greek?

Greek social organizations are not all alike, nor are their members. Fraternities and sororities can be a rich source of friends and support. Some students love them. But other students might find them philosophically distasteful, too demanding of time and finances, and/or too constricting. Members of Greek organizations sometimes associate exclusively with other members, and this exclusivity causes them to miss opportunities to have a more varied group of friends. Greek rush (member recruitment) on your campus might happen before you've had an opportunity to decide whether you want to go Greek or to determine which fraternity or sorority is right for you. There is nothing wrong with delaying a decision about Greek membership. In fact, we would argue that it's better to learn your way around campus and meet lots of different friends before committing to a particular organization. Fraternities and sororities are powerful social influences, so you'll definitely want to take a good look at the upper-class students in them. If what you see is what you want to be, consider joining. If not, steer clear.

If Greek life is not for you, there are many other ways to make close friends. Many campuses have residence halls or special floors for students with common interests or situations, such as first-year students; honors students; students in particular majors; students with strong ethnic or religious affiliations; students who shun tobacco, alcohol, and drugs; students interested in protecting the environment; and so on. Check these out—often they provide very satisfying experiences.

Working on Campus

One of the best ways to develop relationships with instructors and administrators on your campus is to get an on-campus job. Generally, your on-campus supervisors will be much more flexible than off-campus employers in helping you balance your study demands and your work schedule. It's possible that you won't make as much money working on campus as you would in an off-campus job, but the relationships you'll develop with influential people who really care about your success in college and who will write those all-important reference letters make the loss of a little money well worth it.

Involvement off Campus

As a first-year student, much of your time will be spent on campus, either going to class, studying, or hanging out with other students. But there are also ways that you can get involved in the surrounding community. Consider being involved in a community service project. Your college might offer service opportunities as part of first-year courses (**service learning**), or your campus's division of student affairs might have a volunteer or community service office.

While working at an off-campus job is one way to meet new people in the community, it's important that you restrict work to a reasonable number of hours per week (no more than 15). It's also better if your work experiences relate to your intended major, and that's more likely to happen when you work on, rather than off, campus. For instance, if you are a premed major, you might be able to find on-campus work in a biology or chemistry lab. That work would help you to gain knowledge and experience, and to make connections with faculty experts in these fields. Although you might feel that you have to work in order to pay your tuition or living expenses, many college students work too many hours just to support a lifestyle—to buy or maintain a brand new car or new stereo system. It's important to maintain a reasonable balance between work and study. Don't fall into the trap of thinking, "I can do it all." Too many college students have found that doing it all means they don't do anything very well.

Co-op Programs

Many schools have **co-op programs** in which you spend some terms in regular classes and other terms in temporary job settings in your field. Although they usually prolong your education somewhat, these programs have many advantages. They offer an excellent preview of what work in your chosen field is actually like, thus helping you know if you have made the right choice. They give you valuable experience and contacts that help you get a job when you finish school; in fact, many firms offer successful co-op students permanent jobs when they graduate.

Alternating work and school terms might be more agreeable to your schedule than 8 or 10 straight terms of classes, and it might help you keep your ultimate goal in mind. Co-op programs can help you pay for school, too; some co-op students, especially in technical fields, make almost as much, or even more, during their co-op terms as their professors do!

Living Safely on Campus

One of the goals of this chapter is to help you establish the kinds of relationships on campus that will give you a sense of belonging, comfort, and safety. But college is not a cocoon. Campuses are part of the real world and, as such, pose certain dangers and risks. It is therefore very important that you take reasonable steps to ensure your own safety and the safety of your property.

Protecting against Sexual Assault

Anyone is at risk for being raped, but the majority of victims are women. By the time they graduate, an estimated one out of four college women will be the victim of attempted rape, and one out of six will be raped. Most women will be raped by someone they know, a date or acquaintance, and most will not report the crime. Alcohol is a factor in nearly three-fourths of the incidents. Whether raped by a date or a stranger, a victim can suffer long-term traumatic effects.

Tricia Phaup of the University of South Carolina offers this advice on avoiding sexual assault:

▶ Know what you want and do not want sexually.

▶ Go to parties or social gatherings with friends, and leave with them.

▶ Avoid being alone with people you don't know very well.

▶ Trust your intuition.

▶ Be alert to subtle and unconscious messages you might be sending and receiving.

▶ Be aware of how much alcohol you drink, if any.

If you are ever tempted to force another person to have sex:

▶ Realize that it is never okay to force sex on someone.

▶ Don't assume that you know what your date wants.

▶ If you're getting mixed messages, ask.

▶ Be aware of the effects of alcohol.

▶ Remember that rape is morally and legally wrong.

If you have been raped, regardless of whether you choose to report the rape to the police or get a medical exam, it is very helpful to seek some type of counseling to begin working through this traumatic event.

The following people or offices might be available on or near your campus to help you deal with a sexual assault: campus sexual assault coordinator, local rape crisis center, campus police department, counseling center, student health services, women's student services office, local hospital emergency rooms, and campus chaplains.

Personal Safety

You cannot plan for every potential event that might cause injury. Each day we read about new tragedies such as airplane crashes, accidental drowning, or violent

◀ **Going out in groups will help keep you safe.**

© Justin Pumfrey/Getty Images

crimes. But we still fly and swim and go out at night, often finding ourselves alone with individuals we do not know and putting ourselves at risk. Here are some commonsense ways to increase your personal safety on campus:

▶ Find out if your campus has an escort service that provides transportation or an escort during the evening hours. Do you know the hours and days of the service and how to arrange for an escort? Use this service if you must walk alone during evening hours.

▶ Write down and memorize the telephone number for your campus police.

▶ If your campus has emergency call boxes, locate them and learn how to operate them.

▶ Be aware of the dark and isolated areas on campus and avoid them, especially when walking alone.

▶ Don't take drinks from people you don't know at parties and don't leave your drink unattended.

▶ If you're a jogger, avoid jogging alone, and wear reflective clothing for your own safety in traffic.

▶ If you go away overnight or for the weekend, let someone know where you will be and how to reach you in case of an emergency or in case someone becomes concerned about you.

▶ Review your privacy settings on social networking websites and make sure that you are comfortable sharing the information that anyone can see.

▶ Check your blog postings to ensure that you aren't sharing sensitive private information or details that would allow someone to find you easily.

Your behavior both on and off campus should be proactive in terms of reducing the opportunity for a crime or injury to occur. Make safety measures part of your everyday routine.

Protecting Your Property

Most campus crime involves theft. As you and other students bring more valuable items to campus, such as computers, the opportunity for theft grows. Books can be stolen and sold at bookstores, and if not properly marked, will never be recovered. Computers and other electronic items such as PDAs and iPods can be traded for cash. To reduce the chances that your property will be stolen, follow these basic rules:

▶ Record serial numbers of electronic equipment, and keep the numbers in a safe place.

▶ Mark your books on a specific page with your name and an additional identifier, such as a code (but not a PIN, Social Security, or driver's license number). Remember the page where you entered the information.

▶ Never leave books or book bags unattended.

▶ Lock your room, even if you are only going out for a minute.

▶ Do not leave your key above the door for a friend or roommate.

- Report lost or stolen property to the proper authority, such as the campus police.
- Don't tell anyone you don't know well about your valuable possessions.
- Keep your credit or debit card as safe as you would your cash.

▶ WHERE TO GO FOR HELP

On Campus

Counseling Center Professional college counselors help students think and talk about their relationships and then support and advise them regarding the most appropriate courses of action. It is normal to seek such assistance. It's a rare student who doesn't have some relationship challenges in college, whether they are with roommates, friends, family, romantic partners, teachers, supervisors, or other individuals. This kind of counseling is strictly confidential (unless you are a threat to the safety of yourself or others) and usually is provided at no charge, which is a great fringe benefit of being in college. But unless this is an emergency, be prepared to wait for your first appointment; these centers have very heavy caseloads due to an increase in student stressors.

Chaplains An often under recognized resource in terms of getting help on relationship matters is a session (or more) with a campus chaplain. Almost all colleges, both public and private, have religiously affiliated ministerial chaplains, who usually have specialized training in pastoral counseling. They also organize and host a number of group activities in campus religious centers that you might want to take advantage of. Your academic advisor might be able to refer you to an appropriate chaplain or you can seek out the one who represents your faith. Most chaplains are happy to see students for counseling whether or not you attend their church, synagogue, or mosque.

Student Organizations The variety of student groups designed to bring together students to help them with their relationships is virtually unlimited. Everything exists—from Greek letter social fraternities and sororities

to single parents with children to gay/lesbian/bisexual/transgendered students.

Online

Websites like Happygrrls (**www.happygrrls.com/relating/survivingabreakup.html**), AskMen (**www.askmen.com/dating/curtsmith/25_dating_advice.html**), and iVillage (**love.ivillage.com/lnsproblems/lnsbreakingup/topics/0,,4tdj,00.html**) all offer information and resources to help you get through a breakup.

The University of Chicago's "Student Counseling Virtual Pamphlet Collection" (**counseling.uchicago.edu/resources/virtualpamphlets/**) takes you to dozens of websites about problems in relationships. Browse among the many links to see if any information applies to you. Healthy Romantic Relationships during College: (**www.utexas.edu/student/cmhc/booklets/romrelations/romrelations.html**) The University of Texas Counseling Center offers an online brochure that explores the ups and downs of romantic relationships.

My Institution's Resources

_____

_____

_____

_____

_____

▶▶▶ BUILDING YOUR PORTFOLIO
A Day in the Life

To exist is to change, to change is to mature, to mature is to go on creating oneself endlessly.

-Henri Bergson (1859–1941), French philosopher

To complete this portfolio activity electronically, please visit academic.cengage.com/collsucc/Gardner/YCE8e.

Managing family relationships while in college can sometimes be a real challenge! Whether you attend college in your hometown or across the country, relationships with those who are close to you will change. Sometimes parents or other family members have a hard time letting go, and sometimes it is difficult for new college students to start making independent decisions.

1. Create a new entry in your portfolio with the title "A Day in the Life." Record your work for this assignment there.

   _____

   _____

   _____

   _____

   _____

   _____

2. Describe some of the ways your life has changed since coming to college (e.g., more independence, personal responsibility, less free time, etc.). How have you handled these changes? What has been the most difficult aspect of your new college life so far?

3. Have you considered how your family's day-to-day lives might also have changed since you began college? Conduct an in-person or phone "interview" with one (or more) of your family members about how life has changed for them.

   Tip: Set up a mutually convenient time to talk and choose a quiet place, free of distractions.

Here are a few questions to get you started:

   a. What do you feel has changed in your life since I began college?

   b. Is the family routine any different now?

   c. Do you worry about me? If so, what is your biggest concern about my college experience?

   d. Do you feel like we communicate enough (by phone, email, etc.)?

If possible, insert photos of the people you interview here.

4. Reflect on what you learned from the interviews. How can you be sensitive to your family's needs/concerns while recognizing your own changing needs?

_____

_____

_____

_____

_____

Diversity: Appreciating Differences Among Us

In this chapter YOU WILL LEARN

▶ The concepts of culture, ethnicity, race, age, sexual orientation, physical ability, and gender as they relate to diversity

▶ The value of learning about various groups

▶ The role colleges play in promoting diversity

▶ How to identify and cope with discrimination and prejudice on campus

On most campus bulletin boards, you'll find many examples of diversity.

© Blend Images/SuperStock

Juan J. Flores of Folsom Lake College contributed his valuable and considerable expertise to the writing of this chapter.

How Do You APPRECIATE DIVERSITY?

A?B?C?A?B?C?A?B?C?

Read the following questions and choose the answer that most fits you:

1 *What terms do you associate with "diversity"?*

A I think "diversity" just means differences among things or people. You can divide people into any kinds of categories you can think up.

B "Culture" is the only term I can think of.

C Some words like "race" and "ethnicity" come to mind, but there must be others.

2 *Do you consider yourself open to differing values and beliefs?*

A I think I am quite tolerant of others' beliefs and our differences—it's an opportunity to learn something new from someone.

B I haven't been exposed to many people different from myself so it's hard to say.

C I try to be open to people different from myself, but I don't think we have much in common, so I don't have many friends who are different.

3 *We all have prejudices and biases. How have you dealt with yours?*

A I always keep an open mind and hear people out. I remember that it's okay to have differences of opinion among people, as long as you can respect others'

beliefs and not put them down just because they are different from your own.

B What's there to deal with? I just stick with people like myself.

C Keeping an open mind is how I try to deal with it, but it doesn't always seem to work.

4 *How do you seek out opportunities to learn about cultures and groups other than your own?*

A I join various extracurricular groups to explore different viewpoints, beliefs, and people.

B I don't really go outside my comfort zone.

C I tend to stay with my own kind, but I'm sometimes introduced to new cultures and people by my friends and I always find that fun and interesting.

Review your responses. **A** responses indicate that you are open to meeting diverse people and having diverse experiences. **B** responses indicate that you haven't had much experience with people or ideas out of your comfort zone. **C** responses indicate that although you've had some experience with diversity, it's still hard for you to explore different people and ideas. Whatever your current attitude about or experience with diversity, this chapter will give you new ideas about why diversity is so important and how you might go about exploring varied experiences and opportunities while you're in college.

At the core of the United States' value system is the belief that America is a place where all people are welcome. This principle has created the richly diverse society in which we live today. America has been called the "great melting pot," which promoted the blending of all cultures into one American identity, but it has been superseded, in most cases, by the "salad bowl" theory, which emphasizes the importance of retaining individual cultural identity while living among others. Today, ethnic and cultural communities have developed throughout the U. S., each preserving components of a unique heritage and providing support to its residents.

Write • DISCUSS • Compare • Ask • BLOG • Answer • *Journal*

Do you believe the U. S. is more accurately characterized as a melting pot or salad bowl? Why?

Colleges and universities serve as a microcosm of the real world ahead—a world that requires us all to work, live, and socialize with various ethnic and cultural groups. In few settings do ethnic and cultural groups interact in such close proximity to one another as they do on a college campus. Whether you are attending a four-year university or community college, you will be exposed to new experiences and opportunities, all of which enhance learning and a deeper sense of understanding.

Through self-assessment, discovery, and open-mindedness, you can begin to understand your perspectives on diversity. This work, although difficult at times, will enhance your educational experiences, personal growth, and development. Thinking critically about your personal values and belief systems will allow you to have a greater sense of belonging and to make a positive contribution to our multicultural society.

Write • DISCUSS • Compare • Ask • BLOG • Answer • *Journal*

> Defining "diversity" very broadly as differences in race, ethnicity, religion, political preference, etc., is your college or university more or less diverse than your high school? Why?

Keeping an Open Mind

Diversity is the variation of social and cultural identities among people living together, while multiculturalism is the *active* process of acknowledging and respecting social groups, cultures, religions, races, ethnicities, attitudes, and opinions. As your journey through higher education unfolds, you will find yourself immersed in this mixture of identities. Regardless of the size of the institution, going to college brings together people with differing backgrounds and experiences but with common goals and aspirations. Each person brings to campus a unique life story, upbringing, value system, view of the world, and a set of judgments. Familiarizing yourself with such differences can greatly enhance your experiences in the classes you will take, the organizations you will join, and the relationships you will cultivate. For many students, college is the first time they are exposed to so much diversity. Learning experiences and challenges await you both in and out of the classroom. It's a chance to learn, not only about others, but also about yourself.

The Sources of Our Beliefs About Diversity

Many of our beliefs grow out of personal experience and reinforcement. If you have had a negative experience or endured a series of incidents involving members of a particular group, you're more likely to develop **stereotypes**, or negative judgments. Or maybe you have heard repeatedly that everyone associated with a particular

Confessions of a College Student

Name: Daniel R. Anderson

Age: 19

University: University of Delaware

Hometown: West Milford, NJ

Major: Psychology

Favorite book: *To Kill A Mockingbird*

Favorite college course: Education 240 (Philosophical and Legal Perspectives). This course reviews Supreme Court cases dealing with various types of educational issues, such as students' rights, religion in schools, and Title IX. Through class discussion, I have learned so much about education and the way power and control are handed down from administrators to students.

Heroes: Two men have been my heroes since I was a little boy: my two grandfathers. Their hard work and dedication to family caused me look up to them as role models.

Favorite way to relax: Playing soccer with my friends.

Your proudest moment or biggest accomplishment: My induction into the National Honor Society during my junior year in high school.

Favorite food: Cheeseburgers and fries, which I order every time I go out to eat.

Diversity confession: Though religious, cultural, and other kinds of groups may have their own organizations, all groups share similarities that everyone can appreciate and are different in ways that broaden perspectives for those outside their groups. For example, groups of students—whatever their backgrounds—must work together in many classes on projects and assignments. And that requires cooperation among group members on meeting times and dividing responsibilities fairly. I was so surprised that most students working in groups were able to look past each other's differences and focus on the task at hand. Of course, things happen. My first roommate had different habits, religious beliefs, and buddies. It was uncomfortable at first, but we were able to work through our differences and become friends. Diversity works when we seek commonalities among one another while learning from our differences, too.

group behaves in a certain way, and you might buy into that stereotype. A child growing up in an environment where dislike and distrust of certain types of people are openly expressed might subscribe to those very judgments without having any direct interaction with those being judged.

In college you might encounter beliefs about diversity that run counter to your basic values. When your friendships with others are affected by differing values, tolerance is generally a good goal. It can be very enriching and rewarding to talk about diversity with someone else whose beliefs seem to be in conflict with your own. Your goal is not to reach agreement, but to enrich your understanding of why people see diversity differently, why some seem to flee from it and others allow experiences with diversity to enrich their college experience.

◀ **In the best sense, all humanity is one big family.**

© Leland Bobbé/CORBIS

Write • DISCUSS • Compare • Ask • BLOG • Answer • *Journal*

> Write about any specific lessons you learned in your family about the expectations you should have of diverse groups.

Prior to college, you might never have coexisted with most of the groups you now see on campus. Your home community might not have been very diverse, although possibly it seemed so before you reached campus. In college, you have the opportunity to learn from many kinds of people. From your roommate in the residence hall, to your lab partner in your biology class, to the members of your sociology study group, your college experience will be enriched if you allow yourself to be open to the possibility of learning from all cultural groups.

Ethnicity, Culture, and Race

Often the terms "ethnicity" and "culture" are used interchangeably, although in reality, their definitions are quite distinct. Throughout this chapter, we will use these two words together and in isolation. Before we start using the terms, it's a good idea to define them so that you're clear on what they actually mean.

Ethnicity refers to a quality assigned to a specific group of people historically connected by a common national origin or language. For example, let's look at one of the largest ethnic groups, Latinos. Latin America encompasses over 30 countries within North, Central, and South America, all of which share the Spanish language.

A notable exception is Brazil. While the national language is Portuguese, Brazilians are considered Latinos. The countries also share many traditions and beliefs, with some variations. However, we shouldn't generalize with this or any ethnic group. Not every Latino who speaks Spanish is of Mexican descent, and not every Latino speaks Spanish. Acknowledging that differences do exist within ethnic groups is a big step in becoming ethnically aware.

Culture is defined as those aspects of a group of people that are passed on and/or learned. Traditions, food, language, clothing styles, artistic expression, and beliefs are all part of culture. With this definition in mind, we can begin to rethink the common mistake that assigns culture to only ethnic expressions. Certainly ethnic groups are also cultural groups: they share common language, foods, traditions, art, and clothing, which are passed from one generation to the next. But numerous other, nonethnic cultural groups can fit this concept of culture, too. Think of the hip-hop community, where a common style of dress, specific terminology used in hip-hop circles, and musical and artistic expression also constitute a culture.

Although we don't use the term much in this chapter, it's important to understand the idea of **race** as commonly used in everyday language. Race refers to biological characteristics shared by groups of people, including skin tone, hair texture and color, and facial features. Making generalizations about someone's racial group affiliation is risky. For instance, can we say that an individual with black, tightly woven hair is always of African or African-American descent? Certainly not, since a person of Dominican, Puerto Rican, Cuban, or other background can have those features. Even people who share some biological features—such as similar eye shape or dark skin—might be ethnically very distinct. For instance, people of Asian descent are not necessarily ethnically and culturally alike, since Asia is a vast region encompassing such disparate places as Mongolia, India, and Japan. Likewise, people of African descent come from very different backgrounds; the African continent is home to 53 countries and hundreds of different languages, and Africans are genetically very diverse.

All of us come into the world with our own unique characteristics—aspects of our physical appearance and personalities that make us who we are. But people around the world share one attribute in common: we want to be respected even if we are different from others in some ways. Whatever the color of your skin or hair, whatever your life experiences or cultural background, you will want others to treat you fairly and acknowledge and value your contribution to your communities and the world. And, of course, others will want the same from you.

Other Forms of Diversity

When you think of diversity, you might first think of differences in race or ethnicity. But in fact, the following terms also have to do with types of diversity that you might experience in college and in the workplace:

 Age. Although some students enter college around age 18, others choose to enter or return in their 30s and beyond. In 2005, 44 percent of the U. S. adult population (individuals over 25 years of age) were enrolled in adult education programs on college campuses. It's important for students of any age to respect each other. Age diversity in the classroom gives everyone the opportunity to learn from others who have different life experiences. If you don't have the opportunity to interact in class with older students, you might even want to consider participating in volunteer service at a senior center or other location where you could meet and learn from people who are older than you.

Write • DISCUSS • Compare • Ask • BLOG • Answer • *Journal*

Other than your grandparents, do you know others who are significantly older than you? If so, what has been the nature of your interaction and your relationship? If not, how might you meet some older people on campus or in your community?

▶ **Learning and Physical Abilities**. Though the majority of students have reasonably average learning and physical abilities, students with physical and mental disabilities are rising in numbers on most college campuses, as are the services available to them. Physical disabilities can include deafness, blindness, paralysis, or a mental disorder. Many students have some form of learning disability (see chapter 3) that makes college work a challenge.

Those with physical and mental disabilities want to be treated just as you would treat anyone else—with respect. If a student with a disability is in your class, treat him or her as you would any student; your zeal to help might be seen as an expression of pity. A quadriplegic student once asked his teacher how he could explain to another student that he did not want her to help him write his papers. He didn't want to hurt her feelings, but he felt he would learn more by working solo.

If you or a friend have, or think you might have, a learning disability, consult your campus learning center for a diagnosis and advice on compensating for learning problems. Most campuses have a special office to serve students with both physical and learning disabilities.

▶ **Gender**. A basic example of diversity is gender. An old saying goes, "Women are different from men and *viva la difference*!" But are the genders, discounting physical differences, really that different? Or do we believe they are because of any of the following:

▶ The idea that one gender is superior to or more valuable than another

▶ Female or male chauvinism (prejudiced loyalty or support for one's own gender)

▶ The tendency to believe that what is masculine is appropriate only for males or what is feminine is appropriate only for females

▶ A feeling of distrust towards another sex, most frequently operating at unconscious levels

While you're in college, make friends with people of all genders and avoid stereotyping what is "appropriate" for one group or another. And don't limit your own interests. In today's world, there is almost no activity or profession that isn't open to all people.

Write • DISCUSS • Compare • Ask • BLOG • Answer • *Journal*

Can you remember any time in your life when you gave up a dream because you thought it was "inappropriate" for someone of your gender? Can you remember a time when you assumed you wouldn't be good at an activity, a sport, or a course because of your gender? What advice could you give to other students about not letting gender narrow their range of life options?

▶ **Sexual Orientation**. In college you will likely meet both students and professors who are homosexual or bisexual. Because most colleges are inclusive of gay, lesbian, or bisexual people, many individuals who were in the closet in high school will come out in the collegiate environment. Sexual orientation is a highly personal and often emotionally charged characteristic, but whatever your own personal sexual orientation, it is important that you respect all individuals with whom you come in contact. Many colleges and universities have campus codes or "standards of behavior" that do not permit acts of harassment or discrimination based on race, ethnicity, gender, or sexual orientation.

Diversity in Higher Education

Acknowledging the importance of diversity to education, colleges and universities have begun to take the concepts of diversity and apply them to student learning opportunities. We see this in efforts by colleges to embrace an **inclusive curriculum**. Today, you can find courses with a diversity focus in many departments of your college or university, such as Black Studies, Asian Studies, Women's Studies, and Gay and Lesbian Studies. Many of the courses in these departments meet graduation requirements. The college setting is ideal for promoting diversity education because it allows students and faculty of varying backgrounds to come together for the common purpose of learning and critical thinking. According to Gloria Ameny-Dixon, education about diversity can:

▶ Increase problem-solving skills through different perspectives applied to reaching solutions

▶ Increase positive relationships through achievement of common goals, respect, appreciation, and commitment to equality

▶ Decrease stereotyping and prejudice through contact and interaction with diverse individuals

▶ Promote the development of a more in-depth view of the world[1]

College students have led the movement for a curriculum that reflects disenfranchised groups such as women, people of color, the elderly, the disabled, and gays and lesbians. By protesting, walking out of classes, and staging sit-ins at the

[1] Gloria M. Ameny-Dixon, "Why Multicultural Education Is More Important in Higher Education Now Than Ever: A Global Perspective." McNeese State University (www.nationalforum.com).

© Jodi Hilton/Getty Images

▲ **Diversity in values can be expressed when individuals support or reject a cause or an individual.**

offices of campus officials, students have demanded the hiring of more ethnic faculty, the creation of Ethnic Studies departments, and a variety of programs for academic support. These support services have increased academic access for students from ethnic and cultural groups and have helped them stay in school. They exist today in the form of multicultural centers, women's resource centers, enabling services, and numerous academic support programs. **Multiculturalism** in education has continued to gain momentum since it began during the Civil Rights movement of the 1960s. By expressing their discontent over the lack of access and representation in many of society's niches, including higher education, ethnic and cultural groups have achieved acknowledgment of their presence on campus.

We hope you will step out of your comfort zone and include a course or two with a multicultural basis in your schedule. Such courses can provide you with new perspectives and an understanding of issues affecting your fellow students and community members. This also will serve you well in your career path; just as your college or university campus is diverse, so, too, is the workforce you will be entering. The multicultural skills you gain in college can enrich the quality of your entire life.

The Many Forms of Diversity on Campus

Perhaps you have actively begun to notice the diversity around you as well as the many forms it takes on your campus. Be it religious affiliation, sexual orientation, gender, ethnicity, age, culture, or ability, your campus provides the opportunity to interact with and learn alongside a kaleidoscope of individuals.

Student-Run Organizations

Student-run organizations can provide you with multiple avenues to express ideas, pursue interests, and cultivate relationships. According to our definition of culture, all student-run organizations are, in fact, culturally based and provide an outlet for the promotion and celebration of that culture. Let's take, for instance, two very different student groups, a Muslim Student Union and an Animation Club, and apply the components of culture to them. Both groups promote a belief system common among their members: The first is based on religious beliefs and the second on what constitutes animation as an art form. Both have aspects that can be taught and passed on: the teachings of the Muslim faith and the rules and techniques used in drawing. Both utilize language specific to their members. Most campus organizations bring like-minded students together and are open to anyone who wants to become involved.

One of the best things about being on campus is the many events available to you. In order to promote learning and discovery not only inside the classroom but outside as well, colleges and universities provide programming that highlights ethnic and cultural celebrations such as Chinese New Year and Kwanzaa, topics of gender such as Take Back the Night, and a broad range of entertainment, including concerts and art exhibits. These events expose you to new and exciting ideas and viewpoints, enhancing your education and challenging your current views.

Most college students, especially first-year students, are seeking their own niche and their own identity. Coming to college is a trying time filled with anticipation, nervousness, and optimism. Whether you are attending a school close to home or farther away, living at home or on your own for the first time, the adjustment can be overwhelming. Many students have found that becoming involved in campus organizations eases the transition and helps them make connections with their fellow students.

Fraternities and Sororities

Fraternities and sororities provide a quick connection to a large number of individuals, a link to the social pipeline, camaraderie, and support. Most fraternities and sororities differ in their philosophies and philanthropy. Fraternities and sororities created by and for specific ethnic groups have existed for a number of years and were developed by students of color who felt the need for campus groups that allowed students to connect to their communities and cultures while in school. Nu Alpha Kappa Fraternity, Alpha Rho Lambda Sorority, Omega Psi Phi Fraternity, Alpha Kappa Alpha Sorority, Lamba Phi Epsilon Fraternity, and Sigma Omicron Pi Sorority are just some of the many ethnically-based Greek organizations that exist across the country. Such organizations have provided many students with a means to become familiar with their campus and to gain friendships and support, while fostering and promoting their culture and ethnicity.

Career/Major Groups

You can explore diversity through your major and career interests as well. Groups that focus on a specific field of study can be a great asset as you explore your interests.

Interested in helping minority and majority groups interact more effectively? Consider majoring in sociology or social work. Want to learn more about human behavior? Study psychology. Join the club that is affiliated with the major you're interested in. Doing so will not only help you find out more about the major, but will also allow you to make contacts in the field that can lead to career options. Many of these clubs participate in challenges and contests with similar groups from other colleges and contribute to campus activities through exhibitions and events. The Psychology Club; the Math, Engineering, and Science Association; and the Association of Student Filmmakers are examples of such groups.

Political/Activist Organizations

Adding to the diversity mix on campuses are organizations pertaining to specific political affiliations and causes. Campus Republicans, Young Democrats, Amnesty International, Native Students in Social Action, and other groups provide students with a platform to express their political views and share their causes with others. Contributing to the diversity of ideas, organizations provide debating events and forums to address current issues and events.

Special-Interest Groups

Perhaps the largest subgroup of student clubs is the special-interest category, which houses everything from recreational interests to hobbies. On your campus you might find special-interest organizations like the Brazilian Jujitsu Club, the Kite Flyers' Club,

◀ **These flamenco dancers symbolize the rich diversity on college campuses.**

© Chris Nash/Getty Images

WHERE TO GO FOR HELP

On Campus

The majority of colleges and university campuses take an active role in promoting diversity on their campuses. In the effort to ensure a welcoming and supportive environment for all students, institutions have established offices, centers, and resources to provide students with educational opportunities, academic guidance, and support networks. Look into the availability of the following resources on your campus, and visit one or more:

Office of Student Affairs

Office of Diversity

Multicultural Centers

Women's and Men's Centers

Lesbian, Gay, Bisexual, and Transgendered Student Alliances

Centers for Students with Disabilities

Academic support programs for underrepresented groups

Online

Student Now Diversity Resources: **www. studentnow. com/collegelist/diversity.html**. A list of campus diversity resources.

Diversity Web: **www.diversityweb.org**. More resources related to diversity on campus.

Tolerance.org: **www.tolerance.org**. This website, a project of the Southern Poverty Law Center, provides numerous resources about dealing with discrimination and prejudice both on and off campus.

My Institution's Resources

_____

_____

_____

_____

_____

the Flamenco Club, and the Video Gamer's Society. Students can cultivate an interest in bird watching or indulge their curiosity of ballroom dance without ever leaving campus. Many of these clubs will sponsor campus events highlighting their specific interests and talents so that you can check them out. If a club is not available, create it yourself. Involvement helps you gain valuable knowledge, expand your exposure to new ideas, make valuable contacts, and create a support network. Not all learning occurs in the classroom. Being involved enhances your college experience.

Discrimination, Prejudice, and Insensitivity on College Campuses

You might feel uncomfortable when asked about your views of diversity. To be honest, we all house **biases** against certain groups or value systems. Yet it is what we do with our individual beliefs that separates the average person from the racist, the bigot, and the extremist.

Unfortunately, some individuals opt not to seek education for the common good but instead to respond negatively to groups that differ from their own. Documented acts of **discrimination** and **prejudice** on campuses span the country. You might be shocked to hear that these acts of violence, intimidation, and stupidity occur on campuses, where the assumption is that college students are "supposed to be above that."

At a Midwestern university, students arrived on campus to find racial slurs and demeaning images aimed at various ethnic groups spray painted on the walls of the Multicultural Center. In the wake of the terrorist attack on the World Trade Center, many students of Middle Eastern descent were subjected to both violence and intimidation because of their ancestry.

While actions like these are deliberate and hateful, others occur out of a lack of common sense. Consider a campus party intended to celebrate Cinco de Mayo. Party organizers asked everyone to wear *sombreros*. On arrival, guests encountered a mock-up of a border patrol station on the front lawn and were required to crawl under or climb over a section of chain-link fencing. Student groups voiced their disapproval over such insensitivity, which resulted in campus probationary measures for the organization throwing the party. At a Halloween party at a large university, members of a campus organization decided to dress in Ku Klux Klan outfits, while other members dressed as slaves and wore black shoe polish on their faces. The group then simulated slave hangings during the party. When photos of the events surfaced, the university suspended the group from campus, while the community demanded that the group be banned indefinitely.

Write • DISCUSS • Compare • Ask • BLOG • Answer • *Journal*

> Have you ever witnessed or been a victim of harassment based on your gender, race, regional identity, religion, or ethnic group? What can colleges and universities do to reduce the incidence of harassment?

Stereotypes used to identify a school and its sports teams have disturbed ethnic and cultural groups such as Native Americans for a number of years. Mascots incorporating the bow and arrow, the tomahawk, feathers, and war paint have raised awareness about the promotion and acceptance of stereotypes associated with the "savage Indian." Some schools have responded by altering the images while retaining the mascot. Other schools have changed their mascots altogether.

Colleges and universities are working to ensure that a welcoming and inclusive campus environment awaits all students, both current and prospective. Campus resources and centers focus on providing support to and acknowledgment of the diverse student population. Campus administrations have established policies against any and all forms of discriminatory actions, racism, and insensitivity, and many campuses have adopted zero-tolerance policies in order to prohibit verbal and nonverbal harassment, intimidation, and violence. You are encouraged to find out what resources are available on your campus to protect you and other students from discriminatory and racist behavior. You might also want to find out what steps your college or university takes to promote the understanding of diversity and multiculturalism. If you've been a victim of a racist, insensitive, or discriminatory act, report it to the proper authorities.

What You Can Do to Fight Hate on Campus

Hate crimes, regardless of where they occur, should be taken very seriously. A hate crime is any prejudicial activity and can include physical assault, vandalism, and intimidation. One of the most common forms of hate crime on campus is graffiti that expresses racial, ethnic, and cultural slurs. Other incidents on campus have taken more direct and violent forms, such as reported assaults on students of Middle Eastern descent following the terrorist attacks on September 11, 2001.

Whatever form these crimes take on your campus, it is important for you to assess your thoughts and feelings about their occurrence. The most important question to ask yourself is: Will you do something or do you think it is someone else's problem? If you or a group that you belong to is the target of the hate crime, you might feel compelled to take a stand and speak out against the incident. But what if the target is not a group you associate with? Will you feel strongly enough to express your discontent with the actions taken? Or will you feel that it is only the problem of the targeted group?

Many students, whether or not they were directly targeted in a hate crime, find strength in unity, forming action committees and making it clear that hate crimes will not be ignored or tolerated. In most cases, instead of dividing students, hate crimes bring student groups together to work toward denouncing hate. It is important not to respond to prejudice and hate crimes with violence. It is more effective to unite with fellow students, faculty, staff, campus police, and administrators to address the issue and educate the greater campus community.

How can you get involved? Work with existing campus services such as the campus police and the Multicultural Center as well as faculty and administration to plan and host educational opportunities, such as trainings, workshops, and symposiums centered on diversity, sensitivity, and multiculturalism. Have an antidiscrimination event on campus in which campus and community leaders address the issues and provide solutions. Join prevention programs to come up with ideas to battle hate crimes on campus or in the community. Finally, look into the antidiscrimination measures your college is employing and decide if they need updating or revision.

Just because you or your particular group has not been targeted in a hate crime does not mean that you should do nothing. Challenge yourself to become involved in making your campus a safe place for students with diverse views, lifestyles, languages, politics, religions, and interests to come together and learn. If nothing happens to make it known that hate crimes on campus will not be tolerated, it is anyone's guess as to who will be the next target.

Challenge Yourself to Experience Diversity

Diversity enriches us all. Allowing yourself to become more culturally aware and open to differing views will help you become a truly educated person. Understanding the value of working with others and the importance of an open mind will enhance your educational and career goals and provide gratifying experiences, both on and off campus. Making the decision to become active in your multicultural education is just

◀ **Service activities provide a great way to meet different people.**

© Mark Richards/PhotoEdit

that, a decision—one that will require you to be active and to sometimes step out of your comfort zone. There are many ways for you to become more culturally aware, with a variety of opportunities on your campus. Look into what cultural programming is being offered throughout the school year. From concerts to films, guest speakers to information tables, you might not have to go far to gain insight into diversity.

Challenge yourself to learn about various groups in and around your community, at both school and home. These two settings might differ ethnically and culturally, giving you an opportunity to develop the skills needed to function in and adjust to a variety of settings. Attend events and celebrations outside of your regular groups. Whether they are in the general community or on campus, this is a good way to see and hear traditions specific to the groups represented. Being exposed to new experiences through events and celebrations can be gratifying. You can also become active in your own learning by making time for travel. Seeing the world and its people can be an uplifting experience. And finally, when in doubt, ask. If done in a tactful, genuine way, the majority of people will be happy to share information about viewpoints, traditions, and history. It is only through allowing ourselves to grow that we really learn.

▶▶▶ BUILDING YOUR PORTFOLIO
It's a Small World After All!

Studying abroad in Granada, Spain, was a digestive process. The world swallowed me whole. It stripped me of everything I once knew and assumed, and spit me out. The outcome wasn't a whole new person, it was an open slate in which everything I now see and hear is digested in a whole new manner that can't be explained but only experienced by traveling abroad.

-Julie Santos, student, Global & International Studies Program,
University of California, Santa Barbara

To complete this portfolio activity electronically, please visit
academic.cengage.com/collsucc/Gardner/YCE8e.

Diversity, ethnicity, culture, and multiculturalism are terms that were explored in chapter 13. Reading about these engaging and sometimes controversial topics is one thing, but really stepping into someone else's shoes is another. Study abroad and student exchange programs are an excellent (and fun) way of adding new perspectives to your college experience. What better way of learning about other parts of the world than immersing yourself in a foreign culture, language, and people!

Consider the possibilities. . .

1. Create a new entry in your portfolio with the title "A Small World." Record your work for this assignment there.

2. Visit your institution's International Programs/Study Abroad office, or if you are at a college that does not have a study abroad program, search for study abroad opportunities on the web.

   Tip: Look for The Center for Global Education (www.lmu.edu/globaled/index.html) *or the Council on International Education Exchange* (ciee.org/study.aspx).

3. Using a major or career that you selected or are interested in, think about how you would like to spend a summer, semester, or year abroad to learn more about or gain experience in your major field.

4. Based on your research, create a PowerPoint presentation to share with your class, outlining the opportunities to study abroad or participate in an exchange program.

   a. Describe the steps students need to take at your campus to include a study abroad trip in their college plan (e.g., who to contact, financial aid, the best time to study abroad, earning course credit, etc).

   b. Describe the benefits of study abroad (e.g., observing different cultures, good résumé builder).

   c. Include photos of the country or countries you would like to visit.

   d. Include information about your current or intended major and career and how a study abroad or exchange trip would fit into your plans.

   e. Reference web links you found useful in preparing your presentation.

5. Attach your PowerPoint presentation to your portfolio entry.

Staying Healthy

In this chapter YOU WILL LEARN

▶ The importance of managing stress

▶ Warning signs of depression

▶ Strategies for better nutrition and weight management

▶ The many options you have for contraception and safer sex

▶ The realities of alcohol use on campus

▶ The consequences of abusing alcohol, tobacco, and drugs

What choices have you made today to stay healthy?

© Kevin Dodge/Masterfile

Michelle Murphy Burcin of the University of South Carolina at Columbia
contributed her valuable and considerable expertise to the writing of this chapter.

How Do You STAY HEALTHY?

A?B?C?A?B?C?A?B?C?

Check the items below that apply to you or that you believe are important for college success.

1 *When you feel overwhelmed, what are the first steps you take to deal with your stress?*

(A) I usually crawl into bed, sleep for a long while, and try to ignore everything.

(B) I will try to talk to my friends and family, but that only helps sometimes—I guess I need to find a better way to deal with things.

(C) I'll exercise or find another way to relax—this helps me to think up a strategy to deal with my stress.

2 *How are you going to maintain your physical health while in college?*

(A) I've already paid for my food through my tuition—I'm going to eat all that I can while I'm here.

(B) I used to participate in sports before college, but I'm a little intimidated to try out while in college.

(C) I'll make sure to stay away from too much junk food, and I'll keep up with my regular exercise routine because it makes me feel good about myself.

3 *Do you think you have to drink alcohol in order to have fun?*

(A) Of course—college parties are all about drinking.

(B) Usually the parties I go to are a good time, and alcohol is there, but I'm not always drinking.

(C) There are lots of ways to have fun, and alcohol is definitely not the only way.

4 *If you have a question about sex, where can you go on your campus for answers?*

(A) I'm really too embarrassed to ask any questions about sex. That's way too personal.

(B) I'd probably go to the Internet. There are lots of sites that give answers to questions about sex.

(C) I would either go to my campus health center or the counseling office. I guess it would depend on what kind of question I have, but one of these places is probably the best source for answers.

Review your answers. (A) responses indicate that you might not be prepared to make the best decisions about your health. (B) responses indicate that you have some good ideas, but need to think more about how to be healthy in college. (C) responses mean that you have thought a lot about your health and take it seriously. But no matter how you responded—and even if you think you've heard it all before—this chapter will introduce you to new information and new strategies about health in college and in life.

College is a great time to explore. It's an opportunity to exercise your mind and expand your horizons. Unfortunately for too many students, it becomes an opportunity to stop exercising the body and begin expanding the waistline! Because the college environment might be new to you, you could forget to take care of yourself.

Most students can handle the transition to college easily using various coping mechanisms. Others drink too much or smoke too much. Some overeat or develop an eating disorder like bulimia or anorexia. Some become so stressed that their anxiety overwhelms them. Some ignore their sexual health and then have to face a sexually transmitted infection or an unplanned pregnancy.

This chapter explores the topic of **wellness**, which is a catchall term for taking care of your mind, body, and spirit. Wellness means making healthy choices and achieving balance. Wellness includes reducing stress, keeping fit, maintaining sexual health, and taking a sensible approach to alcohol and other drugs.

Stress

In 2006, 32 percent of college students reported stress as the number one impediment to their academic performance, according to the American College Health Association.[1] When you are stressed, your body undergoes rapid physiological, behavioral, and emotional changes. Your rate of breathing can become more rapid and shallow. Your heart rate begins to speed up, and the muscles in your shoulders and forehead, the back of your neck, and perhaps across your chest begin to tighten. Your hands might become cold and/or sweaty. You might experience disturbances in your gastrointestinal system, such as a "butterfly" stomach, diarrhea, or constipation. Your mouth and lips might feel dry and hot, and you might notice that your hands and knees begin to shake or tremble. Your voice might quiver or even go up an octave.

A number of psychological changes also occur when you are under stress. You might experience changes in your ability to think, such as confusion, trouble concentrating, inability to remember things, and poor problem solving. Emotions such as fear, anxiety, depression, irritability, anger, or frustration are common, and you might have insomnia or wake up too early and not be able to go back to sleep.

Write • DISCUSS • Compare • Ask • BLOG • Answer • *Journal*

> How do you feel when you are stressed, both physically and mentally? What specific changes do you notice about your behavior and feelings? How does stress affect your ability to concentrate, your breathing patterns, your patience, and so on?

Stress has many sources, but two seem to be prominent: life events and daily hassles. Life events are those that represent major adversity, such as the death of a parent, spouse, partner, or friend. Researchers believe that an accumulation of stress from life events, especially if many events occur over a short period of time, can cause physical and mental health problems.

The College Readjustment Rating Scale is a life-events scale designed especially for traditional college students. Complete the scale here. If you find that your score is 150 or higher, you have experienced a great deal of stress over the past year. You might consider what help you need or skills you must learn to be able to cope effectively.

The College Readjustment Rating Scale is an adaptation of Holmes and Rahe's Life Events Scale. It has been modified for traditional-age college students and should be considered a rough indication of stress levels and possible health consequences. On this scale, each event, such as one's first term in college, is assigned a value that represents the amount of readjustment a person has to make in life as a result of change. In some studies, people with serious illnesses have been found to have high

---

[1] "American College Health Association National College Health Assessment Spring 2006 Reference Group Data Report," *Journal of American College Health,* Vol. 55, No. 4 January/February 2007.

scores on similar scales. Persons with scores of 300 and higher have a high health risk. Persons scoring between 150 and 300 points have about a 50–50 chance of a serious health change within two years. Subjects scoring 150 and below have a 1 in 3 chance of a serious health change.

To determine your stress score, circle the number of points corresponding to the events you have experienced in the past six months or are likely to experience in the next six months. Then add up the circled numbers.

Event	Points
Death of spouse	100
Pregnancy for unwed female	92
Death of parent	80
Male partner in unwed pregnancy	77
Divorce	73
Death of a close family member	70
Death of a close friend	65
Divorce between parents	63
Jail term	61
Major personal injury or illness	60
Flunked out of college	58
Marriage	55
Fired from job	50
Loss of financial support for college (scholarship)	48
Failing grade in important or required course	47
Sexual difficulties	45
Serious argument with significant other	40
Academic probation	39
Change in major	37
New love interest	36
Increased workload in college	31
Outstanding personal achievement	29
First term in college	28
Serious conflict with instructor	27
Lower grades than expected	25
Change in colleges (transfer)	24
Change in social activities	22
Change in sleeping habits	21
Change in eating habits	19
Minor violation of the law (for example, a traffic ticket)	15

WIRED WINDOW

IT'S CALLED "INTERNET ADDICTION" and researchers have discovered that problems arising from Internet use have more to do with *how people use* rather than *how much time they spend* on the Internet. College students who use the Internet for communicating with others are less likely to be addicted than those who use the Internet for shopping, reading news, and checking sports scores. Communicating via the Internet might allow introverted students to make friends more easily. Students who are more engaged in their studies and in campus life tend to be more successful in college. Yet students who use the Internet extensively tend to have less time for real world social contacts. How do you use the Internet? For this week, keep a record of how much time you spend online and how much time you spend on each of the following activities: Instant Messaging, Facebook, MySpace, e-mail, reading news, shopping, checking sports scores, playing multiplayer games, and/or playing single-player games. How much time did you spend online? How did you spend most of your time online? If you found that you are online more for shopping, reading news, checking sports scores, and/or playing single-player games, do you have strong relationships with friends outside of the wired world? If you didn't like what you discovered, you might want to talk to a counselor at your college to help you manage your Internet activities.

If your score indicates potential health problems, it would be to your benefit to seriously review the stress inoculation and management techniques discussed in this chapter and select and implement some strategies to reduce your stress.[2]

Daily hassles are the minor irritants that we experience every day, such as losing your keys, dropping your soft drink, having three tests on the same day, quarreling with your roommate, or worrying about money.

Managing Stress

The best starting point for handling stress is to be in good physical and mental shape. When your body and mind are healthy, it's like inoculating yourself against stress. This means you need to pay attention to diet, exercise, sleep, and mental health.

Diet and Stress

There is a clear connection between what you eat and drink, your overall health and well-being, and stress. Eating a lot of junk food will add pounds to your body and reduce your energy level. And when you can't keep up with your work because you're sluggish or tired, you might experience more stress. But there is one dietary substance that can be directly linked to higher stress levels, and that is caffeine.

In moderate amounts (50–200 milligrams per day), caffeine increases alertness and reduces feelings of fatigue, but even at this low dosage it might make you perkier during part of the day and more tired later. Consumed in larger quantities, however, caffeine can cause nervousness, headaches, irritability, stomach irritation, and insomnia—all symptoms of stress. Many heart patients have been told to avoid caffeine

[2] Adapted with permission from T. H. Holmes and R. H. Rahe, "The Social Readjustment Scale," in Carol L. Otis and Roger Goldingay, *Campus Health Guide* (New York: CEEB, 1989).

since it tends to speed up heart rates. How much caffeine do you consume? Total your caffeine intake based on these figures:

Product	Caffeine Content (mg per serving)
Coffee (5 oz. cup)	
Regular	65–115
Decaffeinated	3
Tea (6 oz. cup)	
Hot steeped	36
Iced	31
Soft drinks and energy drinks (12 oz. serving)	
Bawls	80
Coca-Cola	46
Dr. Pepper	61
Full Throttle (16 oz)	144
Jolt Cola	72
Mountain Dew	54
Pepsi-Cola	36
Red Bull	80
Water Joe (16.9 oz.)	115
Chocolate bar	6–20
Caffeine gum (2 pieces)	115
Over-the-counter drugs	
NoDoz (2 tablets)	200
Excedrin (2 tablets)	130
Midol (2 tablets)	65

If the amount is excessive (this will vary with individuals; monitor such things as inability to sleep, high-energy mornings with tired afternoons, and so forth), think about drinking water in place of caffeinated drinks, or choose the decaf version of coffee or the soft drink you like.

Exercise and Stress

Exercise is an excellent stress management technique, the best way to stay fit, and a critical part of weight loss. While any kind of recreation benefits your body and spirit, aerobic exercise is the best for stress management as well as weight management. In aerobic exercise, you work until your pulse is in a "target zone" and keep it in this zone for at least 30 minutes. You can reach your target heart rate through a variety of exercises: walking, jogging, running, swimming, biking, or using a stair climber. What makes the exercise aerobic is the intensity of your activity. Choose activities that you enjoy so you will look forward to your exercise time. That way, it's more likely to become a regular part of your routine.

Calculating Your Target Heart Rate Zone

1. Estimate your maximum heart rate:

220 − age = _____ (maximum heart rate)

2. Determine your lower-limit exercise heart rate by multiplying your maximum heart rate by 0.6.

Max Heart Rate × 0.6 =

3. Determine your upper-limit exercise heart rate by multiplying your maximum heart rate by 0.9.

Max Heart Rate × 0.9 =

4. Your Target Heart Rate Zone is the range between your lower and upper limits.

Source: *American College of Sports Medicine Fitness Book: A Proven Step-by-Step Program for Experts.* 3rd edition.

Besides doing wonders for your body, aerobic exercise also keeps your mind healthy. When you do aerobic exercise, your body produces hormones called beta endorphins. These natural narcotics cause feelings of contentment and happiness and help manage anxiety and depression. Your mood and general sense of competence improve with regular aerobic exercise. In fact, people who undertake aerobic exercise report more energy, less stress, better sleep, weight loss, and an improved self-image.

Think about ways you can combine activities and use your time efficiently. Maybe you could leave the car at home and jog to class. Go to the gym with a friend

◀ **Intense aerobic activity will help you manage weight and stress.**

and ask each other study questions as you work out on treadmills. Park at the far end of the lot and walk to classes or take the stairs whenever possible. Remember, exercise does not have to be a chore. Find something you enjoy doing and make it part of your daily schedule. Many campuses have recreation departments that offer activities such as intramural sports, rock climbing, aerobics classes, and much more. The most important thing about exercise is that you stay active and make it part of your day-to-day life.

Sleep and Stress

Getting adequate sleep is another way to protect yourself from stress. According to the National Sleep Foundation, 63 percent of American adults do not get the recommended eight hours of sleep per night. Lack of sleep can lead to anxiety, depression, and academic struggles. Researchers at Trent University in Ontario found that students who studied all week but then stayed up late partying on the weekends forgot as much as 30 percent of the material they had learned during the prior week. Try out the following suggestions to establish better sleep habits:

- If you can't sleep, get up and do something boring.
- Get your clothes and/or school materials together before you go to bed.
- Avoid long daytime naps.
- Try reading or listening to a relaxation tape before going to bed.
- Get exercise during the day.
- Sleep in the same room and bed every night.
- Set a regular schedule for going to bed and getting up.

Modifying Your Lifestyle

Modifying your lifestyle is yet another approach to stress management. You have the power to change your life so that it is less stressful. Teachers, supervisors, parents, friends, and even your children influence you, but ultimately you control how you run your life. Lifestyle modification involves identifying the parts of your life that do not serve you well and making plans for change. For instance, if you are stressed because you are always late for classes, get up 10 minutes earlier. If you get nervous before a test when you talk to a certain classmate, avoid that person before a test. Learn test-taking skills so you can manage test anxiety better.

Relaxation Techniques

Relaxation techniques such as visualization and deep breathing can help you reduce stress. Learning these skills is just like learning any new skill. You need knowledge and practice. Check your course catalog, college counseling center, health clinic, student newspaper, or fitness center for classes that teach relaxation. You'll find books as well as audio tapes and CDs that guide you through relaxation techniques.

Confessions of a College Student

Name: Matt Malanuk

Age: 19

College: Farmingdale State College

Hometown: Nanuet, NY

Major: Construction Management

Favorite college course: English

The people who inspire me most or who I would most like to meet: Bob Vila and Tiger Woods

Heroes: My father and my high school basketball coach

Favorite way to relax: Play a round of golf or go to the driving range with my buddies

Are you the first to go to college in your family? No, my parents and siblings were very helpful to me because they have already been down this road.

Your proudest moment or biggest accomplishment: Graduating high school

Favorite food: Ice cream

Staying healthy confession: Before attending college, I usually went to bed around 10:30 pm. Now that I live in a college dormitory, I tend to stay up until 1 am. Unlike the people hooting and hollering in the middle of the night, I have classes every morning. It has been a tough transition, especially since I will have to wake up every day this summer at 7:30 am.

I was always a big eater, and although I have gained weight in college, playing basketball has kept me in shape, for the most part. Now I am trying to shed some of those pounds. For example, I don't drink soda at all. And now when I get hungry, instead of reaching for a greasy bag of chips, I eat a banana or an apple instead. I also go on 2-mile runs now that the basketball season is over.

Other Ways to Relieve Stress

Your mental health plays a key role in your overall level of stress. Here are several things you can do to improve your mental health:

▶ Reward yourself on a regular basis when you achieve small goals.

▶ Remember that there is a reason you are in a particular situation. Keep the payoff in mind.

▶ Laugh. A good laugh will almost always make you feel better.

▶ Get—or give—a hug.

▶ Pray or meditate.

▶ Do yoga.

▶ Practice a hobby.

▶ Purchase a pet.

▶ Get a massage.

▶ Say "stop!" to yourself whenever things get too intense.

▶ Practice deep breathing.

Write • DISCUSS • Compare • Ask • BLOG • Answer • Journal

Review the preceding list of ways to improve your mental health.
Which of these ideas do you think makes the most sense for you?
Based on your experience, which ideas would you suggest to other
college students? Explain your choices.

Depression

According to the American Psychological Association, depression is one of the most common psychiatric disorders in the United States, affecting more than 15 million adults. The National Institutes of Health report that depression is twice as common in women as in men. Depression is not a weakness; it is an illness that requires medical attention. You will find that many college students suffer from some form of depression. Often these feelings are temporary and may be situational. A romantic breakup, a disappointing grade, or an ongoing conflict with a friend or roommate might create feelings of despair. While most depression goes away on its own, if you or a friend have any of the following symptoms for more than two weeks, it is important to talk to a health care provider:

▶ Feelings of helplessness and hopelessness

▶ Feeling useless, inadequate, bad, and guilty

▶ Self-hatred, constant questioning of thoughts and actions

▶ **Seek help for depression by talking with a counselor.**

© Mug Shots/CORBIS

▶ Loss of energy and motivation

▶ Weight loss or gain

▶ Difficulty going to sleep or excess need for sleep

▶ Loss of interest in sex

▶ Difficulty concentrating for a length of time

Suicide

College students are at especially high risk for suicide as well as depression. The Centers for Disease Control and Prevention (CDC) report that students ages 15 to 24 are more likely than any other age group to attempt suicide. Most people who commit suicide give a warning of their intentions. The following are common signs of possible suicide:

▶ Recent loss and a seeming inability to let go of grief

▶ Change in personality—sadness, withdrawal, apathy

▶ Expressions of self-hatred

▶ Change in sleep patterns

▶ Change in eating habits

▶ A direct statement about committing suicide ("I might as well end it all.")

▶ A preoccupation with death

If you or someone you know threatens suicide or displays any of these signs, it's time to consult a mental health professional. Most campuses have counseling centers that offer one-on-one sessions as well as support groups for their students. Finally, remember there is no shame attached to high levels of stress or other anxiety-related issues. Proper counseling, medical attention, and, in some cases, prescription medication can help students cope with stress.

Write • DISCUSS • Compare • Ask • BLOG • Answer • *Journal*

> Why do you think that college students are at especially high risk for depression and suicide? Is there anything that colleges and universities can do to decrease this risk, or is this all up to the students themselves?

Nutrition and Weight Management

"You are what you eat" is more than a catchphrase; it's an important reminder of the vital role diet plays in our lives. You've probably read news stories about how there are more and more obese young people than ever before in our history. The CDC reports that the rates of obesity have more than doubled in the U.S. since 1990: in 1990, an estimated 11.6 percent of U.S. citizens were obese; in 2004, an estimated 24.5 percent were classified as obese. One expert, Dr. James Hill, Director of Human Nutrition at the University of Colorado, predicts that, "If obesity is left unchecked, almost all Americans will be obese by 2050." Many attribute this to the explosion of fast food restaurants, which place "flavor and filling" before health. A Tufts University researcher found that 60 percent of college students eat too much saturated fat, which increases the risk for heart disease. Also, most of us do not consume sufficient amounts of fiber and whole grains. As a result, we are more likely to have long-term health problems, such as diabetes, heart disease, and cancer.

So what to do? It's not easy at first, but if you commit to a new eating regime, you will not only feel better, you'll be healthier . . . and probably happier. Your campus might have a registered dietitian available to help you make healthy changes in your diet. Check with your student health center. Meanwhile, here are some suggestions:

▶ Restrict your intake of red meat, real butter, white rice, white bread, and sweets. "White foods" are made with refined flour, which has few nutrients. Instead, go for fish, poultry, soy products, and whole-wheat or multigrain breads. And remember that brown bread is not necessarily whole wheat.

▶ Eat plenty of vegetables and fruits daily. These are important building blocks for a balanced diet, and they contain lots of fiber (to help fight off cancer and heart disease). Instead of fruit juices, which contain concentrated amounts of sugar, opt for the actual fruit instead. When you sit down to eat any meal (including breakfast), make sure you have at least one fruit and/or vegetable on your plate.

▶ Avoid fried foods—french fries, fried chicken, and so forth. Choose grilled meats instead. Avoid foods with large amounts of sugar, such as donuts.

▶ Keep your room stocked with healthy snacks, such as fruit, vegetables, yogurt, pretzels, and graham crackers.

▶ Eat a sensible amount of nuts and all the legumes (beans) you want to round out your fiber intake.

▶ Watch your portion size. Avoid "super-sized" fast-food items and "all-you-can-eat" buffets.

▶ Eat breakfast! Your brain will function at a more efficient level with a power-packed meal first thing in the morning. Eating breakfast can also jump-start your metabolism. If you are not normally a breakfast eater, try eating just a piece of fruit or half of a bagel. You will notice a big difference in your energy level during your early morning classes. Watch out for sugar-coated cereals. Go for healthier options that are loaded with fiber. *The New York Times* reported in 2004 that many college students are eating cereal for more than just breakfast. In fact, cereal-themed restaurants are opening near some campuses. If you have cereal for lunch or dinner, remember that you need to balance the rest of your day with nutrient-packed foods.

▶ Always read the government-required nutrition label on all packaged foods. Check sodium content (sodium will make you retain fluids and increase your weight) and the number of fat grams. Strive for a diet with only 20 percent fat.

Figure 14.1 shows the Healthy Eating Pyramid, designed by Walter Willett, Chairman of the Department of Nutrition at Harvard's School of Public Health. The

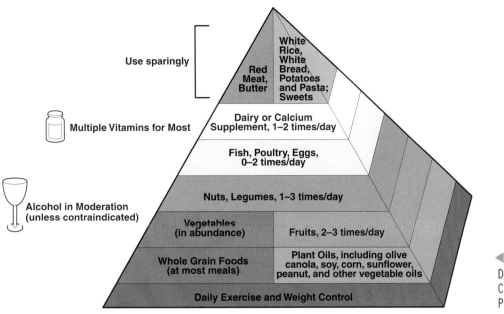

◀ **Figure 14.1**
Daily Exercise and Weight Control Healthy Eating Pyramid

Healthy Eating Pyramid puts exercise and weight control at the base, recommends eating whole-grain foods at most meals, and encourages eating vegetables "in abundance." This pyramid emphasizes eating lots of plant oils, like olive, canola and soy, and gives fish and poultry a higher profile than red meat, which you should eat sparingly.

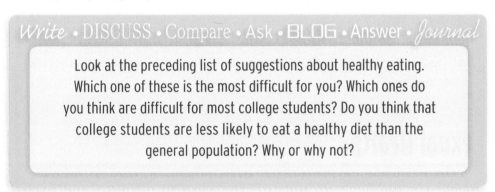

Write • DISCUSS • Compare • Ask • BLOG • Answer • *Journal*

Look at the preceding list of suggestions about healthy eating. Which one of these is the most difficult for you? Which ones do you think are difficult for most college students? Do you think that college students are less likely to eat a healthy diet than the general population? Why or why not?

Obesity

People have been joking about the "freshman 15" forever, but it's no joke that new college students tend to gain weight during their first term. Nutrition experts at Tufts University reported that the average weight gain is 6 pounds for men and about 4.5 pounds for women during the first year of college. Increased stress, lifestyle changes, new food choices, changes in physical activity, and alcohol consumption can all cause weight gain. Try eating smaller meals more often, getting regular exercise, keeping a food journal (to keep track of what you are actually consuming), and being realistic about dieting.

Eating Disorders

An increasing number of college students are obsessed with their body and food intake. This obsession can lead to conditions such as anorexia, bulimia, or binge eating disorder, all of which affect women disproportionately to men. Anorexia is characterized by self-induced starvation, extreme preoccupation with food, and a body weight less than 85 percent of the healthy weight. Bulimia is characterized by cycles of bingeing (eating large amounts of food) and purging by vomiting, abusing laxatives and/or diuretics, exercising excessively, and fasting. People with a binge eating disorder do not purge the calories after the binge. Individuals with binge eating disorder tend to eat secretively and are often clinically obese.

Some of the signs and symptoms of an eating disorder are:

▶ Intense fear of gaining weight

▶ Restricting food or types of food, such as food containing any kind of fat

▶ Weighing less than 85 percent of recommended body weight based on height or failure to make appropriate weight gain for a period of growth

▶ Stopping or never getting a monthly menstrual period

▶ Seeing one's body as fat, even though it is underweight

▶ Overexercising

▶ Secrecy around food and denial of a problem with eating

Anyone who is struggling with an eating disorder should seek medical attention. Eating disorders can be life-threatening if they are not treated by a health care professional. Many colleges and universities have eating disorder case management teams to help individuals on their campus. Contact your student health center for more information, or contact the National Eating Disorder Association (**www.nationaleatingdisorders. org** or 1-800-931-2237) to find a professional in your area who specializes in eating disorder treatment.

Sexual Health

Numerous studies report that about 75 percent of traditional-age college students have engaged in sexual intercourse at least once.

Regardless of whether you are part of this percentage, it can be helpful to explore your sexual values and to consider whether sex is right for you at this time. If it is the right time and you do not wish to become pregnant or impregnate someone, you should choose a birth control method and adopt some strategies for avoiding sexually transmitted infections (STIs). What matters most is that you take care of yourself and your partner.

Negotiating for Safer Sex

If you are sexually active, it's important that you talk with your partner about ways to protect against sexually transmitted infections and unwanted pregnancy. Communicating with your partner about safer sex can be difficult and even embarrassing initially, but this communication can make your relationship stronger and more meaningful. The national organization Advocates for Youth offers these suggestions to help make this conversation easier and more effective.

◀ **Sex includes communication.**

▶ Use "I" statements when talking. For example, "I feel that abstinence is right for me at this time." Or, "I would feel more comfortable if we used a condom."

▶ Be assertive! Do not avoid talking about sex because you fear your partner's reaction.

▶ Be a good listener. Let your partner know that you hear, understand, and care about what she or he is saying and feeling.

▶ Be patient with your partner, and remain firm in your decision that talking is important.

▶ Understand that success in talking does not mean getting a partner to agree to do something. It means that you both have said what you honestly think and feel and that you have both listened respectfully to one another.

▶ Avoid making assumptions. Ask open-ended questions to discuss relationship expectations, past and present sexual relationships, contraceptive use, and testing for STIs.

▶ Do not wait until you become sexually intimate to discuss safer sex with your partner. In the heat of the moment, you and your partner might be unable to talk effectively.

Sexually Transmitted Infections

The problem of STIs on college campuses has received growing attention in recent years as epidemic numbers of students have become infected. In general, STIs continue to increase faster than other illnesses on campuses today, and approximately 5 to 10 percent of visits by U.S. college students to college health services are for the diagnosis and treatment of STIs. The belief that it won't happen to you and you can't catch these sorts of infections is inaccurate and potentially more dangerous than ever before. If you choose to be sexually active, particularly with more than one partner, exposure to an STI is a real possibility.

Table 14.1   Sexually Transmitted Infections

SEXUALLY TRANSMITTED INFECTION	FEMALE SYMPTOMS	MALE SYMPTOMS	NUMBER OF NEW CASES IN THE UNITED STATES ANNUALLY	CURABLE OR TREATABLE
AIDS(Acquired immunodeficiency syndrome)	Symptoms appear several months to several years after contact with HIV; unexplained weight loss; white spots in mouth; yeast infections that do not go away	Symptoms appear several months to several years after contact with HIV; unexplained weight loss; white spots in mouth	40,000	Treatable
Chlamydia	Yellowish discharge; bleeding between periods; burning or pain during urination	Painful and frequent urination; watery, puslike discharge from penis	3 million	Curable
Genital HPV (Human Papillomavirus)	Small, bumpy warts on the sex organs and/or anus; burning or itching around sex organs	Small, bumpy warts on the sex organs and/or anus; burning or itching around sex organs	5.5 million	Treatable
Gonorrhea	Thick yellow or gray discharge; abnormal periods or bleeding between periods; cramps or pain in lower abdomen	White, milky discharge from penis; painful, burning urination; swollen or tender testicles	800,000	Curable
Hepatitis B	Symptoms appear 1–9 months after contraction; flulike feelings that go away; tiredness; dark urine	Symptoms appear 1–9 months after contraction; flulike feelings that go away; tiredness; dark urine	120,000	Treatable
Herpes	Burning sensation and redness at the site of infection; painful blister that will crust over, dry up, and disappear	Burning sensation and redness at the site of infection; painful blister that will crust over, dry up, and disappear	1 million	Treatable
Syphilis	Painless chancre; rash or white patches on skin; lymph nodes enlarge	Painless chancre; rash or white patches on skin; lymph nodes enlarge	70,000	Curable in early stages
Trichomoniasis	Yellowish, unpleasant-smelling discharge accompanied by a burning sensation during urination	Watery, white drip from the penis; burning or pain during urination; need to urinate more often	5 million	Curable

Adapted from www.plannedparenthood.org and www.ashastd.org

Sources: Rebecca J. Donatelle and Larraine G. Davis, *Access To Health, 8th ed.* (San Francisco: Benjamin Cummings, 2004); Linda L. Alexander, et al., *New Dimensions in Women's Health, 3rd ed.* (Sudbury, MA: Jones and Bartlett, 2004).

STIs are usually spread through genital contact. Sometimes, however, STIs can be transmitted through mouth-to-mouth contact. There are more than 20 known types of STIs; Table 14.1 breaks down the most common on college campuses.

As you can see from the table, many of the sexually transmitted infections have similar symptoms or no symptoms at all. Many women show no symptoms and are therefore considered "asymptomatic." Most health care professionals recommend that women who are sexually active be screened for all of the possible STIs during their yearly pap smear. These screenings are not part of the regular annual exam and must be specifically requested.

Not all STIs are curable. This means that medications will help alleviate the symptoms but the virus will stay in an individual's system. Sexually transmitted infections that are left untreated can progress to pelvic inflammatory disease (PID), which is now thought to be the leading cause of infertility in women.

One particularly common STI is the Human Papillomavirus (HPV). In fact, the Centers for Disease Control estimate that 20 million people in the U.S. had Human Papillomavirus (HPV) in 2005. HPV is a sexually transmitted infection closely linked to cervical cancer. Gardasil, a new vaccine on the market, provides protection against four types of HPV that cause 70 percent of cervical cancer cases. For more information about this vaccine or to receive the three injection series, contact your college or university health services or local health care provider.

Options for Safer Sex

You can avoid STIs and unwanted pregnancies by avoiding sex entirely. Apparently, 25 percent of college students choose this option, according to national research. For some people, masturbation is a reasonable alternative to sex with a partner.

If you're in the remaining 75 percent, you'll be safer (in terms of STIs) if you have only one partner. Yet, you might feel that you're at a point in your life where you would prefer to have multiple relationships simultaneously. But whether you're monogamous or not, you should always protect yourself by using a condom.

In addition to being a contraceptive, the condom can help prevent the spread of STIs, including HIV. The condom's effectiveness against disease holds true for anal, vaginal, and oral intercourse. The most current research indicates that the rate of protection provided by condoms against STIs is similar to its rate of protection against pregnancy (90–99 percent) when used correctly and consistently for each and every act of intercourse or oral sex. Note that only latex rubber condoms and polyurethane condoms—not lambskin or other types of "natural membrane" condoms—provide this protection. The polyurethane condom is a great alternative for individuals with latex allergies. Use only a water-based lubricant (such as KY Jelly) to keep the condom from breaking.

Birth Control

Sexually active heterosexual students have to plan to prevent an unwanted pregnancy. Planning is the key. What is the best method of contraception? It is any method that you use correctly and consistently each time you have intercourse. Table 14.2 compares the major features of some of the most common methods of birth control.

Always discuss birth control with your partner so that you both feel comfortable with the option you have selected. For more information about a particular method, consult a pharmacist, your student health center, a local family planning clinic, the local health department, or your private physician. The important thing is to resolve to protect yourself and your partner each and every time you have sexual intercourse.

What if the condom breaks or if you forget to take your birth control pill? Emergency contraception pills can reduce the risk of pregnancy if started within 72 hours after unprotected vaginal intercourse. According to Planned Parenthood Federation of America, if the pills are taken within 72 hours of unprotected intercourse, they can reduce the risk of pregnancy by 75 to 89 percent. Emergency contraception does come with side effects, such as nausea, vomiting, and cramping. In rare cases, serious health complications can result from emergency contraception. Be sure you ask your provider what symptoms to watch for. Most campus health centers and local health clinics are now dispensing emergency contraception to individuals in need.

Table 14.2 Methods of Contraception

METHOD	HOW EFFECTIVE IS THIS METHOD?	DOES IT PROTECT AGAINST HIV AND STIS?	AVERAGE COST	DO I NEED A PRESCRIPTION?
Abstinence	100%	Yes	Free	No
Cervical Cap	84%	No	$13–25	Yes
Contraceptive Injection	99%	No	$20–40 (visit to clinician); $30–75 (injection)	Yes
Diaphragm	94%	No	$13–25	Yes
Female Condom	95%	Yes	$2.50 per condom	No
Intrauterine Device (IUD)	99%	No	$175–400 (exam, insertion, and follow-up visit)	Yes
Male Condom	97%	Yes	$.50 and up per condom	No
Norplant	99%	No	$500–750 (exam, implants, and insertion); $100–200 (removal)	Yes
NuvaRing	99%	No	$30–35 monthly	Yes
Ortho Evra (The Patch)	99%	No	$30–35 monthly	Yes
Oral Contraceptive (The Pill)	99%	No	$15–35 monthly	Yes
Spermicide	94%	No	$4–8 per kit	No
Tubal Ligation (Female Sterilization)	99%	No	$1,000–2,500	Yes
Vasectomy (Male Sterilization)	99%	No	$240–520	Yes

Adapted from www.plannedparenthood.org

Source: Rebecca J. Donatelle and Larraine G. Davis, *Access To Health, 8th ed.* (San Francisco: Benjamin Cummings, 2004).

Making Decisions about Alcohol

Even if you don't drink, you should read this information because 50 percent of college students reported helping a drunken friend, classmate, or study partner in the past year. A number of surveys have confirmed that your peers aren't drinking as much as you think they are, so there's no need for you to try and "catch up." Most students who try to estimate college drinking are off by almost half. In the final analysis, it's your decision to drink or not to drink alcoholic beverages; to drink moderately or to drink heavily; to know when to stop or to be labeled as a drunk who isn't fun to be around. Between 10 and 20 percent of people in the United States become addicted to alcohol at some point in their lives. Alcohol can turn people into victims even though they don't drink, such as those killed by drunk drivers or family members who suffer from the behavior of an alcoholic. Over the course of one year, about 20 to 30 percent of students report serious problems related to excessive alcohol use. You might have heard news reports about college students who died or were seriously or permanently injured as a result of excessive drinking. Just one occasion of heavy or high-risk drinking can lead to problems.

Drinking and Blood Alcohol Content

How alcohol affects behavior depends on the dose of alcohol, which is best measured by blood alcohol content, or BAC (see Table 14.3). Most of the pleasurable effects of alcoholic beverages are experienced at lower BAC levels, when alcohol acts as a behavioral stimulant. For most people, the stimulant level is around one drink per hour. Usually, problems begin to emerge at doses higher than .05 when alcohol acts as a sedative and begins to slow down areas of the brain. Most people who have more than four or five drinks on one occasion feel "buzzed," show signs of impairment, and are likely to be higher risks for alcohol-related problems. However, significant impairment at lower doses can occur.

How fast you drink makes a difference, too. Your body gets rid of alcohol at a rate of about one drink an hour. Drinking more than one drink an hour might cause a rise in BAC because the body is absorbing alcohol faster than it can eliminate it.

Professionals can estimate BAC from your behavior. When someone is stopped for drunk driving, police might videotape the person completing a series of tasks such as walking on a line and tipping his or her head back, or touching the nose with eyes closed. The degree of impairment shown in these tests can be presented as evidence in court.

Alcohol and Behavior

At BAC levels of .025 to .05, a drinker tends to feel animated and energized. At a BAC level of around .05, a drinker can feel rowdy or boisterous. This is where most people report feeling a buzz from alcohol. At a BAC level between .05 and .08, alcohol starts to act as a depressant. So as soon as you feel that buzz, remember that you are on the brink of losing coordination, clear thinking, and judgment!

Driving is measurably impaired at BAC levels lower than the legal limit of .08. In fact, an accurate safe level for most people might be half the legal limit (.04). As BAC

Table 14.3   **Correlation of Blood Alcohol Content (BAC) with Behavior**

BAC RANGE	COMMON EFFECTS ON BEHAVIOR	MAJOR DANGERS
0.00 to 0.04	Increased energy, animation	No impairment
.05 to .08	Feeling a buzz; slowed reflexes	Four times the risk of auto accident*
.09 to .20	Impaired walking, poor social judgment, slurred speech, nausea, fighting, vandalism, sexual aggression, blackout	25 times the risk of auto accident*; risk of indiscriminate sex
.20 to .30	Vomiting, stupor, passing out	Death from suffocation or choking on vomit
.31 to .45	Coma, shock from alcohol poisoning	Brain damage; death
.45 or higher	The fatal blood alcohol level for 50% of people	When higher than .45, death becomes more and more certain.

*Compared to a driver with a BAC of less than .01

Source: Robert Julien, *A Primer of Drug Action*, 9th ed. (New York: Worth, 2001).

levels climb past .08, you will become progressively less coordinated and less able to make good decisions. Most people become severely uncoordinated with BAC levels higher than .08 and might begin falling asleep, falling down, or slurring their speech.

Warning Signs, Saving Lives

Most people pass out or fall asleep when the BAC is above .25. Unfortunately, even after you pass out and stop drinking, your BAC can continue to rise as alcohol in your stomach is released to the intestine and absorbed into the bloodstream. Your body might try to get rid of alcohol by vomiting, but you can choke if you are unconscious, semiconscious, or severely uncoordinated.

Worse yet, at BAC levels higher than .30, most people will show signs of severe alcohol poisoning, such as an inability to wake up, slowed breathing, fast but weak pulse, cool or damp skin, and pale or bluish skin. People exhibiting these symptoms need medical assistance immediately. If you ever find someone in such a state, remember to keep the person on his or her side with the head lower than the rest of the body. Check to see that the airway is clear, especially if the person is vomiting or if the tongue is blocking the back of the throat.

Helping an Intoxicated Friend

There are many home remedies (such as coffee, water, cold showers) for helping to sober someone up, but none have been proven to truly work. Time is the only remedy because your liver can only metabolize one ounce of alcohol per hour. Harvard University has developed the following guidelines for helping an intoxicated friend:

▶ Never leave a drunk person alone.

▶ Keep the person from driving, biking, or going anywhere alone.

▶ If your friend wants to lie down, turn the person on his or her side to prevent the inhalation of vomit.

▶ Don't give the person any drugs or medications to try to sober him or her up.

▶ You can't prevent the alcohol from being absorbed once it has been consumed so giving a drunk person food will only increase the risk of vomiting.

▶ Do not assume that a drunk is just "sleeping it off" if he or she cannot be awakened. This person needs urgent care.

Heavy Drinking: The Danger Zone

We know that many students have been subjected to what they might regard as exaggerated scare tactics by well-intentioned educators. However, there are many compelling warning indicators related to heavy drinking. Think about the following statistics and their possible application to you and your friends; the effects of heavy drinking are nothing less than a tragedy for many college students:

▶ 1,700 college students between the ages of 18 and 24 die each year from alcohol-related unintentional injuries, including motor vehicle crashes.

Table 14.4   Annual Consequences of Alcohol and Other Drug Use Among All Students, All Drinkers, and Heavy Drinkers

CONSEQUENCES	PERCENT EXPERIENCING CONSEQUENCE		
	ALL STUDENTS	ALL DRINKERS	HEAVY DRINKERS
Had a hangover	59.7	81.1	89.5
Performed poorly on a test	21.8	31.4	40.8
Trouble with police, etc.	11.7	17.4	23.7
Property damage, fire alarm	7.8	11.8	16.5
Argument or fight	29.5	42.0	52.2
Nauseated or vomited	47.1	63.9	73.5
Drove while intoxicated	32.6	47.0	57.3
Missed a class	27.9	40.9	52.9
Been criticized	27.1	37.2	45.3
Thought I had a problem	12.3	16.4	21.6
Had a memory loss	25.8	37.3	48.0
Regretted action later	35.7	49.8	60.4
Arrested for DWI, DUI	1.7	2.4	3.3
Tried, failed to stop	5.8	8.1	16.6
Been hurt, injured	12.9	18.8	25.2
Taken advantage of sexually	11.4	15.9	19.9
Took sexual advantage of someone	6.1	9.0	11.9
Tried to commit suicide	1.6	1.9	2.6
Thought about suicide	5.1	6.7	8.2

Source: Adapted with permission from C. A. Presley, P. W. Meilman, J. R. Cashin, and R. Lyeria, *Alcohol and Drugs on American College Campuses: Use, Consequences, and Perceptions of the Campus Environment, Volume IV: 1992–94* (Carbondale: The Core Institute, Southern Illinois University).

▶ 599,000 students between the ages of 18 and 24 are unintentionally injured each year while under the influence of alcohol.

▶ More than 696,000 students between the ages of 18 and 24 are assaulted each year by another student who has been drinking.[3]

Heavy, or binge, drinking is commonly defined as five or more drinks for males and four or more drinks for females on a single occasion. Presumably, for a very large person who drinks slowly over a long period of time (several hours), four or five drinks might not lead to a BAC associated with impairment. However, research suggests that in many cases the BAC of heavy drinkers exceeds the legal limit for impairment (.08).

The academic, medical, and social consequences of heavy drinking can seriously endanger quality of life. Research based on surveys conducted by the Core Institute at Southern Illinois University (**www.siuc.edu/~coreinst**) provides substantial evidence that heavy drinkers have significantly greater risk of adverse outcomes, as shown in Table 14.4. Among other problems, the Core data identify heavy drinking with increased risk of poor test performance, missed classes, unlawful behavior, violence, memory loss, drunk driving, regretful behavior, and vandalism, compared with all drinkers and all students. At the same time, college health centers nationwide are

[3] Hingson, R., et al. "Magnitude of Alcohol-Related Mortality and Morbidity among U.S. College Students Ages 18–24: Changes from 1998–2001." *Annual Review of Public Health* 26 (2005): 259–79.

reporting increasing occurrences of serious medical conditions—even death—resulting from excessive alcohol use:

- Alcohol poisoning causing coma and shock
- Respiratory depression, choking, and respiratory arrest
- Head trauma and brain injury
- Lacerations
- Fractures
- Unwanted or unsafe sexual activity causing STIs and pregnancies
- Bleeding intestines
- Anxiety attacks and other psychological crises
- Worsening of underlying psychiatric conditions such as depression or anxiety

If you engage in heavy drinking so long that your body can tolerate large amounts, you might become an alcoholic. According to the medical definition, someone is alcohol dependent or alcoholic if he or she exhibits three of the following symptoms:

1. A significant tolerance for alcohol
2. Withdrawal symptoms such as "the shakes"
3. Overuse of alcohol
4. Unsuccessful attempts to control or cut down on use
5. Preoccupation with drinking or becoming anxious when you do not have a drink
6. Making new friends who drink and staying away from friends who do not drink or who do not drink to get drunk
7. Continued heavy drinking despite experiencing alcohol-related social, academic, legal, or health problems

Consequences for All

All Core Institute surveys conducted since the early 1990s have consistently shown a negative correlation between grades and the number of drinks per week—and not just for heavy drinkers. Findings, as shown in Figure 14.2, are similar for two-year and four-year institutions.

As shown in Table 14.5, frequent heavy drinkers suffered a higher rate of problems than heavy drinkers, while heavy drinkers suffered more problems than light to moderate drinkers. The Core Institute reports the following percentages of students who have experienced adverse effects as a result of others' drinking:

Study interrupted: 29%

Space messed up: 25%

Felt unsafe: 22%

Unable to enjoy events: 19%

Interfered with in other ways: 32%

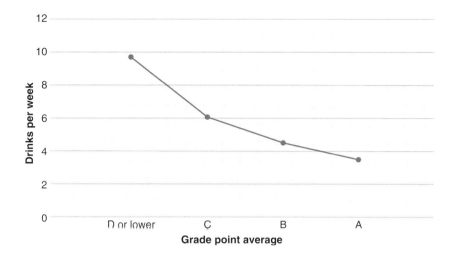

◀ **Figure 14.2**
Negative Correlation between
Drinks per Week and Grade
Point Average

Adapted with permission from
C. A. Presley, P. W. Meilman,
J. R. Cashin, and R. Lyeria,
*Alcohol and Drugs on American
College Campuses: Use,
Consequences, and Perceptions
of the Campus Environment,
Volume IV: 1992-94* (Carbondale:
The Core Institute, Southern
Illinois University).

Table 14.5   **Percentage of Students Reporting Alcohol-Related Problems: Light to Moderate Drinkers, Heavy Drinkers, and Frequent Heavy Drinkers**

PROBLEM	LIGHT TO MODERATE DRINKERS	HEAVY DRINKERS	FREQUENT HEAVY DRINKERS
Got behind on schoolwork	9	25	48
Missed a class due to drinking	10	33	65
Argued with friends while drinking	10	24	47
Got hurt or injured	3	11	27
Damaged property	3	10	25
Got in trouble with campus police	2	5	15
Had five or more alcohol-related problems since the beginning of the school year	4	17	52

Source: Data from Henry Weschler et al., "Changes in Binge Drinking and Related Problems Among American College Students Between 1993 and 1997: Results of the Harvard School of Public Health College Alcohol Study," *Journal of American College Health* 47 (1998): 57-68.

Tobacco–The Other Legal Drug

Tobacco use is clearly the cause of many serious medical conditions, including heart disease, cancer, and lung ailments. Over the years, tobacco has led to the deaths of hundreds of thousands of individuals. Unfortunately, cigarette smoking is on the rise among college students. The College Tobacco Prevention Resource estimates that approximately 30 percent of college students are current users, meaning they have used a tobacco product in the past 30 days. However, the greatest concern about college students and smoking is "social smoking." These are students who smoke only when hanging out with friends, drinking, or partying. The CDC reports that among 18 to 24-year-olds, 28.7 percent of college students fall into the "social smoker" category.[4] Most college students feel they will be able to give up their social smoking

[4] CDC, "Prevalence of Current Cigarette Smoking among Adults and Change in Prevalence of Current and Some Day Smoking—United States, 1996–2000." *Morbidity and Mortality Weekly Report* 52:14 (April 2003): 303–07.

habit once they graduate but, after four years of college, find that they are addicted to cigarettes. A national tobacco study reported that almost 40 percent of college students either began smoking or became regular smokers after starting college.[5]

Write • DISCUSS • Compare • Ask • BLOG • Answer • *Journal*

> In your opinion, given the cost and the dangers of smoking, what are the reasons that some college students continue to smoke?

The College Tobacco Prevention Resource reports that about 3.7 percent of college students use smokeless tobacco and that one "dip" delivers the same amount of nicotine as three to four cigarettes. Smokeless tobacco contains 28 known cancer-causing substances and is associated with the same health risk as cigarette smoking.

Because more women than men now smoke, the rate of cancer in women is rapidly approaching or surpassing rates in men. One explanation as to why more women smoke than men is the enormous amount of pressure on young women to stay thin. While there is some evidence that smoking increases metabolism and suppresses the appetite, the problem of being two or three pounds heavier cannot begin to compare to the dangers of smoking. It has been noted that a female smoker has her first heart attack 19 years before a nonsmoking female.

Chemicals in tobacco are highly addictive, making it hard to quit. Although young people might not worry about long-term side effects, increased numbers of respiratory infections, worsening of asthma, bad breath, stained teeth, and the huge expense should be motivations to not start smoking at all. Smoking and the use of hormonal birth control can be a deadly combination. A recent study conducted at Boston University School of Medicine showed that women who smoke and use hormonal birth control are nearly 10 times more likely to have a heart attack than women who do not smoke or use one of these methods of birth control. A final reason for smokers to quit is the cost (see Table 14.6). Many institutions and local

Table 14.6   The Cost of Smoking

HALF-PACK-A-DAY SMOKER
$4.49/pack × 3.5 packs/week = $15.72/week
$15.72/week × 52 weeks/year = $817.44/year
$817.44/year × 4 years of college = $3,269.76
In 25 years you will have spent $81,744 on cigarettes.
PACK-A-DAY SMOKER
$4.49/pack × 7 packs/week = $31.43/week
$31.43/week × 52 weeks/year = $1,634.36/year
$1,634.36/year × 4 years of college = $6,537.44
In 25 years you will have spent $163,436 on cigarettes.

[5] Rigotti, N., Lee, J., and Wechsler, H. "U.S. College Students' Use of Tobacco Products: Results of a National Survey." *Journal of the American Medical Association* 284:6 (2000): 699–705.

hospitals offer smoking cessation programs to help individuals addicted to nicotine to quit smoking. Contact your campus health center for more information about taking this step toward quitting.

Prescription Drug Abuse and Addiction

Researchers at the University of Michigan reported in January of 2005 that seven percent of college students have used prescription stimulants for nonmedical purposes at some point and four percent have used them in the past year. Three classes of prescription drugs are the most commonly abused: opioids, central nervous system (CNS) depressants, and stimulants. Abuse of anabolic steroids is on the rise, and college students' nonmedical use of prescription pain relievers is also increasing. Some individuals might engage in "doctor shopping" to get multiple prescriptions for the drugs they abuse.

Opioids include morphine, codeine, and such branded drugs as OxyContin, Darvon, Vicodin, Demerol, and Dilaudid. Opioids work by blocking the transmission of pain messages to the brain. Chronic use can result in addiction. Taking a large single dose of an opioid can cause a severe reduction in your breathing rate that can lead to death.

Taken under a doctor's care, central nervous system (CNS) depressants, such as Valium, Librium, Xanax, and Halcion, can be useful in the treatment of anxiety and sleep disorders. The flip side is that exceeding the recommended dosage can create a tolerance and the user will need larger doses to achieve the same result. If the user stops taking the drug, the brain's activity can rebound and race out of control, possibly leading to seizures and other harmful consequences.

Stimulants, such as ephedrine, Ritalin, and Dexadrine, enhance brain activity, causing an increase in alertness, attention, and energy accompanied by elevated blood pressure and increased heart rate. Legal use of stimulants to treat obesity, asthma, and other problems has dropped off as their potential for abuse and addiction has become apparent.[6]

Ritalin is prescribed for a condition called ADHD (Attention Deficit Hyperactivity Disorder) but is gaining recognition on college campuses as a "cramming drug." This prescription drug costs only about $.50 per tablet but sells on the street for as much as $15.00. College students are using Ritalin to stay awake for long periods of time to study for exams. Many students think that since it is a prescribed drug, it must be harmless. The U.S. Department of Education's Higher Education Center for Alcohol and Other Drug Abuse and Violence Prevention lists the following as possible adverse effects from abusing Ritalin: nervousness, vomiting, changes in heart rate and blood pressure, dependency, fevers, convulsions, headaches, paranoia, hallucinations, and delusions.

Another class of drugs that is of concern in the college setting is anabolic steroids. When most people think of steroids, they think about college and professional athletes. But, it is important for all college students to know and understand the dangers of these

---

[6] Adapted from "Prescription Drugs: Abuse and Addiction." National Institute on Drug Abuse, part of the National Institutes of Health, a division of the U.S. Department of Health and Human Services.

synthetic substances. According to the National Institute on Drug Abuse, steroids are taken orally or injected into the body in cycles lasting weeks or months. Steroid abuse has many major side effects, including liver tumors, cancer, jaundice, fluid retention, high blood pressure, kidney tumors, and severe acne. Most anabolic steroid users are male and therefore have gender-specific side effects including shrinking of the testicles, reduced sperm count, infertility, baldness, development of breasts, and increased risk for prostate cancer. Abusers also put themselves at risk for contracting HIV or other blood-borne viruses when using or sharing infected needles.

The abuse rate for steroids is fairly low among the general population. In 2003, the Monitoring the Future Survey found that 1.8 percent of young adults ages 19–28 reported using steroids at least once during their lifetimes. One-half (0.5) percent reported using steroids at least once in the past year and 0.2 percent reported using steroids in the past month.[7]

Over-the-Counter Drugs and Supplements

Drugs that can be purchased without a prescription are generally safe when taken according to directions on the bottle or package. But never take more than the recommended dose without consulting your physician.

Drugstores and health food stores also carry many supplements in pill or liquid form that are labeled "natural." This label does not mean that the product has been tested, is safe, or is worth your money. The Food and Drug Administration (FDA) does not regulate supplements as they do food or other medication, so it is very important to do thorough research and to consult your physician before starting any over-the-counter regimen.

Illegal Drugs

Illegal recreational drugs, such as marijuana, cocaine, methamphetamine, Ecstasy, and heroin, are used by a much smaller number of college students and far less frequently than alcohol. Yet these drugs are significant public health issues for college students. The penalties associated with the possession or abuse of illegal drugs tend to be much more severe than those associated with underage alcohol use.

Athletic departments, potential employers, and government agencies do routine screenings for many of these illegal drugs. Future employability, athletic scholarships, and insurability might be compromised if you have a positive drug test for any of these substances. A brief summary of five of the most prevalent drugs follows.

Marijuana. The effects of marijuana can linger for three to seven days, depending on the potency and the smoker. Chronic use of marijuana can lead to a lethargic state in which users can forget about current responsibilities (such as going to class). Long-term use carries the same risks of lung infections and cancer that are associated with smoking tobacco.

---

[7] "2004 Monitoring the Future Survey," funded by the National Institute on Drug Abuse, National Institutes of Health, DHHS, and conducted by the University of Michigan's Institute for Social Research. For more data, visit **www.drugabuse.gov**.

Ecstasy. MDMA, or Ecstasy, as it is known, is a synthetic—or manmade—drug. While many young people believe that MDMA is safe and offers nothing but a pleasant high for the $25 cost of a single tablet (how bad can it be if it's that cheap?), the reality is far different. Taken orally, the effects of MDMA last approximately four to six hours. Many will take a second dose when the initial dose begins to fade. Some tablets contain drugs in addition to MDMA, including amphetamine, caffeine, destromethorpin, ephedrine, and cocaine. MDMA significantly depletes serotonin, a substance in the brain that helps regulate mood, sleep, pain, emotion, and appetite, as well as other behaviors. It takes the brain time to rebuild the serotonin needed to perform important physiological and psychological functions. Of great concern is MDMA's adverse effects on the pumping efficiency of the heart. Heavy users can experience obsessive traits, anxiety, paranoia, and sleep disturbance. Another study indicates that MDMA can have long-lasting effects on memory.[8]

Heroin. Numerous reports have suggested a rise in heroin use among college students. A highly addictive drug with the potential to be more damaging and fatal than other opiates, heroin is the most abused and most rapidly acting of this group. One of the most significant—and surest—effects of heroin use is addiction. The human body begins to develop tolerance to the drug on first use. Once this happens, the abuser must use more of the drug to achieve the same intensity. Within a short period of time, users must take the drug more and more often to alleviate the symptoms of addiction. Heroin can be injected, smoked, or snorted. Injection is the most efficient way to administer low-purity heroin. However, the availability of high-purity heroin and the fear of infection by sharing needles has made snorting and smoking the drug more common. Some users believe that snorting or smoking heroin will not lead to addiction. They are 100 percent wrong.

Chronic users can develop collapsed veins, infection of the heart lining and valves, abscesses, and liver disease. In addition, users are at risk for pulmonary complications, including various types of pneumonia. In addition to the effects of the drug itself, users who inject heroin or share needles also put themselves at risk for contracting HIV, Hepatitis B and C, and other blood-borne viruses. A heroin overdose is known to cause slow and shallow breathing, convulsions, coma, and possibly death.

Cocaine. Cocaine, or crack, produces an intense experience that heightens senses. A crack high lasts only a few minutes; then the good feelings are gone. During the crash, the user might feel tired and unmotivated and find it impossible to sleep. Cocaine is highly addictive. In some instances, users have died of cardiac arrest while taking the drug.

Meth (Methamphetamine). Methamphetamine is particularly dangerous because it costs so little and is so easy to make. Much of it is being produced in makeshift labs in homes or college residences, which not only means that the quality varies from batch to batch, but that it's virtually impossible to tell what else is in the mixture.

The drug can initially produce euphoria, enhanced wakefulness, increased physical activity, and decreased appetite. Prolonged use can lead to binges, during which

---

[8] Excerpted from "Ecstasy: What We Know and Don't Know About MDMA: A Scientific Review." National Institute on Drug Abuse, part of the National Institutes of Health (NIH), a division of the U.S. Department of Health and Human Services.

▶ **It's healthy to talk openly about how drugs and alcohol abuse your body and mind.**

© Stephen Simpson/Getty Images

users take more meth every few hours for several days until they run out of the drug or become too disorganized to continue. Chronic abuse can lead to psychotic behavior, characterized by intense paranoia, visual and auditory hallucinations, and out-of-control rages that can be coupled with extremely violent behavior. Researchers have found that many former meth users experience long-term brain damage, and it is unknown whether the damage can ever be reversed.

WHERE TO GO FOR HELP

On Campus

Counseling Center Professionals here will offer individual and group assistance and lots of information. Remember, their support is confidential and you will not be judged.

Health Center/Infirmary On most campuses, the professionals who staff the health center are especially interested in educational outreach and practicing prevention, but you should be able to receive treatment as well.

Health Education and Wellness Programs College campuses assume and recognize that for many students, problems and challenges with alcohol, other drugs, and sexual decision making and its consequences are part of the college universe. Fellow student peer health educators who are trained and supervised by professionals can provide support. Taking part in such peer leadership is also a great way to develop and practice your own communication skills.

Campus Support Groups Many campuses provide student support groups led by professionals for students dealing with problems related to excessive alcohol and drug use, abusive sexual relationships, and so forth.

Online

Advice about college student health issues: **www.goaskalice.com.** This website sponsored by Columbia University has answers to many health questions.

Dealing with stress: **www.stress.org.** Want to combat stress? Find out how at the American Institute of Stress website.

Advice from the American Dietetic Association: **www.eatright.org.** This website provides information on healthy eating and nutrition.

How tobacco affects your health: **www.cancer.org.** To learn more about the health effects of tobacco, visit the American Cancer Society.

The Center for Young Women's Health: **www.youngwomenshealth.org/collegehealth10.html** This website has helpful advice on sexual health as well as other issues.

National Clearinghouse for Alcohol and Drug Information: **www.health.org.** or 800-729-6686. This organization provides up-to-date information about the effects of alcohol and drug use.

DrugHelp: **www.drughelp.org.** This is a private, nonprofit referral service for drug treatment.

Methamphetamine addiction: **www.methamphetamineaddiction.com/** Learn more about the dangers of methamphetamine at this website.

The Centers for Disease Control and Prevention: **www.cdc.gov.** This website is an excellent resource for all of the topics in this chapter.

If you have questions about suicide prevention, contact the National Suicide Prevention Lifeline at 1-800-273-TALK or on the website (**www.suicidepreventionlifeline.org**).

Here are some other valuable resources:
National Clearinghouse for Alcohol and Drug Information: **www.health.org**
National Eating Disorders Association: **www.nationaleatingdisorders.org**
U.S. Government's Nutrition Information: **www.nutrition.gov**
Shape Up America: **www.shapeup.org**
National Health Information Center: **www.healthfinder.org**
Planned Parenthood Federation of American: **www.plannedparenthood.org**
U.S. Food and Drug Administration: **www.fda.gov**

My Institution's Resources

_____

_____

_____

_____

_____

_____

_____

_____

▶▶▶ BUILDING YOUR PORTFOLIO
Are you "Technostressed"?

Imagine if every Thursday your shoes exploded if you tied them the usual way.
This happens to us all the time with computers, and nobody thinks of complaining.

–Jef Raskin (1943–2005), American human-computer interface expert

To complete this portfolio activity electronically, please visit
academic.cengage.com/collsucc/Gardner/YCE8e.

Ever-changing, ever-improving technology is a wonderful part of our modern world, but it can also be an additional stressor on our everyday lives. It seems the list of hot new gadgets grows longer every day. How does being a constantly accessible, multitasking marvel with continuous reminders of what you haven't done yet affect your stress level? Do you occasionally find yourself overwhelmed or even a bit lonely when you are face to face with your computer instead of your friends, families, or coworkers? The hurried, plugged-in life can be exhausting and nerve-racking, especially if you get an incomprehensible error message on your computer screen the night before a big paper is due!

So, how are you plugged in?

1. Create a new entry in your portfolio with the title "Technostressed." Record your work for this assignment there.

2. Describe all the ways your life is affected by technology. How are your health and well-being affected, both positively and negatively, by the things you list?

   Tip: Think of how you use technology for entertainment, and also for class or work.

My Gadgets & Gizmos	Positives Aspects	Negative Aspects
Example: Instant Messenger	Ability to communicate anywhere in the world, in a matter of seconds, 24/7	Staying up late, talking to my friends = no sleep!

Sometimes it seems like all of the technology that is supposed to make our lives easier actually adds to the balancing act. Here are a few tips for reducing your stress level and avoiding a technology takeover.

▶ Schedule some downtime *offline* for yourself.

▶ Don't become a text-message junkie.

▶ Don't try to multitask 24/7! Take advantage of time to exercise, eat, or just take a break without the demands of e-mail and cell phones.

▶ Recognize the warning signs of Internet addiction, for example the following:

    ▶ Using the Internet to escape from problems or responsibilities

    ▶ Missing class, work, or appointments to spend time online

    ▶ Always allowing the Internet to substitute for face-to-face interaction with others

Epilogue: It Ain't Over 'Til It's Over

The great baseball player Yogi Berra is often quoted as having said, "It ain't over 'til it's over!" So here you are at the end of the course. This course is over—or is it? One thing is for sure: College isn't over for you and what you learned in this course isn't over. But finishing this course has to feel good. Because there has been so much research done on students like you, we can confidently tell you that successful completion of this course is a good predictor for overall success in college.

When you finish any of your courses in college, it is a good time to reflect, step back, and ask yourself some thoughtful questions like.

▶ What did I learn in this course?

▶ Can I apply what I learned to other courses?

▶ Will I use what I learned both in and out of class?

▶ What did I learn that I am most likely to remember?

▶ Do I want to stay in touch with this professor?

▶ Did I improve my basic skills?

▶ How do I feel about what I accomplished?

▶ Did I do better than I thought I would?

▶ What did I do that helped me progress, and how can I repeat those kinds of successful efforts in other courses?

▶ What challenges do I still face?

Whether you are finishing this course at the end of your first term in college or at the end of your first year in college, there are many success strategies that you learned in this course that will continue to help you as you move through the rest of your college experience.

Some Parting Suggestions

Keep in Touch with Professors We suggest that you consider keeping in touch with the professor of this course. Educators who volunteer to teach a college success course or first-year seminar really do care about students and enjoy staying in touch with them over time and noting their progress. You will also want to stay in touch with your other professors. Later in college you may need to ask them to write reference letters for you as you seek employment or admission to graduate school. When a professor becomes part of your larger support group, this is a form of networking.

Using Campus Resources You should also keep using the campus's services and resources that you learned about in this course such as the learning center or career center. Remember, these services are most heavily utilized by the best students, and you want to be one of those. Those students continue to seek help. It's a lifelong behavior pattern of successful people.

Practice Study Strategies in All Your Courses It's important for you to keep on practicing the success strategies that were presented in this book. Usually, you don't learn these in just one term. And, if you don't keep practicing them, you get rusty. Using these strategies is like learning anything else in life such as riding a bike or roller skating. Practice is absolutely essential. But we also realize that you may not yet have been ready to attempt some of the strategies we endorsed in this book. So maybe the next term, or the next year, will be a better time to revisit some of these ideas. We also suggest that you hang on to all your books so you can revisit them. We know that students like to resell their books. And if you do resell them, you could get library copies at some point in the future. But your books could be valuable resources for you when you might need to revisit course topics in the future. There may also be friends or family members who'll be coming to college. You could share these materials with them.

Planning Your Summer We would also like to suggest that you begin thinking about what you are going to do this summer. We realize that students may have learned in high school that "summer school" was for dummies or slackers. But in college, nothing could be further from the truth. We now know from national research on college students' progress, that continuous enrollment is a good thing; it keeps students in the swing of things, they don't fall out of practice, and they are more likely to keep on going and going—and graduate.

An alternative to summer school is to do something in the summer that is connected to your education—or sponsored by your college, like an internship, practicum, or study abroad. Continuing your learning in summer maintains your fast pace of uninterrupted development and doesn't allow you to backtrack and get out of practice. Also, students who take the initiative to attend summer school or who have held summer jobs or internships will often be more attractive to future employers.

Planning Your Remaining Time in College As you end this course, we suggest that you once again think seriously about your major. That decision is really important because eventually you have to get a degree in something, even if it's an interdisciplinary degree. And you want to feel good and comfortable about your major. And, even more important, your chosen major is connected to that all-important idea that we stressed in the first chapter of this book: purpose—that is your purpose for being in this college at this time in your life. One of the ways that U. S. colleges are different from higher education institutions in most of the rest of the world is that we give our students far more opportunities to change majors. So this is something we encourage you to revisit now. This course may have given you some new insights into yourself and what might really motivate you now and in the future.

Now is also a good time to ask yourself about your academic advisor. Are you getting what you need from this important relationship? If not, don't hesitate to request a change.

It's possible that you haven't used the career center yet, even though you learned about it in this course. Now, as this course is coming to a close, would be a great time to pay a visit to the career center to learn about possible internships, summer employment, and additional help if you haven't decided on a major.

Ending a course like this is a good time to take stock of your accomplishments this term. By all means, you should pat yourself on the back. But you also may want to take a hard look at those things that didn't go so well. Learn from your mistakes and apply what you learn to future successes.

Let's circle back to that concept of purpose. Here at the end of the term, how is the "fit" between you and this college, between you and your major? Is this campus meeting your expectations and your needs? Are you getting a clearer idea of why you are here—as opposed to why some other people in your life may want you to be here? Even if you're still unsure, we hope you'll give yourself more time to get adjusted to this college thing, to get more comfortable, to find a sense of "fit," and to accomplish some things for yourself that you can be really proud of.

We wrote this book to help students like you. Much of what we know about what students need in order to be successful, we learned from our students. Thanks for giving us a chance to help you as you began *Your College Experience.* You've already come a long way from where you started, and there are many great college experiences ahead waiting for you. So practice the strategies we tried to teach you in this book and remember, if millions of students before you have made it, you can too.

Sincerely,

John N. Gardner
A. Jerome Jewler
Betsy O. Barefoot

Glossary

Abstract A paragraph-length summary of the methods and major findings of an article in a scholarly journal.

Abstract conceptualization A learner's ability to integrate observation into logically sound theories; this is one of the four stages of Kolb's Inventory of Learning Styles

Abstract-concrete One of two basic divisions in Kolb's Inventory of Learning Styles.

Accommodators Individuals who prefer hands-on learning. Accommodators are good at making things happen and work well with other people, although they can be pushy and impatient. This is one of the categories in Kolb's Inventory of Learning Styles.

Active experimentation A learner's ability to make decisions, solve problems, and test what he or she has learned; this is one of the four stages of Kolb's Inventory of Learning Styles.

Active learning Learning by doing, for example writing, speaking, creating, participating in class.

Active-reflective One of two basic divisions in Kolb's Inventory of Learning Styles.

Aesthetic Emphasizing beauty, art, and good taste.

Annotate To add critical or explanatory margin notes as you read or review a textbook.

Argument Reason and information brought together in logical support of an idea.

Assimilators People who like to think about abstract concepts. Assimilators enjoy courses that are highly theoretical, such as physics. This is one of the categories in Kolb's Inventory of Learning Styles.

Attention deficit hyperactivity disorder A disorder characterized by difficulty organizing tasks, completing work, and following directions.

Aural learner A person who prefers to learn by hearing information. This is one of the preferences described by the VARK Learning Styles Inventory.

Autonomy Independence. College students usually have more autonomy than they did in high school.

Behavioral interview An interview in which the interviewer questions the candidate about past experience and how it helped the candidate learn and grow.

Bias A negative, preconceived opinion of some person or group. The opinion may manifest itself either in attitude or in acts of discrimination.

Biorhythms The internal biological clocks that drive our daily patterns, influencing when we are most active and alert.

Brainstorming The process of writing down everyone's ideas without comment or criticism so that the team members build on each other's ideas.

Chunking A previewing technique that involves making a list of terms from a reading assignment, dividing the list into groups of five, seven, or nine terms, and learning one group at a time.

Citation A source or author of certain material. For instance, when browsing for sources on the Internet, it is important to use only material that has citations explaining who wrote it, where it came from, and who posted it.

Co-curricular experiences Learning that occurs outside of the classroom, through on-campus clubs and groups, co-op programs, internships, or other means.

Cognitive restructuring Using positive thinking and self-talk to improve one's performance, for example on an exam.

Collaboration Working with others in the learning environment to enhance understanding for everyone.

Concrete experience Abilities that allow learners to involve themselves fully in new experiences; this is one of the four stages of Kolb's Inventory of Learning Styles.

Content skills Cognitive, intellectual, or "hard" skills, acquired as one gains mastery in an academic field. Content skills include writing proficiency, computer literacy, and foreign language skills.

Context A frame of reference that helps you refine your search for information. When conducting research, it is important to establish a context for the research, such as limiting your search to historical documents, statistics, or opinion pieces.

Convergers People who enjoy the world of ideas and theories but are able to apply them to practical situations. Convergers often major in health sciences or engineering. This is one of the categories in Kolb's Inventory of Learning Styles.

Co-op program Also called cooperative education—a program that provides an opportunity to work in academic major-related settings off campus while enrolled in college.

Cornell format A note-taking and organizing format in which one side of the page is reserved for note-taking and the other side for recall after class.

Credit history The record of an individual's or a company's past borrowing and repaying.

Culture Those aspects of a group of people that are passed on and/or learned.

Developmental arithmetic disorder A learning disability characterized by difficulty recognizing numbers and symbols, memorizing mathematical facts, aligning numbers, and understanding abstract mathematical concepts.

Developmental writing disorder A learning disability that involves some or all of the areas of the brain that involve vocabulary, grammar, hand movement, and memory.

Discipline An area of academic study, such as history, mathematics, or nursing.

Discrimination Treating people differently depending on their race, ethnicity, gender, socioeconomic class, or other identifying characteristic, rather than on merit.

Divergers Individuals who are good at reflecting on situations from many viewpoints. These people are good at brainstorming and are imaginative and people-oriented, but sometimes have difficulty making decisions. This is one of the categories in Kolb's Inventory of Learning Styles.

Drop date The date by which you can drop a course without penalty, providing that you follow proper procedures.

Dyslexia A developmental reading disorder that is sometimes characterized by an inability to distinguish or separate the sounds in spoken words.

Ethnicity A reference to a quality assigned to a specific group of people historically connected by a common national origin or language.

Examples Stories, illustrations, hypothetical events, and specific cases that provide support for the ideas in a presentation or written work.

Explanatory writing Writing that is "published," meaning that others can read it.

Exploratory writing "Freewriting" that is generally in draft form and is not ready for others to read.

Expressive language disorder The inability to express oneself using accurate language or sentence structure.

Extraverts Individuals who are outgoing, gregarious, and talkative, and who like to act and lead. This is one of the preferences described by the Myers-Briggs Type Indicator.

Fallacies Errors in thinking such as using false cause, attacking the arguer instead of the argument, and appealing to authority rather than relying on logic.

Faulty reasoning Illogical thinking that depends on fallacies such as false cause and hasty generalization.

Feeling types Warm, empathetic, and sympathetic individuals who value harmony above all else. This is one of the preferences described by the Myers-Briggs Type Indicator.

Financial aid Money that is available through grants or loans to pay the costs of college attendance.

Freewriting Writing that is temporarily free of mechanical processes, such as punctuation, grammar, spelling, context, and so forth. Freewriting is similar to writing in a stream-of-consciousness style.

Galloping New Ignorance (GNI) The erroneous assumption that anything that exists in electronic form must be true and useful information.

Grade Point Average (GPA)   The average grade of a student, calculated by dividing the grades received by the number of credits earned.

Humanities   Branches of knowledge that investigate human beings, their culture, and their self-expression. Distinguished from the physical and biological sciences and, sometimes, from the social sciences, the humanities include the study of languages and literatures, the arts, history, and philosophy.

Idioms   Peculiar and unique phrases that cannot be understood from the individual meanings of the words. "Pull the wool over one's eyes" is a common English language idiom.

Inclusive curriculum   A curriculum that offers courses that introduce students to diverse people, worldviews, and approaches. For instance, an inclusive curriculum might include majors in the areas of gender studies, ethnic and cultural studies, and religious studies.

Information age   The period of time in which we live, characterized by the central role of information in the economy, the necessity to have information retrieval and information management skills, and the explosion of available information.

Introverts   Quiet, sometimes shy people who prefer to reflect carefully and think through a problem before taking action. This is one of the preferences described by the Myers-Briggs Type Indicator.

Intuitive types   Individuals who are excited by the meaning behind the facts and the connections between concepts. This is one of the preferences described by the Myers-Briggs Type Indicator.

Job-shadow   To observe someone as he or she works, with permission.

Judging types   People who strive for order and control in their environment, making plans and decisions quickly. This is one of the preferences described by the MyersBriggs Type Indicator.

Key word   A critical task word on an essay test that tells you how the question is to be answered. Examples of key words are analyze, describe, and justify.

Kinesthetic learner   A person who prefers to learn through experience and practice, whether simulated or real. This term also refers to someone who learns best by doing something rather than reading about it or listening. This is one of the preferences described by the VARK Learning Styles Inventory.

Learning disabilities   Disorders that affect people's ability to either interpret what they see and hear or to link information from different parts of the brain. Dyslexia is a common learning disability.

Learning styles   Particular ways of learning. For example, one person's learning style may be to "split" information into small parts and another's may be to "lump" concepts together.

Long-term memory   Memories that you retain, divided into the categories of procedural, episodic, and semantic memory.

Mapping   A previewing technique that use a wheel or branching structure to display main ideas and secondary ideas from your reading.

Marking   The act of making marks in textbooks while reading. Marking can take the form of making text notations, underlining, highlighting, and writing margin notes.

Mind map   A personal study device consisting of words and drawings on a single page that summarizes information about a topic.

Mnemonics   Techniques to aid the memory, including acronyms, rhymes, or other bits of language that help you remember lists or phrases.

Multiculturalism   The active process of acknowledging and respecting the various social groups, cultures, religions, races, ethnicities, attitudes, and opinions within an environment.

Multitasking   Performing many tasks at once, such as eating lunch, studying, and making phone calls simultaneously.

Network   To develop a chain or web of contacts and advisors who can help you achieve your academic and career goals.

Outsourcing   The movement of jobs to individuals and companies outside of one's own. This includes hiring contractors who are not part of a company's full-time staff.

Perceiving types   Individuals who are comfortable adapting to change and are prone to keeping their options open to gather more information. This is one of the preferences described by the Myers-Briggs Type Indicator.

Plagiarism   A form of academic misconduct that involves presenting another's ideas, words, or opinions as one's own.

Prejudice   Judging someone based on little knowledge; for example, prejudging someone based solely on his or her ethnic or racial background.

Prewriting   Also called rehearsing, prewriting is preparing to write by filling your mind with information from other sources. It is generally considered the first stage of exploratory writing.

Primary sources   The original research or document on a topic. For example, The Gettysburg Address is a primary source document about the Civil War.

Procrastination   Putting off doing a task or assignment.

Race   A term that refers to biological characteristics shared by groups of people and includes hair texture and color, skin tone, and facial features.

Read/write learning preference   A preference for learning information that is displayed as words. This is one of the preferences described by the VARK Learning Styles Inventory.

Reflective observation   A learner's ability to reflect on his or her experience from many perspectives; this is one of the four stages of Kolb's Inventory of Learning Styles.

Returning student   Students for whom several or many years have elapsed between previous and current attendance in college. Also called nontraditional students.

Sensing types   Individuals who are practical, factual, realistic, and down-to-earth. This is one of the preferences described by the Myers-Briggs Type Indicator.

Service learning   Mandatory, unpaid service embedded in courses across the curriculum.

Short-term memory   How many items you are able to perceive at one time. Short-term memories disappear after about 30 seconds unless they are transferred to long-term memory.

Sorting   Part of applying information literacy to searching the Internet. Sorting is a way of sifting through available information and selecting the most relevant material.

Statistics   Data used to support ideas in a speech or written work.

Stereotype   An oversimplified set of assumptions about another person or group.

Subject   A way of searching on the Internet that looks for information only by checking subject headings, rather than the entire document.

Supplemental Instruction (SI)   Classes that provide further opportunity to discuss the information presented in lecture.

Syllabus   Written class requirements or a course outline given by instructors on the first day of class to all students.

Systematic thinking   Examining the outcome of abstract and creative thinking in a demanding and critical way in order to narrow down the list of possible solutions. Tactile learner A person who learns best by using the sense of touch, for example, by typing notes after a lecture.

Thinking types   Logical, rational, and analytical individuals who tend to be critical and objective without involving their own or other people's feelings. This is one of the preferences described by the Myers-Briggs Type Indicator.

Transferable skills   General skills that apply to or transfer to a variety of settings. Examples of transferable skills include excellent public speaking skills, using available software to maintain homepages, and providing leadership while working in a team environment.

Visual learner   A person who learns best by reading words on a printed page or by viewing pictures, maps, charts, or videos.

Visual learning preference   A preference for learning through charts, graphs, symbols, or other visual means. This is one of the preferences described by the VARK Learning Styles Inventory.

Wellness   The process of taking care of one's self by making healthy choices and achieving balance in mind, body, and spirit.

Index

Credits

TEXT CREDITS

This page constitutes an extension of the copyright page. We have made every effort to trace the ownership of all copyrighted material and to secure permission from copyright holders. In the event of any question arising as to the use of any material, we will be pleased to make the necessary corrections in future printings. Thanks are due to the following authors, publishers, and agents for permission to use the material indicated.

Chapter 3. 44–45: Copyright Version 5.1 (2004) held by Neil D. Fleming, Christchurch, New Zealand and Charles C. Bonwell, Green Mountain Falls, Colorado 80819 U.S.A. Reprinted by permission of Neil D. Fleming.

49: From The Modern American College by Chickering. Copyright © 1981 Jossey-Bass. Reprinted with permission of John Wiley & Sons, Inc

Chapter 14. 280: Adapted from "Holmes-Rahe Social Readjustment Rating Scale," Journal of Psychosomatic Research, vol. II, 1967. Used by permission of Elsevier.

289: The Food Pyramid reprinted with the permission of Simon & Schuster Adult Publishing Group from Eat, Drink and Be Healthy: The Harvard Medical School Guide to Healthy Eating by Walter C. Willett, M.D., p. 17, Figure 2. Copyright © 2001 by President and Fellows of Harvard College.

297: Data from C. A. Presley, P.W. Meilman, J.R. Cashin and R. Lyeria, Alcohol and Drugs on American College Campuses: Use, Consequences and Perceptions of the Campus environment, Volume IV: 1992–94, Carbondale: The Core Institute, Southern Illinois University.

299: Data from C. A. Presley, P. W. Meilman, J.R. Cashin and R. Lyeria, Alcohol and Drugs on American College Campuses: Use, Consequences and Perceptions of the Campus Environment, Volume IV: 1992–94, Carbondale: The Core Institute, Southern Illinois University

PHOTO CREDITS

Chapter 1. 1: © John Boykin/PhotoEdit; **3:** © Tom Stewart/zefa/CORBIS; **7:** © Michael Newman/PhotoEdit; **9:** © image100/Alamy

Chapter 2. 17: © Gary Gerovac/Masterfile; **23:** © Erin Gilcrest; **31:** © David Young-Wolff/PhotoEdit

Chapter 3. 41: © Sam Pellissier/SuperStock; **50:** © Bill Aron/PhotoEdit; **53:** © Lisa Peardon/Getty Images; **55:** © Christina Micek; **60:** © Carlo Allegri/Getty Images Entertainment; **60:** © Mitchell Gerber/CORBIS

Chapter 4. 63: © Andrew Douglas/Masterfile; **66:** © David Fischer/Getty Images; **68:** © Christina Micek; **72:** © ThinkStock/SuperStock; **73:** © iStockPhoto

Chapter 5. 83: © AFP/Getty Images; **86:** © David Young-Wolff/PhotoEdit

Chapter 6. 107: © Rhoda Sidney/PhotoEdit; **111:** © Image Source/SuperStock; **116:** © Don Smetzer/PhotoEdit; **117:** © Steve Smith/SuperStock; **123:** © Myrleen Ferguson Cate/PhotoEdit

Chapter 7. 127: © Tony Freeman/PhotoEdit; **131:** © Digital Vision/Getty Images; **132:** © Sidney Shaffer/Getty Images; **140:** © Jon Feingersh/CORBIS

Chapter 8. 145: © Gabe Palmer/CORBIS; **149:** © David Young-Wolff/PhotoEdit; **150:** © age/fotostock/SuperStock; **157:** © BananaStock/SuperStock; **161:** © Mark Richards/Photo Edit; **162:** © Big Cheese Photo/SuperStock

Chapter 9. 169: © Vince Bucci/Getty Images; **173:** © Christina Micek; **177:** © David Pollack/CORBIS; **181:** © Robert Daly/Getty Images; **182:** © image100/SuperStock; **184:** © Christina Micek

Chapter 10. 191: Courtesy of the National Aeronautics and Space Administration.; **193:** © David Zimmerman/Masterfile; **195:** © PureStock/Alamy; **196:** © Mark Richards/PhotoEdit; **197:** © Anton Vengo/SuperStock; **208:** © Will & Deni McIntyre/CORBIS

Chapter 11. 213: © Lester Lefkowitz/CORBIS; **217:** © PhotoAlto/SuperStock; **220:** © Sheri Blaney/Cengage; **227:** © Bob Daemmrich/PhotoEdit; **228:** © SW Productions/Getty Images; **234:** © White Packert/Getty Images

Chapter 12. 241: © Bill Aron/PhotoEdit; **243:** © Cindy Charles/PhotoEdit; **245:** © David Young-Wolff/PhotoEdit; **247:** © Myrleen Ferguson Cate/PhotoEdit; **249:** © Bonnie Kamin/PhotoEdit; **251:** © age/fotostock/SuperStock; **255:** © Justin Pumfrey/Getty Images

Chapter 13. 261: © Blend Images/SuperStock; **265:** © Leland Bobbé/CORBIS; **269:** © Jodi Hilton/Getty Images; **271:** © Chris Nash/Getty Images; **275:** © Mark Richards/PhotoEdit

Chapter 14. 277: © Kevin Dodge/Masterfile; **283:** © Stockbyte/SuperStock; **286:** © Mug Shots/CORBIS; **291:** © Mary Kate Denny/PhotoEdit; **304:** © Stephen Simpson/Getty Images

All Student Profile photos courtesy of students.